DIRECTOR'S AND OFFICER'S
COMPLETE LETTER BOOK

DIRECTOR'S AND OFFICER'S COMPLETE LETTER BOOK

THIRD EDITION

by Prentice Hall Editorial Staff

L. Edward Purcell, Editor

PRENTICE HALL
Englewood Cliffs, New Jersey 07632

Prentice-Hall International (UK) Limited, *London*
Prentice-Hall of Australia Pty. Limited, *Sydney*
Prentice-Hall Canada, Inc., *Toronto*
Prentice-Hall Hispanoamericana, S.A., *Mexico*
Prentice-Hall of India Private Limited, *New Delhi*
Prentice-Hall of Japan, Inc., *Tokyo*
Simon & Schuster Asia Pte. Ltd., *Singapore*
Editora Prentice-Hall do Brasil, Ltda., *Rio de Janeiro*

© 1991 by
PRENTICE HALL
Englewood Cliffs, NJ

10 9 8 7 6 5 4 3 2 1

Library of Congress Cataloging-in-Publication Data

Director's and officer's complete letterbook: complete letter book/
by Prentice-Hall editorial staff; L. Edward Purcell, editor. — 3rd ed.
     p.   cm.
   Includes index.
   ISBN 0-13-218132-0
     1. Commerical correspondence.   I. Purcell, L. Edward.
   II. Prentice-Hall, Inc.
   HF5726.D57   1991
   651.7'5—dc20   91–3742
                                                              CIP

ISBN 0-13-218132-0

PRENTICE HALL
Business Information Publishing Division
Englewood Cliffs, NJ 07632

Simon & Schuster. A Paramount Communications Company

Printed in the United States of America

As long as there are postmen,
life will have zest.

—Will James

Note on the Editor

L. Edward Purcell is a writer, editor, and consultant with wide experience as a business journalist and in working with corporations. He has been a marketing and public relations consultant for several businesses, and has worked as executive editor for a large national public interest group.

He is the author of several books, and has written many articles in regional and national business magazines and trade journals on a wide range of topics. In addition, he has worked directly for corporations in the areas of computer software, biotechnology, construction, heavy equipment manufacture, insurance, real estate, wholesale supply, restaurant and food supply, and marketing. He has edited a book on purchasing, written a guide to print buying, and has been a publications consultant to a national organization of auditors, comptrollers, and treasurers.

He is married and lives in Kentucky.

Introduction

This is the third revised version of the highly popular, time-saving *Director's and Officer's Complete Letter Book*.

Many corporate officers, directors, and executives have improved their personal productivity by turning to the model letters in this book as a shortcut to more effective and efficient business correspondence. The volume is designed to assist directors and officers in the letter-writing tasks they face each day as part of their corporate responsibilities.

This new edition has been expanded to include a total of 200 basic sample letters and nearly 600 additional alternative versions covering all approaches to high-level corporate and executive letter writing.

Fully three-fourths of the book's model letters are new and have never been published before. In addition, several of the new letters are authentic examples of real business correspondence, written by actual directors and officers of American businesses who have granted permission to reproduce letters from their correspondence files. Letters retained from earlier editions of *The Director's and Officer's Complete Letter Book* have been revised and updated to encompass recent changes in business technology and procedure.

The book covers a full range of business activities, and the model letters are organized into categories typical of commerce in the United States. For example, in Chapter 2 there is a series of letters suitable for dealing with a top-level executive search firm, in addition to letters about hiring and firing, such as "Turning Down a Job Applicant." Chapter 4 on customer relations has letters such as "Explaining a Company Policy," which was actually written by the Chairman of the Board of an investment firm. Chapter 5 has sales and marketing letters, including "Contacting an Inactive Account" and "Follow-up Sales." Chapter 7 has model letters for dealing with stockholders, including a sample "Annual Meeting Announcement," and so on.

Each of the sample letters is followed by a brief "Tips and Comment" section, which discusses the business context in which the letter might be used and special hints for that specific case.

There are also several alternative letter texts, demonstrating some of the possible variations on the main sample. The alternatives have essentially the same purpose as the main sample letter but employ a differing tone or approach in order to provide a range of formality and style from which to choose. The alternatives, for example, might reflect variations in corporate culture, the personality of the writer, the size of the company, or how well the writer knows the recipient.

In all, there are seventeen chapters, covering almost every phase of business, plus a valuable Master Checklist for Letter Writing and extensive additional sections on the mechanics of letter writing and the proper forms of address.

The sample letters are not intended as prescriptions for an officer or executive's letter writing, but rather as models in the best sense: demonstrating the style, tone, form, and general approach of effective business letters. They should help define purpose and technique, as well as provide examples that can be adapted to a writer's own needs.

In an age of rapidly advancing communications technology, when fax machines are everywhere and voices are only a fiber-optic phone call away, it may well be asked what role remains for letters? The answer is simple: there are still many occasions when there is no substitute for a written communication between business people. Many times, a formal document is desirable or even required in order to do business. The recipient may need a letter for further reference. A situation may demand the considered thought and attention that letter writing provides.

In short, the business letter is not only alive and well, but thriving in the modern business environment. Most of the new technology (word processing, for example) serves only to make letter writing more efficient and effective.

Unfortunately, much business correspondence today still reads as if it were conducted only between white, Anglo-Saxon males in high starched collars who dictate to female stenographers wearing white blouses and long skirts. Except where specifically required, this archaic formality should yield to a relaxed, clear style of business correspondence. The samples in this book attempt, wherever appropriate, to exemplify this principle.

What should modern executives keep in mind when consulting these samples and preparing to write their own letters? The following are some basic guidelines:

- Clarity is the cardinal virtue of all business correspondence—letters are written to improve communications and understanding, not muddy the waters.
- Keep the firmest possible grasp on the context of the letter—why it is being written and what goal it is intended to achieve.
- Even the most formal letter should exhibit evidence that the writer is a real human being—business does not require impersonality.

- Courtesy is never amiss, even if the situation is less than friendly—courtesy greases the wheels of commerce.
- Style and tone should be appropriate for the occasion—the right "voice" makes a letter effective.
- Care with technicalities and mechanics will be repaid—a good-looking letter with non-sexist language and the proper forms of address will be better received (even if only subconsciously) than a sloppy, insensitive one.

Above all, a good business letter is written with a clear and precise understanding of its *purpose*. In more routine cases, the purpose is clear and an almost automatic part of a particular business situation: asking the cost of goods, for example. Yet writing a good letter becomes more and more important as the purpose becomes more subtle and the circumstances less obvious. Letters intended to exert control or to persuade or to clarify complex dealings must bring to bear all the talents of the business executive.

This book is meant to help.

A Guide to Using This Book: How to Find The Letters You Need

In order to locate a sample letter, ask: "What is the business activity associated with writing this letter?"

The sample letters in *The Director's and Officer's Complete Letter Book* are organized and arranged into chapters that correspond to specific categories of business activity:

1. All-Purpose Management: Letters for Daily Executive Business
2. Hiring and Firing: Letters About Employment
3. People at Work: Letters Dealing with Employees
4. The Customer Is Usually Right: Letters to Clients and Customers
5. Making the Deal: Sales and Marketing Letters
6. Money Matters: Letters About Finance
7. The Owners: Letters to Stockholders
8. Changing Corporate Control: Letters Concerning Mergers and Acquisitions
9. Credit and Collections: Letters to Extend and Letters to Collect
10. Buying Goods and Services: Letters for Purchasing
11. Dealing with Government: Letters to Officials
12. In the News: Letters to the Media
13. The International Marketplace: Letters for Doing Business Abroad
14. Local Responsibilities: Letters Concerning Community Affairs.
15. Courtesy and Feelings: Social and Personal Letters
16. Part of the Profession: Letters About Professional Activities

Individual letters within these chapters have their own descriptive titles, such as "Cover Letter for Enclosures," "Making a Job Offer," "Performance Appraisal Letter," "Follow-up Sales Letter," and so on.

The tools for finding specific sample letters are the Contents and the Index:

Contents. The Contents describes each chapter with a title that tells you what category of business activity it covers. Even more specifically, the Contents also gives a description of each individual sample letter within the chapter ("Welcoming a New Client," "Contacting an Inactive Account," "Direct Mail Sales Letter," and so on).

The Contents, therefore, is the first place to consult when looking for a specific sample letter.

For example, if you need to write a letter to sell your company's product to a client, you should look for an appropriate model in Chapter 5, "Making the Deal: Sales and Marketing Letters" which contains sample letters of the kind written by executives and company officers when they want to make sales or to contact potential customers. If you are faced with buying supplies for your company, look at Chapter 10, "Buying Goods and Services: Letters for Purchasing, " which includes sample letters that might be written when buying materials or services.

By using the Contents with its general descriptions of business activity and detailed descriptions of individual letters, you should be able to locate rapidly the model letter you need.

Index. In the back of the book, the Index lists all the individual sample letters under broad subject headings. If you look under an appropriate subject, the page numbers for sample letters are given.

For example, if you need a letter thanking an employee for a good suggestion, then you would look in the Index for "Employee Suggestions" or "Thanks" and find a page reference to a letter called "Thanks for an Employee Suggestion" in Chapter 4. Or, if you need a letter advising a client on an investment, you would consult the Index under "Advice" or "Investments" and find a reference to the letter called "Giving Specific Advice" in Chapter 6.

The subject headings in the Index are arranged alphabetically.

Contents

Chapter Three—PEOPLE AT WORK:
Letters Dealing Employee Relations   63

Chapter Four—THE CUSTOMER IS USUALLY RIGHT:
Letters to Clients and Customers   91

Chapter Eight—CHANGING CORPORATE CONTROL:
Letters Concerning Mergers
And Acquisitions   197

Chapter Nine—CREDIT AND COLLECTIONS:
Letters About Loans, Accounts,
And Overdues   215

Chapter Thirteen—THE INTERNATIONAL MARKETPLACE:
Letters for Doing Business
Abroad   315

Chapter Fourteen—LOCAL RESPONSIBILITIES:
Letters Concerning
Community Affairs   339

Chapter Fifteen—COURTESY:
Social and Personal Letters 365

Chapter Sixteen—PART OF THE PROFESSION:
Letters About Professional
Activities 395

Chapter Seventeen—GREAT LETTERS FROM THE PAST

DIRECTOR'S AND OFFICER'S COMPLETE LETTER BOOK

1

ALL-PURPOSE MANAGEMENT: LETTERS FOR DAILY EXECUTIVE BUSINESS

High-level business executives must deal with a host of day-to-day matters that are apparently simple, recurring, and routine. Few of these letters will be earth-shattering in impact, but the wise executive who wants to save time and to work efficiently will focus attention on such day-to-day letters. These communications establish a tone and standard for good business, and they provide an opportunity for the individual executive to infuse a sense of personality into otherwise routine matters. To save time, many of these letters (as demonstrated in the following examples) may be created once, set up in a standard form, and used over and over again. If the original is thoughtfully written, then the initial effort will have positive effects over a long period of time with a minimum of further effort. Letters designed to pass on information or give instructions call for clarity and conciseness, as demonstrated in the following examples.

Letter of Appreciation

LEASE-TECH
P.O. BOX 78
WEBSTER GROVES, MO

May 9, 19—

Mrs. Karen H. Samuels
Samuels Advertising, Inc.
333 Revlore Building
Webster Groves, MO

Dear Mrs. Samuels:

I want you to know what a delight it has been to work with you and your company during the past six months.

Your campaign on our behalf has not only been exciting, but it has gotten results. Our business is up by 20 percent, which I attribute almost entirely to the new print ads.

I can tell you that this is the first time in my experience that an ad agency really made a difference.

Moreover, it has been a personal pleasure to work with you. You listen well and respond to what you hear—that's pretty rare in the advertising world.

I'm looking forward to a continued relationship.

Yours truly,

Phyllis K. Gann
President

Tips and Comment:

If a business relationship goes especially well, a letter of appreciation will go far toward making it even better. Everyone wants to be loved—even in a business situation—and an expression of approbation is always welcome. Such letters will vary in tone, depending on the personal relationship of the writer and recipient. A letter to someone you don't know well should be warm and exude genuine appreciation, but it need not be effusive or inappropriately cozy.

Alternative A:

I'm certain you will be happy to hear that we think your service on the Hastings account was the best we have ever received. We could not be more pleased with your performance.

I hope that we can continue to work together in the future whenever a suitable project appears.

I'll be certain to stay in touch.

Alternative B:

Thanks for your continued support during our shake-down period at the Jamestown plant. We managed to get the new equipment on-line a day sooner than scheduled, due mostly to the quick adjustment phase.

I will be happy to communicate my positive feelings to any of your other clients or potential clients.

Rest assured that if we need similar service in the future, we will call you first.

Alternative C:

This is just to let you know again how much I appreciate working with you. We have undertaken a lot of joint ventures during the last year, and I think I haven't paused often enough to tell you how I value your help and appreciate the support.

It looks as though there will be few chances to work with you during the next six months, but as soon as something promising comes up, I'll let you know.

Meanwhile, thanks again.

Complimenting Outside Staff

WINE INSTITUTE
717 MARKET STREET
SAN FRANCISCO, CA

December 13, 19—

Peter Simon, Sales Manager
Hotel Fountleroy
231 King Street
San Francisco, CA

Dear Mr. Simon:

We have been holding our monthly meetings in the Banquet Room of your hotel for more than a year, and this seems like an appropriate time to compliment you and your staff for the excellent food and service we have had at every one of our meetings.

Please give all your workers in the Banquet Room and your chef and his staff our sincere thanks and appreciation.

Sincerely,

Fred C. Dobbs
Executive Director

Tips and Comment:

Letting people know when their service is appreciated is simple, courteous, and usually guarantees continued good service in the future. Such letters need not be overdone—a letter that expresses more than is properly due may be suspected of insincerity—but honest appreciation is always welcome, especially by the people who really do the work.

Alternative A:

Thanks to your efficient staff, our monthly meetings have been pleasant and enjoyable ever since we began to hold them in your Banquet Room.

Please let everyone involved know how much the Institute appreciates the fine service.

Alternative B:

I don't want the end of the year to go by without letting you know how much the members of the Wine Institute have enjoyed our monthly meetings at your hotel. Some of the places we had tried before failed to deliver, but you and your staff have been tops.

We certainly intend to continue to meet at the Fountleroy.

Tell all your people we like the service.

Alternative C:

It's not often one encounters first-rate service month after month, so I want to tell you how much we have appreciated the conditions at your hotel.

Our monthly meetings, which we've held in the Banquet Room for more than a year now, have been highlighted by good food and fast, efficient service, and we've never had a single problem with scheduling.

Thanks to everyone on your staff, from the busboys to the chef.

Thanks to a Speaker

BPI COMMUNICATIONS, INC.
475 TERRACE AVENUE
MINNEAPOLIS, MN

October 12, 19—

William R. Bradley, Ph.D.
School of Communications
West Rockover, PA

Dear Dr. Bradley:

Your lecture, "The Next New Wave of the Future," at our company symposium last week was informative and interesting. In fact, your imaginative presentation was the highlight of the meeting.

The audience enjoyed the sneak preview of future global communications, and the standing ovation you received reflected their appreciation.

All of us at the symposium thank you for an outstanding presentation. We hope you will be able to come again next year.

Cordially,

Harvey S. Doke
President

Tips and Comment:

A follow-up letter to a speaker is routine. However, if the presentation was really good, a special note of gratitude is appropriate, particularly if a return engagement is desired. Be specific about the best points of the presentation and the reaction of the audience.

Alternative A:

I want you to know how stimulating we all found your speech at our company symposium last week. The halls and offices have been abuzz with comment on what you told us.

Thanks for doing such a great job.

Can you put us on your schedule again for next year?

Alternative B:

Your superb presentation at the BPI Communication Annual Business Symposium was the high point of the week. All of us thought you gave everyone in the room much to think about.

The consensus is that we would like you to consider speaking at the next meeting of our trade association, which is scheduled for early in the new year.

Will you be free in January for a trip to Puerto Rico? Let me know if you are available.

Alternative C:

Great job! I've seldom heard a talk that set me thinking so much. In fact, I still find myself mulling over what you said.

Could you suggest any books or articles for further reading? I hate to let these ideas go at this stage, and I'd appreciate being able to educate myself more.

Have you thought of going on the lecture circuit in a big way? If you're interested, give me a call, since I have many contacts in the field.

Thanks again.

Complaint to a Service Provider

FARMERS TRUST AND SAVINGS BANK
510 ELM STREET
WILLIAMSBURG, IA

January 11, 1989

Mr. James Troppett
President
Computer Assist, Inc.
P.O. Box 334
Cedar Valley, IA

Dear Jim:

Congratulations! For two years running your firm has caused me grave concern and great consternation.

Why do you want to do this to me?

What are you trying to do to this bank?

Why do I ask these questions? Let me explain!

At year-end 1987, CAI converted their payroll clients to another processor during the last month of the year. I reported the hardship this created, plus made my feelings known on this issue with customer representative Alissa May Parks. I did not send a letter but indicated my displeasure orally. I'm sure it is well documented in our file. Enough said.

This year, we converted our general ledger format to the Financial Control System (FCS). Again, this conversion was made during the last month of 1988.

Will I ever learn?

But wait! During April of 1988 this bank made a commitment to convert to FCS. We selected a time period in October. We had an understanding it was compatible with CAI scheduling. September arrives, and I'm told we'll have to back up implementation to December.

What to do?

Well, we decided to proceed in December. We felt we had the assurance that we would have help all along and got the feeling this was "old hat" for CAI. During December, Mary Jones provided exceptional and knowledge-able service during the pre–year-end conversion phase. We had excellent contact. After year-end, it seems we lost all face-to-face communication.

What went wrong?

1. Our income statement did not zero out.
2. We did not have the personal contact of a representative to reinforce our working knowledge of the system. We were led to believe that this would happen with our year-end entries and reports. (The manual is great but when we decided on a December conversion we felt we would be receiving the face-to-face reinforcement and support.)
3. If I had $1.00 for every computer sheet you've run for the re-run retro statement I could pay your bill for a month! (And I don't think I'm exaggerating!)
4. We had our CPAs scheduled to review the bank tax records last Friday. They kept their appointment but they did not have an accurate statement based on year-end entries. They did this manually from the last year-end statement. This took one of them two and a half hours to calculate by hand. This is all something that could have been handled by a working computerized general ledger system!

Do you know how much they charge? Answer: PLENTY!

Jim, when representatives of competing data processing bureaus or in-house systems come marching through they tell me that we are paying premium dollars. But I also tell them I believe we are getting premium service. Problems such as this make me wonder!

What can be done?

Potential solutions:

1. never NEVER ever EVER again do a conversion in December.

2.
3.

I don't know; I'll have to think about it and fill in the blanks later.

Jim, can you understand why I ask these questions?

You need to understand I'm the guy with mud on my face. Prior to this conversion, my staff addressed the problem of December conversions, but I pooh-poohed them. I truly felt that with the competence of your staff assisting mine, and your previous experience with FCS, we could surmount any year-end conversion concerns.

Sincerely,

John R. Jones
President
(Courtesy of John R. Jones, Williamsburg, Iowa)

Tips and Comments:

Sometimes, getting the attention of the reader is the first goal of a letter. While it is not a good idea to be too cute, something out of the ordinary will often get the best results, or at least lead to a fruitful discussion of the problem. In the foregoing real-life example, the writer used an unusual format and approach, but it seems almost certain the recipient sat up and took notice. In other situations, a simpler, more straightforward letter of complaint may be sufficient. Be certain to state clearly the exact nature of the difficulty and what is expected by way of correction.

Cover Letter for Enclosures

TREES UNLIMITED
45 FORESTRY DRIVE
TIMMER, WI

February 3, 19—

Mr. Samuel L. Powers
Corner Nursery
23 West Mail Street
Hanover, IN

Dear Mr. Powers:

Enclosed is our spring wholesalers' catalog, which lists all of our products and prices.

This catalog replaces the one you now have. Please use the new version for pricing and odering stock.

If I can be of any help, please let me know.

Sincerely,

John Goody
District Manager

Tips and Comment:

Cover letters are among the most routine of all business correspondence, yet they should always be accurate and succinct. They are usually more of a polite reflex than a vital message—presumably the recipient will understand the enclosures and the reason they are sent—but some occasions call for extended explanation. Avoid the archaic "Please find enclosed..." formula and be direct.

Alternative A:

Enclosed are the contracts for the Lothario Project.

Note that changes have been made on page A-2 as you requested.

Unless there are further changes, please have these documents signed and distributed to the proper places.

Alternative B:

Enclosed is a copy of the engineer's report, as you requested.

Please call me with any comments after you review the data.

Alternative C:

Enclosed is a copy of my letter to John. As you can see, we are in trouble on this one, and I don't see how we can recoup our position in time.

If you have any bright ideas, let me know.

Verifying Information

MONARCH CORPORATION
34 FLOWERS ROAD
GRANGER, FL

September 19, 19—

Ms. Laraine Hodges
Supervisor
Janklow and Co.
P.O. Box 1234
Bentonville, TX

Dear Ms. Hodges:

The Monarch Corporation operates three Janklow programs as part of our Florida manufacturing operations.

Recently, we learned from one of your salespeople that Janklow intends to replace the programs with new products.

In order to plan a smooth continuation of our work, I would like to confirm this information and ask if you have a projected date for the change.

It seems likely that we would be interested in the replacement programs, but consideration will call for long-range planning.

I hope you can supply the information. Thanks.

Sincerely,

Alan Alden
Manager

Tips and Comment:

Verifying or requesting information is a common form of business correspondence. The usual rules apply to such letters: state your need with clarity and work to eliminate any confusion about what you are after. It is the responsibility of the writer to establish a clear channel of communication. A certain amount of ordinary courtesy will also work toward assuring a reply.

Alternative A:

Do six-pound packages of Agropro come with the retail price printed on the box, or do retailers need to mark them?

We need to know this in order to service our distribution network, and we do not as yet have any samples from the factory.

We would appreciate any guidance you can supply on this matter.

Alternative B:

I have recently learned that Gompers, Inc. makes a four-pronged widget for electronic capacitors.

Is this true, and if so, what are your unit prices?

My company uses approximately 3,000 four-pronged widgets per year, and we are looking for a new source of component supply.

I'd be happy to discuss this with a sales representative.

Alternative C:

Can you verify that Model 34 units should be run at no more than 30 percent rated capacity during prolonged sessions?

We have been having trouble with our Model 34, and one of our operators had word-of-mouth information that we want to nail down.

Any technical help you can offer will be very much appreciated.

Confirming Arrangements or Reservations

RAM-TECH, INC.
ONE PARK PLAZA
NEW YORK, NY

October 13, 19—

Mr. Jan Herder
Customer Service Representative
Hilton Hotel
Sunset, NJ

Dear Mr. Herder:

Please confirm a reservation for Ram-Tech, Inc. for a meeting room on Thursday, November 15, from 9:30 A.M. to 4:00 P.M.

I need to have a contract for the room, catered lunch, and coffee breaks, as we discussed on the phone yesterday.

Thanks for your help.

Sincerely,

Robert F. Quimby
Sales Manager

Tips and Comment:

It is simple routine to send letters confirming or requesting confirmation of arrangements, and these can usually be entrusted to subordinates for drafting. However, executives and managers should check even such routine letters to be certain the form is correct and the information accurate. If an office sends out a good many such confirmation letters it may repay the effort to devise a standard form letter.

Alternative A:

This is to confirm your reservations for a party of 50 at 6:00 P.M. on Wednesday, December 5.

We will serve cocktails and snacks at 6:00 P.M., followed by a prime rib dinner at 7:30 P.M.

The price per person will be $27.50, plus a 15 percent gratuity. No cancellations will be taken after November 30.

Alternative B:

I'd like to confirm my reservation for three nights at the hotel, May 3–5, with a meeting room for May 5.

Please let me know in writing.

Alternative C:

This is to confirm our use of the concert hall on the evening of Tuesday, January 22.

We will require set-up by 5:30 P.M. and will vacate the hall by 11:15 P.M.

Please let me know if any other arrangements need to be made.

Setting Up a Meeting

REGINA MEMORIAL HOSPITAL
23 HOSPITAL DRIVE
ALLAMAKEE, IA

October 23, 19—

Ms. Wendy Keynes
Chief Administrator
Battelle Hospital
333 Lantern Way
Cairo, IL

Dear Ms. Keynes:

I will be traveling through Cairo on November 7, and I would very much like to stop and meet with you concerning the latest Medicare rulings on compensation.

You have been referred to me by John Parent in Dubuque as a real expert on this.

We have been having great difficulty with getting the forms through in less than three months. I hope you can give me some guidance.

I can arrange to be at the hospital any time between 10:00 A.M. and 3:30 P.M.

Truly yours,

Karyn J. Matthews
Administrator

Tips and Comment:

When making arrangements for a business meeting, it is important to be accurate and precise about dates, times, and places, as well as making clear the circumstances of the meeting and the subject matter. This sample not only broaches the time and place, but gives the recipient a good idea of what will be discussed. The writer has also included a personal reference.

Alternative A:

Since we will both be at the Annual Conference in Seattle next week, I suggest we meet for a half hour or so to discuss the next stage in the planning phase.

According to the pre-meeting schedule, there is an open period at 3:00 P.M. on Thursday. Let's plan to meet then.

I'll call your room or leave a message for you when I arrive at the hotel.

Alternative B:

Please schedule a meeting with the Budget Committee for next Wednesday, June 23, in Conference Room B of the headquarters building at 2:00 P.M.

We will discuss the impact of the latest change in Burnham's income. You should have received a report on this previously.

It is expected that the meeting will last at least two hours.

If you cannot attend, please let me know as soon as possible.

Alternative C:

I think we need to talk privately when I'm in town for next week's Board meeting.

Can you meet me at the Lamplighter for drinks and dinner on the 5th?

I'll confirm this when I see you at the meeting, but I wanted to get it set up ahead of time.

Agenda Letter

TRULLOW PRODUCTS
P.O. BOX 3421
WEST REDDING, MS

June 6, 19—

Mr. James F. Oppos
Jitterbug, Inc.
23 Edgewood
Inglewood, AR

Dear Jim:

The schedule for the meeting next month is:
- 8:00 A.M. — Breakfast
- 9:30 A.M. — Opening discussion
- 12:00 noon — Lunch
- 1:30 P.M. — Reply discussion
- 4:00 P.M. — Adjourn

The agenda for the discussions will be:
- Interlocking economic factors
- Sales projections
- Optional expansion
- Capital projections
- Counter proposals
- Criteria

This should be a crucial meeting and discussion.

Truly yours,

Kenneth L. Pratt
President

Tips and Comment:

Pay special attention to the format of agenda letters. Techniques such as bullets, numbered points, indentation, underlining, and boldface may be manipulated to add clarity and impact to agenda letters. Most formal business meetings go better when attendees follow an agenda, and meetings go better still if participants receive the agenda before the meeting by means of a letter or memo.

Alternative A:

When we meet next week in Dallas, the discussions will include:

1. Financing the addition of four new salespeople
2. How to handle the profits from the Hancher contract
3. Morale problems in the Dallas office

If we can reach agreement and solutions on these points, it will be a successful meeting.

Alternative B:

Here's the agenda for the meeting with Hamilton Associates:
Our schedule for the project
—begin date
—first level analysis
—preliminary report
—final report
—The nature of the final report
—Planning for the next stages.
I'd like you to coordinate the presentation visuals.

Alternative C:

Even though we know what is coming up, here is a formal agenda for the meeting (it can't hurt to have a plan):
—Mop up on Phase 1 of the Suitland Project
—Marketing plans for next year
—Discussion of John's proposal
—Cash flow and investment after Suitland
Let me know if there is anything else to talk about.

Giving Instructions

GEMTECH, INC.
HEADQUARTERS OFFICE
393 PLEASANT DRIVE
WADLEY, AL

July 26, 19—

Ms. Jane M. Doe
Systems Manager
Gemtech, Inc.
Mississippi Division
Passavent, MS

Dear Jane:

Please assign an Engineering Order number to every charge over $10 and return the printout. For charges under $10, accumulate until the total exceeds $10 or combine with other charges that have the same order number.

You need not return the printout if any have no costs to transfer out of overhead.

We can communicate more cheaply than by toll calls—for example, by WATS line, telex, or mailgram. Please use toll calls only as a last resort.

Yours truly,

John Doe
Group Manager
(Courtesy of Robert S. Burger, Burger Associates, Glen Mills, PA.)

Tips and Comment:

Letters of instruction, especially within the same company, are similar to memos. They may dispense with some of the standard formal courtesies of external letters, but the tone should be carefully controlled to give the correct impression of the nature of the message. This example, drawn from a business writing class, employs a generally neutral tone, giving little hint of approval or disapproval and aiming at transmitting clear, unambiguous directions. Even the implied criticism of previous methods of communication is couched in value-free terms.

Alternative A:

The third shift at the Decatur plant has slipped slightly below the benchmark for defect rates on the 101/DR. Our analysis shows that the balancing wedges are consistently off by .03 degrees in slightly more than 32 percent of the production runs.

If you adjust the machines for the extra humidity, we believe the problem will be solved.

Be certain to monitor the production on the third shift closely and report your findings.

Alternative B:

You should be using four-color process on all divisional price lists.

The task force report of last month specified this change, and we want to see it put in place as soon as possible.

Please review the report and plan to alter the procedure as soon as possible.

Alternative C:

Please make a change from Express Mail to commercial overnight courier. We have discovered that the overall savings is worth the slight inconvenience.

We have set up a headquarters account to which all shipments may be billed.

This change should also cut the downtime.

Schedule Letter

AMERITECHNOL, INC.
INDUSTRY ROAD
ANY CITY, NH

March 10, 19—

Mr. James Doe
Factory Service, Inc.
111 West Grand
Any Town, NH

Dear Mr. Doe:

Before you publish the October schedule, please reschedule:

1. 02312 DOR Org and Corr Input due from 1600 to 1400. The current schedule wastes two hours. The users (IC and Polymers Accounting, C&F Accounting, and Corporate Accounting) should turn around their corrections within two hours. The reduction of input to the next edit will shorten keypunch and computer turnaround time.
2. 00485 A/P Freight Trial Balance Report due from Day 10 to Day 8 Charlie Guilden says he needs this report to apply adjustments to the DORs. The final adjustments are due out at 0800 on Day 9 and we need at least a two-day backup.

Also, please review and revise the budget schedule to eliminate the computer-time conflict we experienced during the February closing.

Sincerely,

John Doe
(Courtesy of Robert S. Burger, Burger Associates, Glen Mills, PA)

Tips and Comment:

Most businesses run on schedules. The writer of this schedule letter (an actual business person) chose to structure the presentation of the revised schedule carefully so that no ambiguities could creep in. The numbered points make the presentation clear. The changes are stated exactly, along with the rationale for the alterations.

Alternative A:

The schedule for the meeting to be held in Boston on May 4 is:

10:00 A.M.—Opening statements

11:00 A.M.—Production presentation

12:00 noon—Lunch

1:00 P.M.—Sales presentation

2:00 P.M.—Summary

2:30 P.M.—Adjournment

You may schedule your travel times accordingly.

Alternative B:

Here is a draft schedule for Phase 1 of the Hurstville project. Please review it and let me know if I can distribute the information to the staff.

March 1—Begin research at Hurstville site

March 15—Research complete; begin data analysis

April 5—Data analysis complete; begin consultation

April 15—Begin final report

May 1—Final Phase 1 report submitted

Mary thought we should allow more time for the data analysis, but I think we can do it on this schedule.

Alternative C:

I'd like to suggest the following:

Begin input—June 3

   Analyze graphs—June 15

   Meeting in Richmond—July 7

   Implementation—August 1

If we push this any further into the fall, we will have severe problems with the weather. But, if we adhere to this schedule, our machines will be clear long before the first storms.

Report to a Client

STANDARD LABORATORIES
ANY TOWN, NY

October 12, 19—

Mr. John D. Doe
Ajax Company
Any City, NJ

Dear Mr. Doe:

We find that the 44 percent formaldehyde solution returned from Ajax's storage tank is contaminated with a urea-type compound, and when butyl alcohol is added, a butylated urea-type formaldehyde forms.

Your formaldehyde contained 4,800 ppm nitrogen-containing compounds (as NH_3) versus 1.7 ppm in a Gowansburg sample.

On standing, a globule of gummy material settles out of the turbid solution resulting from mixing your sample with an equal amount of butyl alcohol. When the globule is air-dried, it becomes a polymeric film. An infrared spectrum suggests the film is a butylated urea-type resin.

If we can be of further help, please contact us.

Truly yours,

James F. Doe, Ph.D.
Chief Chemist
(Courtesy of Robert S. Burger, Burger Associates, Glen Mills, PA)

Tips and Comment:

A report letter forms the standard "product" of many types of service companies. In this model letter, drawn from a real-life example, the report is highly technical, yet the essential information is expressed so clearly as to make the gist of the report understandable to any layperson. The letter writer achieves this clarity by using technical terms only when absolutely necessary—the names of chemicals and compounds, for example—and by constructing a clear narrative of the testing procedure.

Alternative A:

Our market survey analysis of sales of your projected widgets shows a significant probability that the widgets would sell in Manville at a rate of 45 percent of those contacted.

We surveyed 1,000 households, selected at random, and asked a series of questions about widget-buying habits and what qualities consumers look for in widgets (see attached questionnaire).

The response rates to all questions indicate a favorable response to medium quality widgets in the $4.50 to $5.25 price range. The enclosed tables show the exact figures.

Please call on us for any further explanation.

Alternative B:

I have completed the study and present my findings in the attached report.

In short form, my conclusion points to a defect in your mid-level organization. The office managers are, in general, unable to complete the necessary steps called for in your operating plan. It is my opinion that no amount of pressure on the office managers will improve their performance significantly. I think the solution will be to restructure the preliminary stages and allow more time for the intermediate steps.

Call me when you have read the report, if more explanation is needed.

Alternative C:

The results of our work indicate you should begin to move swiftly into print media rather than direct mail.

Over 85 percent of your identifiable customers are subscribers to either the daily press or a weekly news magazine, but only 15 percent acknowledge that they open and read their own mail (most is intercepted by office staff). The high expense of direct mail would be wasted on this potential audience.

Internal Report Letter

AMALGAMATED TECHNOLOGIES
56 TRIDENT ROAD
ANY TOWN, DE

September 10, 19—

Mr. James Doe
Vice-President for Operations
Amalgamated Technologies
Techno Drive
Any City, MD

Dear Mr. Doe:

Of my four recommendations, Plant Manager Rudy Santos implemented 3 and 4 immediately but is still considering 1 and 2, which are critical.

Rudy asked whether anything could be done about occasional delays in getting special export containers for shipping light ends. Tom Crow asked Export Manager Jay Balderston to determine where the delays occurred, and Jay has corrected the problem.

Rudy also says he needs an updated Inventory Control Manual. We have recently written a new one that we will distribute to all inventory users.

The attached was delayed because I was involved in Distribution's training program for new customer-service people and heavy operational support.

Sincerely,

John Doe
(Courtesy of Robert S. Burger, Burger Associates, Glen Mills, PA)

Tips and Comment:

Report letters should follow the same guidelines as other messages intended to convey information concisely and clearly: be accurate, direct, and complete. This sample manages to explain, without becoming overly defensive, why suggested changes are still pending and why the report was delayed. A clean explication of the facts and sequence of events is substituted for excuses, and the overall effect is convincing.

Alternative A:

We have taken the steps you requested and changed the procedures in processing the closing statements.

So far, the results have been mixed. Our speed has increased but the rate of errors continues to be unacceptably high.

I will review the entire process again with the staff and emphasize the need to clear up the problem. It's costing the company money.

Alternative B:

The revised staging of components was put in place last week, and we have already seen improvements in the degrading rates, including the final end-of-the-week run.

I compiled the enclosed report over the weekend.

While it may be too soon to say with total certainty, I think the degrading problem is solved. Our follow-up study this week should tell us definitively.

Alternative C:

As the enclosed table shows, our retention rates are now holding steady and may even have begun creeping upward. This appears to be a direct response to the February mailing.

If the trend continues, we should reinstitute the program and put it into the mail again (with new lists) in June.

I will ask Helen to do a budget breakdown for the projected costs and have it to you by the 3rd.

Solving a Problem

TECHO-ALLIED, INC.
123 RIVER STREET
ANYTOWN, PA

March 15, 19—

Mr. James F. Doe
Plant Manager
Techo-Allied, Inc.
Industrial Drive
Any City, NJ

Dear Jim:

I recommend we test the process of steam-blowing filter cake in the Schenk Filter as a less costly alternative to solvent washing for RCRA compliance.

Our current procedure, nitrogen blowing, does not produce a filter cake acceptable for landfill; its organic leachability exceeds RCRA specs. Solvent washing is more effective but would require a much larger investment.

Steam-blowing the filter cake should make the polyol less viscous and may remove enough of it to meet RCRA regulations; it should at least reduce solvent-washing costs. Also, steam costs less than nitrogen.

Economic calculations and experimental criteria are attached.

Sincerely,

John Doe
Chief Process Engineer
(Courtesy of Robert S. Burger, Burger Associates, Glen Mills, PA)

Tips and Comment:

This sample letter aims at solving a technical processing problem that has significant financial and operational repercussions. The writer has wisely chosen to avoid technical jargon, and he explains the solution to the problem with great clarity, leaving no doubt about what action he recommends.

Alternative A:

The registration problems can be solved by replacing the pin-guide system on Unit No. 10. This should alleviate the lateral play in the unit and allow for the necessary adjustments during the run.

The cost of a new pin system is about $4,000, but if we can reduce the spoilage rates significantly the expenditure will be repaid within the next six months.

Please contact the equipment supplier and get a firm price and delivery date.

Alternative B:

We have pinpointed the balance problems to the machine on Line A. This is an old piece of equipment and apparently it will not hold tolerances during a complete cycle.

You will need to replace either the grommets or the demi-widgets. The downtime will probably run two days, but we cannot continue to produce so many out-of-balance bungees.

Let me know if you need a back-up on this.

Alternative C:

The report from Fred shows yet another sale lost this month due to fouled up records. We must take action immediately to solve this problem.

I suggest that we switch immediately to the ARCHIVE software. I know it will cause some confusion at first, but in the long run it will straighten out the front-end difficulties.

We have the program cued up here and can transmit it to you whenever you are ready. Let's try to have it in place by the 15th.

Follow-Up to a Meeting

CONGRO MANUFACTURING
78 CONGRO PLACE
ANYTOWN, NJ

March 12, 19—

Division Managers:

Representatives from Plan Betterment, Engineering Services, and Power Plan Additions met March 10 to identify specific problems with the system and plan corrective action. To make the system work:

Engineering Services will

- list the index numerically and check for multiple listings for identical drawings at different revision levels
- retain all drawing numbers even when drawings are redone
- hire two summer engineering students to correct the mistakes in location codes, descriptions, etc.
- improve cross reference among RS&T, FF and manufacturer's drawing numbers
- identify all changes on the updated Master Drawing List with an asterisk ahead of each number that changes are made for.

Plant Betterment will

- help Engineering Services draft a letter with instructions on how to identify revised drawings (see attached flow diagram)
- prepare a purchase order for a microfilm hard copy machine for each fossil plant.

Bob Hughes says the fossil plants' present systems will be converted to STAIRS—a system that uses a computer to sort key words and easily locates drawings within minutes—when manpower committed to the Somerville project become available.

Truly yours,

John Doe
(Courtesy of Robert S. Burger, Burger Associates, Glen Mills, PA)

Tips and Comment:

This letter, sent as a follow-up after an important company meeting, serves to reinforce the decisions made and the assignments that resulted. The format is exceptionally clear, leaving no doubt about who is to do what. Letters (or memos) such as this one are important when representatives from several divisions or corporate sub-organizations make decisions during group discussions. The letter aids the memories of the people who attend the meeting and clarifies what actions need to take place.

Alternative A:

Our meeting on the 12th was productive. I came away with a new understanding of the way the widget system should work.

John will take responsibility for writing the new operations manual, and Helen will provide the technical backup.

We will shoot for a finished draft by the end of next month.

Alternative B:

Our long-term marketing strategy session on Wednesday produced a list of potential clients and an overall approach.

Media will follow up on the budget planning with projections for the next six months.

Creative will coordinate with Technical to be certain we have the key points at the heart of the copy.

I will assemble the presentation of the plan before the Board meeting in June.

Alternative C:

Here are the assignments we agreed on:

1. Harry's group will re-draw the schematics for the HD-102.
2. John will check the operating ranges with the OEM people.
3. My staff will coordinate.

Conference Report Letter

MANAGEMENT GROUP, INC.
NEW ENGLAND DIVISION
333 GLENDOVER AVENUE
ANYTOWN, NH

October 4, 19—

Ms. Jane Doe
Senior Vice President
Management Group, Inc.
24 Downs Trace
Any Town, GA

Dear Jane:

Three facts surfaced during the Intercomm Users Group Conference that will interest our group:

Release 8.0 will replace 7.1 (our current version) on October 15.

SAINT, a new software package, allows users to interactively design, modify, and delete screen maps.

An *information retireval system* designed by Insurance Systems of America supports most database systems.

Also, I believe we should consider STORBE (a program-analysis and fine-tuning package) and Enhanced Log Analysis for our cost-reduction program.

These conferences are informative and provide industry-wide contacts. I recommend we continue to attend.

Sincerely,

John Doe
Divisions Systmes Manager
(Courtesy of Robert S. Burger, Burger Associates, Glen Mills, PA)

Tips and Comment:

The foregoing example, actually written by an executive as part of a course on business writing, demonstrates a commendably brisk approach to reporting on an outside conference. The style is clear, concise, direct, and informative. It also demonstrates the use of "bullets" to summarize several points. This technique allows the writer to highlight specific points and draw special attention to information that might have less impact if presented in a more conventional fashion.

Alternative A:

The conference on collection and credit techniques for accounting firms was excellent, and I came away with several good ideas that we should consider.

I am forwarding a full report along with my recommendations.

Note particularly the section on third-level follow-ups, which is where we have had trouble.

Alternative B:

The conference in San Francisco on the new federal regulations was a disappointment. The conference planners failed to take into account the needs of companies like ours, and consequently, most of the sessions focused on formatting rather than reporting, which is where we need help.

This is the third conference in a row by this group that has been a waste of our time and money, so I recommend we look for another source of information.

Alternative C:

Here are the highlights of the conference:

- Discovery of a new performance pattern makes the usual routine of H-34 obsolete.
- A new procedure should be put in place immediately—the speakers all recommended L-546.
- The rerouting of hyper fluids is no longer necessary under the new industry protocols.

I'd like you to contact the people at Hurley and begin the changeovers.

Management Report Letter

AMALGAMATED FLUIDS CORPORATION
124 WEST REARDON STREET
ANYTOWN, LA

July 15, 19—

Mr. James Doe
Task Force Director
Amalgamated Fluids Corporation
22 Lakeland Drive
Any City, TX

Dear Jim

The 500-ton tank backlog problem has been solved, but we must watch order buildup and empty tank availability closely to prevent if from recurring.

We established a 60-day partial moratorium on orders, effective August 1; increased the empty-return rate; increased production and shipped according to a priority list; and cut backlog by 200 tanks immediately by using Gulf Atlantic, Houston.

Our success was due to the combined efforts of the task force and Cromwell Works personnel.

Truly yours,

John Doe
Sales Service Coordinator
(Courtesy of Robert S. Burger, Burger Associates, Glen Mills, PA)

Tips and Comment:

Reporting on changes in management or procedures is a frequent duty, especially in companies with many divisions and operating units. As this actual example from a writing class for executives shows, the ideal is to be exquisitely clear about what has happened. It is tempting to over-explain, but the writer in this case has resisted that impulse and produced a letter that presents all the pertinent facts with a minimum of distraction.

Alternative A:

We have solved the persistent problem of the high defect rate from Site No. 2.

Jim Burns, the site manager, discovered that one of the main press rams was misaligned, a fact that did not show up during the usual diagnostics.

A day's work on the calibrations has resulted in a defect rate of no more than 4 percent, well within our tolerance level.

We should notify all site managers to double-check the press rams if their defect rates begin to creep up.

Alternative B:

Please make a change in the billing procedure for WX-1 accounts.

Instead of posting the accounts on the 15th of each month, from now on post on the 10th.

This will allow us more leeway in preparing the end-of-the-month summaries.

Alternative C:

The faulty report for the last quarter can be traced to keyboarding errors in the Milford data-processing section.

We have made an adjustment in the work schedules in the section, and I think this will solve the problem.

Please keep me informed if you spot any further difficulties.

2

HIRING AND FIRING: LETTERS ABOUT EMPLOYMENT

Jobs and job-seeking are central issues in business life: Most executives make job-related decisions about others and, sooner or later, explore new opportunities for themselves. The fact that job-related letters may be emotion-laden or contain hidden agendas makes them particularly difficult to write and requires exquisite attention to both tone and content. The following examples cover a range of situations and provide guides on how to approach what may be tricky requirements. Many of these letters call for a subtlety not needed in other kinds of letters. The good executive will understand the nuances involved.

Letter of Application

HAROLD J. BRODSKY
1432 56TH AVENUE
SUMMIT, NJ

May 23, 19—

Mr. Jerome K. Kunstler
Managing Partner
The Group
P.O. Box 3
Summit, NJ

Dear Mr. Kunstler:

I am applying to you in response to your advertisement in the recent Sunday *New York Times* for an account executive.

As you will see from the enclosed résumé, I have eight years experience as a successful account executive in the New York-New Jersey area, in addition to a B.A. and M.A. in business and public relations.

I am quite happy in my current position, but the job with your firm sounds interesting.

I will look forward to hearing from you.

Yours truly,

Harold J. Brodsky

Tips and Comment:

Few things are more difficult than a cold letter of application for a job: the writer feels naked, anxious, and vulnerable. However, most recipients will be more interested in the facts of the résumé and the writer's career than the letter itself. Unless the circumstances are unusual, such letters are really little more than cover letters. Do not attempt to make cold letters too cute or attention-grabbing; just keep them accurate, clear and businesslike. Make certain to draw the reader's attention, however, to pertinent information such as experience and education.

Alternative A:

This is an application for your open position in the Westover office, which you advertised in yesterday's paper.

I have three years experience in widget sales, and I believe I would fill the qualifications you list.

Enclosed is my résumé.

Please let me know if you are interested.

Alternative B:

I wish to apply for the post of Assistant Manager that was listed in the "Billboard" section of last week's *Business News*.

This is exactly the sort of job I have been looking for, and the qualifications fit my experience and education very well. It would be an exciting prospect.

I am including a résumé and would be happy to discuss this with you on the phone or in person.

Alternative C:

Professional reading sometimes pays off. The notice in last week's *Widget Review* that you are seeking a new manager not only caught my eye, but fired my imagination.

I have several years experience in managing a small widget operation (see the enclosed résumé) and believe I am ready to move on to bigger challenges.

I'd be very pleased to speak to you about the possibilities.

Letter of Recommendation

ESTATE REALTY
SUITE 4
THOMPSON BUILDING
TACOMA, WA

December 10, 19—

To Whom It May Concern:

I am happy to give the highest recommendation to Jane T. Haley, who worked in my office under my direct supervision for five years.

Jane was an extremely competent office manager who speeded the work of our office and oversaw thirteen other workers. Jane's attention to detail and schedules kept our paper-laden business on track and functioning smoothly.

We were very sorry to lose her, but her mother's health demanded that Jane relocate to your area.

You could do no better than place Jane in a position of trust and responsibility.

Sincerely,

Edward F. Gompers
President

Tips and Comment:

Letters of recommendation for former employees should be honest in fact and sincere in tone. If you hesitate to recommend someone, then decline to write the letter. A positive letter should state the relationship with the employee and make clear the opportunities you had to observe the quality of their work. It is also a good idea to say why the worker left.

Alternative A:

It is a pleasure to recommend John McManus. He worked in our sales office for three years and was a consistently high producer.

Moreover, he was a delight to be with and a favorite among his fellow workers, all of whom were sad when he felt it necessary to leave the region.

I would not hesitate to hire John again.

Alternative B:

Harvey Sloan is a fine systems analyst who compiled a strong reputation while working for our company.

He was in my department, and I observed his skills on a weekly basis. His performance appraisals were consistently high, and he had moved steadily upward in the employee salary structure.

It is my impression that he was well liked by his colleagues, although his duties often placed him in a position of potential conflict. I assume, therefore, that his abilities include on-the-job diplomacy.

Please feel free to contact me for further comments.

Alternative C:

Karen Hutchins worked in my department from 19—to 19—. She was responsible for coordinating correspondence from five offices, and she supervised approximately five other employees.

Based on her generally superior performance, I would not hesitate to recommend her for a similar position.

Ms. Hutchins's minor physical disability in no way detracted from her abilities to perform her job well.

Turning Down a Job Applicant

KAISER INDUSTRIES CORPORATION
300 LAKESIDE DRIVE
OAKLAND, CA

January 30, 19—

Ms. Shirley Thomas
321 Overlook Blvd.
Westchester, WY

Dear Ms. Thomas:

Thank you for your recent inquiry about employment with Kaiser Industries Corporation.

We have reviewed your qualifications with the various Kaiser affiliated companies and regret to report that there are no appropriate openings. However, we are taking the liberty of retaining your résumé in our active files in the event of future openings in your field.

We appreciate your interest, and we sincerely hope that we will be able to offer you more encouragement at a later date.

Yours truly,

Susan G. Knoss
Personnel Director

Tips and Comment:

A corporation may receive a large volume of job applications (depending on the size of the company, the state of the economy, and conditions in a specific industry), only a small portion of which will be viable. A standard reply may be devised to turn down unsuccessful applicants. In every case, however, care must be taken to be frank about why the applicant was rejected and even more so about future prospects. In the case of the foregoing letter, the company genuinely believes a job may open up and wants to keep the applicant's credentials on hand. In all situations, it is best to be honest about prospects.

Alternative A:

Thank you for your application, but we have no openings now, nor do we think there will be any in the near future.

Just in case, we will keep your résumé on file.

We appreciate your inquiry and wish you success in your job search.

Alternative B:

I've looked over your résumé with great interest, and I regret that we don't have any openings right now that you are qualified for.

However, I'm impressed with your background, and I'd like to keep in touch with you since we may be expanding some of our operations within the next six months. I can't promise anything, but I'd like you to keep me informed of your address.

I'm sorry we are not in a position to offer you anything now.

Alternative C:

Thank you for your letter and résumé.

I regret to tell you that after screening applications for our current opening, your name is not among the final candidates.

Good luck in your continued job search.

Letter of Resignation

WEATHERBY LEASING, INC.
14 REVAMP ROAD
IRONTON, OH

July 23, 19—

Mr. Larry Weatherby
President
Weatherby Leasing, Inc.
14 Reamp Road
Ironton, OH

Dear Larry:

I resign from my position as Executive Vice President of Weatherby Leasing, effective on August 15, 19—.

As you know, I have been looking for some time for an opportunity to invest in my own business, and such a chance has now materialized.

I will be moving to Cleveland and beginning a leasing corporation there. My new business will in no way compete with Weatherby Leasing.

My work here has been challenging and interesting, and I am grateful to have had the chance to work with you.

Best wishes for the future of the company.

Yours truly,

Kenneth O. Agee
Executive Vice President

Tips and Comment:

Letters of resignation spring from several sources, some pleasant and some not so pleasant. When the split is amicable, a friendly and courteous letter is an agreeable way to announce the change. If you wish to maintain good relations with the soon-to-be former employer, a simple explanation of the reasons for the resignation will be effective, as in the foregoing letter. If the resignation is a euphemism for a firing, a letter of resignation should be brief and to the point. At best a forced resignation is only a sop to the affected employee's ego.

Alternative A:

This is to inform you that I have accepted today the offer of Weatherby Leasing to become Executive Vice President, and therefore I must resign my position here.

The opportunity to work here has been fruitful and positive, and I leave with only the best wishes for the continued success of the company. The chance to move into a position of more management responsibility is too good to deny, however.

Alternative B:

I hereby resign from my position with Weatherby Leasing, effective immediately.

I will make tomorrow my last day in the office, although as we discussed, my pay and benefits will continue through the end of the month.

Alternative C:

It is with a great deal of sadness that I submit my resignation. I have enjoyed knowing the employees here during my brief stay, and I have also enjoyed learning a new set of processes.

Unfortunately, my family situation makes it impossible to continue.

Please schedule a meeting with me soon to discuss the details of my departure.

Asking for a Resignation

POTENTIAL UNLIMITED, INC.
40 TOWER PLACE
LAWRENCE, KS

June 27, 19—

Mr. Brandon H. Moore
Potential Unlimited, Inc.
40 Tower Place
Lawrence, KS

Dear Brandon:

As we discussed earlier today, I want you to submit your resignation from Potential Unlimited to be effective immediately.

You will receive severance pay equal to a month's salary, in addition to a sum equal to your accumulated sick leave and vacation.

The company will also continue to carry your health insurance as part of our group plan for six months, although you will be responsible for paying the full amount of the monthly premium.

I expect you to have vacated your office completely by tomorrow.

Sincerely,

Frederick J. Lancer
Managing Partner

Tips and Comment:

The typical business firing takes the guise of asking for a resignation, but the effect is the same: a forced departure by an employee. The firing is done usually in person with a formal letter following. These letters should make no pretence and sign no false notes. They are not easy or pleasant to write, but beating around the bush will only make everything harder. Speak straight and leave no doubt about the meaning of the request. It is also a good time to set out any severance arrangements so both parties have the conditions in writing.

Alternative A:

This is a formal request for your resignation, the details of which we discussed earlier today.

I will expect you to work through the end of this month in the office, and you will continue as a consultant until the completion of the Hayes project.

You will receive a lump sum equivalent to six-months salary on the last day of this month.

Alternative B:

Please have your letter of resignation on my desk by the end of business today.

As we discussed, you will continue to work until the end of this week, but will clear your office by 5:00 P.M. on Friday.

The terms of departure are set forth on pp. 15—23 of the employee manual, and we will abide by all the rules specified there.

Alternative C:

This is a formal notice that, after several discussions, we have agreed that your resignation will be to the mutual benefit of the company and you.

Since little could be accomplished by prolonging your departure, I suggest you resign immediately.

We can discuss further the financial details.

Accepting a Resignation

PACIFIC TECHNOLOGIES CORPORATION
23 WEST BEACH
BLOOMINGTON, CA

April 29, 19—

Ms. Janice Pratt
MIS Manager
Pacific Technologies Corporation
23 West Beach
Bloomington, CA

Dear Jan:

I'm very sorry to have to accept your resignation, but I can only applaud your ambition and wish you the best of success in your new spot.

We are unhappy to lose a person of your ability.

I understand that May 20 will be your termination date, and we will arrange all the paperwork and final compensation for that day.

Please keep in touch in the future.

Yours truly,

Howard B. Olds
Service Division Manager

Tips and Comment:

A letter accepting an employee's resignation is usually little more than a *pro forma* response, especially if the resignation has been demanded by the company. However, if the parting is by positive mutual agreement or the employee is leaving for a better opportunity than the current company can offer, then the letter of acceptance can function as a genuine expression of regret and appreciation for past services. As always in business letters that touch on emotional issues, guard against striking false notes.

Alternative A:

I hereby accept your resignation as MIS Manager.

I wish you every success in the future, and hope that your next assignment works out to your satisfaction.

Please confirm the details of severance with the Personnel Office.

Alternative B:

I accept your resignation, but I would like to learn more about the reasons for your decision to leave.

Will you please call my secretary and schedule an appointment for sometime before your final day?

I hope you will be frank and forthcoming.

Alternative C:

I agree that you cannot turn down the new opportunity offered to you and I only regret that we cannot foresee any similar possibilities here.

I therefore reluctantly accept your resignation as of the first of the month.

Please check with Charlie to see that he understands the details of your part of the current project.

Applicant's Inquiry to Search Firm

JOHN G. MCNAMARA
3 THE PINES
ELMHURST, NE

July 22, 19—

Ms. Jean Hansen
Account Executive
Execu-Search, Inc.
23 Madison Avenue
New York, NY

Dear Ms. Hansen:

After several years as Operations Manager at the Omaha plant of the Datacrunch Company, I am interested in seeking a new position elsewhere in the country.

I have no problems with Datacrunch; I just am ready to relocate and move on to a position of larger responsibility.

Can you assist me in a search? I know from colleagues in the computer manufacturing field that you have a strong reputation, and I'd like to take advantage of your wide contacts.

Enclosed are a complete résumé and a profile of the sort of job I'm looking for.

Please contact me at my home address (listed above), and please keep this inquiry confidential.

Sincerely,

John G. McNamara

Tips and Comment

It is a matter of some subtlety to place yourself in the hands of an executive search firm. Several points need to be made clear in the initial letter: that you are the one starting the job search; that you are ambitious for more challenge; and that you want to keep the search quiet. A full résumé should be included as well as a description of the sort of job you seek.

Alternative A:

I have been president of my current company for five years, but my family and I agree that the time has come to consider a change. I am therefore beginning a quiet survey of possible new positions.

I'd like your help again in conducting a search among those firms who may need a senior officer with my background.

I'm enclosing a full résumé.

Alternative B:

I understand you maintain listings of job opportunities and specialize in placing executives in new positions.

Since I have recently begun a job search, I'd like to discuss the possibility of using your services.

I am enclosing my résumé and a profile of the sort of job I'm looking for. Please let me know if we can be of mutual benefit.

Alternative C:

Sometime during the next nine months my current position will be eliminated due to a corporate merger. Since I have no control over the timing of the change, I want to begin a serious job search now.

Your reputation among some of my friends is quite high, and so I turn to you for assistance in looking for a new position.

I feel no restrictions as to location, but I would prefer the Northeast.

Enclosed is a detailed résumé and a description of my current responsibilities.

Corporate Letter to Executive Search Firm

INTERNATIONAL COMPUTERS CORPORATION
ICC BUILDING
DALLAS, TX

September 15, 19—

Ms. Joan Hansen
Account Executive
Execu-Search, Inc.
23 Madison Avenue
New York, NY

Dear Ms. Hansen:

International Computers Corporation is beginning a search for a new Plant Manager for one of our major production facilities, located in Kansas City, Missouri.

We seek a senior manager with wide experience in plant operations and at least five years in computer manufacturing. Age, gender, and race are, of course, not part of the criteria.

The position will come open soon after the first of the year, and we want to have someone in place no later than March 1.

The compensation package includes a salary of $120,000 per year, in addition to the usual bonuses, insurance, stock options, personal car, and housing allowance.

Please contact me if you think you can assist our search.

Yours truly,

Thomas H. Watson
Divisional Director

Tips and Comment:

Locating the right candidate for a job opening may involve the help of an executive search firm. A letter of inquiry to such a firm should include the general outlines of the job and the qualifications sought among possible candidates. It might be assumed that more details could be supplied later.

Alternative A:

We are seeking a replacement for one of our division managers, and would like you to help conduct a national search.

The candidate we are after will have at least a Ph.D. in metallurgy and ten years experience in manufacturing and fabrication.

We would prefer someone close to the location of the plant, in order to cut down on relocation time and expense.

The job will pay approximately $75,000 per year.

Please let me know if you can help.

Alternative B:

My company has an opening for a MIS supervisor with at least two years experience in an IBM environment.

We would like to look at four or five candidates within the next two months.

Please check your files and let me know if you have anyone we should talk to.

Alternative C:

After attempting our own search for a new president, we have decided to begin again. Can you provide some assistance?

Our efforts were mainly through personal networks, which failed to yield any outstanding candidates.

Please contact me at the above address.

Invitation to a Job Applicant

INTERNATIONAL COMPUTERS CORPORATION
ICC BUILDING
DALLAS, TX

October, 23, 19—

Mr. John G. McNamara
3 The Pines
Elmhurst, NE

Dear Mr. McNamara:

International Computers Corporation is about to begin a search for a new Plant Manager in our Kansas City plant.

You have come to our attention as someone with the skills and experience we seek in filling this important job.

If you are interested, I'd be pleased to hear from you and to read your résumé.

I can be reached at the above address at ICC headquarters in Dallas. The number is 800/555-1212.

Yours truly,

Thomas H. Watson
Divisional Director

Tips and Comment:

Feeling out a possible job applicant is delicate business. Initial letters should be cautious (the candidate may not be what you want at all on closer inspection) but encouraging. An almost neutral tone is best, with few details in the first contact letter, leaving concrete matters until later in the process.

Alternative A:

Your name has been mentioned prominently as among those who might be both looking for a new opportunity and qualified for our presidency. It is, I assure you, a very short list already.

If you are interested and would like to speak further, please call or write me.

The Board and I hope to move rapidly toward a new appointment, since John Bowers is due to announce his retirement within a few days.

Alternative B:

We have received your name from our search agency in connection with an opening in our organization.

A preliminary review of possible candidates shows you have the background we seek, and if you are interested, I'd like to arrange an interview for next week.

Please call my office for an appointment.

Alternative C:

Because we plan to install a great deal of new equipment in our plant over the coming months, we are expanding our process engineering staff.

If you are currently looking for a new job, I'd like to discuss our openings with you.

Please let me know.

Follow-Up to Interview

JOHN G. MCNAMARA
3 THE PINES
ELMHURST, NE

December 15, 19—

Mr. Thomas H. Watson
Divisional Director
International Computers Corporation
ICC Building
Dallas, TX

Dear Mr. Watson:

I arrived home from our meeting with a sense of having answered many of my questions about the way ICC works in general and the operations of the Kansas City plant in particular.

I appreciate your candor and courtesy during my stay.

While the position of plant manager is certainly interesting, I am still a little hesitant about considering the job further without more discussions with my family. We plan to talk it all over during the holiday season.

I should also point out that the salary and benefits package lacks anything in the way of performance bonus, a point I would like to discuss further if the process goes beyond this stage.

Thanks again for your kindness.

Yours truly,

John G. McNamara

Tips and Comment:

The follow-up stage in the employment process can be delicate. A letter after an interview gives the prospective employee a chance to make general inclinations known and to point out any potential problems. It is all part of the negotiation procedure and must be handled with care and acute concern for clear communications. Consider every word and phrase carefully when writing a follow-up.

Alternative A:

The meeting with the Board on Tuesday was an interesting and stimulating experience.

You obviously have a situation fraught with potential.

One of my lingering concerns, however, is about a relocation and the effect it will have on my husband's career.

I'll think over what was said and call you later in the week.

Alternative B:

Thank you for the time spent with me in your office on Thursday.

I am definitely interested in the job, and I'd welcome the chance to discuss some ideas with you about how to solve the problems you pointed to.

Please let me know if we can speak again.

Alternative C:

The tour of the plant and the briefing on the proposed equipment were interesting and informative.

I am traveling this week to interview in Akron, and I will be better armed to understand the situation there after my time with you.

Thanks again for your courtesy.

Making a Job Offer

INTERNATIONAL COMPUTERS CORPORATION
ICC BUILDING
DALLAS, TX

February 1, 19—

Mr. John G. McNamara
3 The Pines
Elmhurst, NE

Dear John:

Based on our conversations over the last few weeks and after a poll of the search committee, I am pleased to offer you the position of Plant Manager of ICC's Kansas City plant.

If you accept, we will ask you to sign a contract for the position. The basic compensation will be $120,000 per year plus bonus options (to be spelled out in the contract) in the maximum amount of $50,000 per year.

You will, in addition, receive full health and life insurance benefits, the use of a company-owned car, and six weeks paid vacation per year.

We would like you to start orientation here in Dallas on March 1.

Please let me know formally of your decision.

Yours truly,

Thomas H. Watson
Divisional Director

Tips and Comment:

A job-offer letter should be specific about the terms and conditions of employment and indicate at least in general any unusual aspects of the appointment. In some cases, the offer letter may form part of the legal basis for the job, and it is in all cases an important document for both sides. Cordiality is encouraged, but not mandatory.

Alternate A:

This is a formal offer to you of the position of secretary in my office.

I was much impressed with your personal skills and experience, and I'd like to have you as part of our team.

The salary will be $315 per week (paid semi-weekly), and you will have the chance to participate in our company insurance programs.

The hours are 9:00 A.M.. to 5:00 P.M., Monday through Friday, with a week's paid vacation after one year of employment.

Please let me know if you accept.

Alternative B:

It was a pleasure to interview you last Thursday, and based on my impression from that meeting, I'm happy to offer you the job.

The conditions would be as we discussed, plus I'd like to increase the salary to $30,000 per year if you can—in return—begin immediately.

Call me if you have any questions before deciding.

Alternate C:

It's not often that I meet someone of your charm and obvious talents.

I wish to offer you the position we discussed (at the salary mentioned), and I hope you accept with no further ado.

I understand your hesitation about the staffing situation, but I think we can work out a solution.

Accepting a Job Offer

JOHN G. MCNAMARA
3 THE PINES
ELMHURST, NE

February 4, 19—

Mr. Thomas H. Watson
Divisional Director
International Computers Corporation
ICC Building
Dallas, TX

Dear Mr. Watson:

I am happy to accept your offer of the position of Plant Manager at the ICC operation in Kansas City.

The terms of employment and compensation are acceptable as outlined in our conversations and confirmed in your letter of February 1.

I will plan to arrive at headquarters in Dallas for orientation on March 1, as you requested.

Needless to say, I am looking forward to what I hope will be a long and fruitful association with ICC.

Let me know if there are any pre-employment details to take care of.

Sincerely,

John G. McNamara

Tips and Comment:

Accepting the offer of a new job is usually the occasion for anticipation and pleasure. A new vista stretches before both the employer and the employee. A formal letter of acceptance might include confirmation of the job title, salary and compensation, and other details. An acceptance letter might also specify the starting date and place.

Alternative A:

As I indicated in our phone conversation yesterday, I am willing to take on the job of president of the corporation. I will plan to be in Dallas for a formal announcement on May 4. Please have the Public Relations department get in touch with me before planning the press conference.

The compensation will be as we discussed, including the stock options and the bonus-for-performance clauses. Please have a contract drawn as soon as possible so my attorney can review it.

My husband joins me in expressing our pleasure at the prospect of a move to Dallas.

Alternative B:

Thank you for the formal offer of the job. I am happy to accept.

I will need a month to disengage from my current responsibilities and I would like to take a few days off, so I will not plan to be on the spot until Monday, June 9.

If you will have someone from the benefits office call me, we can work out the details of my insurance package.

I'm looking forward to the the new challenge.

Alternative C:

I will be happy to become the new process engineer in your division, and I formally accept your offer.

As you say, it should be an interesting next two or three years with the new equipment due to come on line.

I appreciate your frankness and courtesy during our conversations, and I look forward to working with you.

3

PEOPLE AT WORK: LETTERS DEALING WITH EMPLOYEE RELATIONS

As top-level managers, many executives are called on to write letters about a host of vital employment matters. Any communication from the highest levels about terms of employment, contract offers, changes in work requirements, or job performance will be read with great care by the recipients. These issues are so important that they get everyone's attention immediately. Letters in this category should be direct in tone with few ambiguities. The following time-saving examples show how to deal with such situations in ways that communicate clearly and yet forcefully.

Announcing New Employee Benefits

ALL-AMERICAN TOBACCO COMPANY
WINSTON-SALEM, NC

January 15, 19—

Dear Fellow Employee:

We are pleased to announce that beginning February 1 the Company will sponsor ten college scholarships for children of regular employees and former employees (both retired and deceased). The scholarships may be used at any accredited college or university in the United States.

The scholarship recipients will be chosen by the National Merit Scholarship Corporation on the basis of scholastic aptitude, leadership, involvement in school-related activities, and good citizenship. No Company officer or employee will play any part in the selection of the scholars.

Each scholarship will be a four-year award, covering the undergraduate years. The amount of the scholarship will be determined by the National Merit Scholarship Corporation and will be based on the winner's financial need in order to attend the college of his or her choice.

The awards for this year will be announced at the end of April.

A leaflet describing the scholarship program is enclosed. If you have a child who intends to enter college this fall and who would like to apply for a Company Scholarship, please request application forms from the Scholarship Program Director in the Personnel Department.

Sincerely,

Walt Rawley
Executive Vice President

Tips and Comment:

A letter is a good medium to announce an improvement in company employee benefits. A notice on bulletin boards might get the information out just as well, but a letter has more impact, and even a form letter indicates a desire by the company to communicate directly with each individual employee.

Alternative A:

It is with greatest pleasure that I am able to let you know that the management and Board of Directors have approved a new scholarship program for children of current and retired employees.

Beginning in the fall of this year, our company will provide ten full scholarships for employee children. The scholarships may be used at any accredited college or university in the country.

The selection of the ten winners will be made by the College Scholarship Service of Princeton, New Jersey, and will be based on high school academic record, extra curricular activities, and community involvement.

If you have a child who is eligible to apply, please contact Mr. Wendover in the Personnel Department. He has the application forms.

Alternative B:

The All-American Company believes that education is the cornerstone of a better future. In keeping with this belief, the Company is announcing today a new program of full college scholarships for children of employees.

We have contracted with an accredited outside agency to select the winners of the scholarships, and we urge any employee who has children bound for college to make an application. The enclosed brochure gives details.

Look for a public announcement of the program on the evening news tomorrow.

Change in Benefits Policy

PLANT-A-GROW CORPORATION
ONE GREENLEAF LANE
AIKEN, GA

December 15, 19—

Mr. James R. Truitt
Vice-President
Plant-a-Grow Corporation
One Greenleaf Lane
Aiken, GA

Dear Jim:

This is to announce to you a change in the company's benefits policy, one brought on by a change in the federal law.

As mandated by P.L. 1011, after January 1, 19—, highly compensated employees of corporations may no longer receive a benefits package that differs significantly from that offered to any other employee.

This means, of course, that the special insurance, which has been part of your package, must be converted to some other form of compensation.

Since the problem exists for several of our senior executives, the Board has decided to convert all disallowed benefits into straight cash increases in salary.

In your case, this will mean a conversion of $30,000 per year.

The Board realizes this change may have important tax consequences for senior employees, but we have no choice if we are to stay within the law.

Yours truly,

Manfred J. Oppenheimer
Chairman of the Board

Tips and Comment:

Announcing a change in benefits, especially if the change is not positive, is a less pleasant task than announcing improvements. A personal letter makes a good medium, nevertheless, and may help to cushion the blow. It is, perhaps, incumbent on the company to explain the change and why it will occur, but a model letter will strive to do so without sounding defensive.

Alternative A:

After a review of sales projections for the coming year and an analysis of sales for the last six months, it has become clear that we must tighten our collective belts in order to ride out what appears to be a long downturn in activity.

Therefore, we are reluctantly asking all outside sales people to turn in their company cars as of November 1.

From now on, we will pay mileage to you at the rate of 25 cents a mile for use of your private automobiles while on company business.

We hope this will not be a burden.

Alternative B:

Owing to continued increases in premium costs, we are changing our health insurance policy and the benefits offered to you as an employee.

Beginning with the first of the year, the health package will no longer include dental coverage for families, although dental coverage will continue for individual employees.

There will be no change in the company policy of paying for the full cost of health insurance.

Alternative C:

On the advice of our consultants, the company is announcing a change in sick leave policy.

After the first of next month, all sick leave will accrue at the rate of one and one half days for each pay period worked.

Sick leave may be accumulated by employees up to a total of 30 days.

Announcing a Company Offer to Employees

BEST MOTOR COMPANY
THE AMERICAN ROAD
DEARBORN, MI

August 23, 19—

To: The Employees of Best Motor Company Represented by the UAW

When I wrote to you on June 28 at the start of our UAW negotiations, I told you that we would dedicate our full efforts to make free collective bargaining work. In keeping with this pledge, we have today made a proposal to the Union that, in my opinion, should form the basis of a sound and fair settlement of all the issues in these negotiations.

The offer, to cover a three-year term, contains across-the-board wage increases amounting to an average increase in the base rate of seven dollars an hour annually, and continuation of the cost-of-living allowance. Further, it contains a new Short Week benefit, improvements in the SUB Plan, and increased retirement benefits. An early edition of your plant newspaper will describe in detail the entire proposal.

Considering the ongoing challenge to the American auto industry from the Japanese and the growing possibility of relaxation of their voluntary import restrictions, I know you will appreciate the Company's proposal.

At Best, we have come a long way toward meeting this challenge in recent years, but there is more to do and we must do it together. Only with the best efforts of ALL of us can we all survive and prosper.

I sincerely hope that within the framework of our proposal there will be a prompt and peaceful conclusion to our current negotiations.

Sincerely,

James Abercromby
President

Tips and Comment:

Announcing a company position on something as delicate and important as a new labor contract calls for the full exercise of communications skills. The letter must be clear and specific about the situation but also take care not to misrepresent any of the important issues. It is an opportunity in this example to make the company's case to the broad union membership and to remind union workers of the need for a united front in the face of off-shore competition. Since this letter will be received at least in part by some workers who will be cynical about the sentiments of management, care must be taken to not indulge in empty rhetoric, but rather to explain the offer realistically and persuasively.

Alternative A:

The Company has today made a full offer to the representatives of the Union. The details will be explained in a special edition of the plant newspaper. They include across-the-board wage increases as well as continuation of the cost-of-living allowance.

We also have included several new provisions such as a Short Week benefit, improvements in the SUB Plan, and increased retirement benefits.

The negotiations so far have proceeded in an atmosphere of positive cooperation, and both sides must continue to work together.

The importance of meeting the challenge from the import of Japanese cars and, increasingly, the manufacture of automobiles in this country in non-union Japanese-owned plants is uppermost in our minds.

We think with a solid, new contract that is fair to both parties, Best Motor Company and the UAW can prosper together.

Alternative B:

I wish I could talk to each of you individually about the offer the Company has just made to the Union.

I think it is a fair and reasonable offer that provides increased wages and several new benefits.

I know it is a strong offer from the viewpoint of the Company and grows out of our desire to continue the strong recovery we have experienced in partnership with the UAW.

Every day our newspapers and television news shows carry stories of the increased activity of the Japanese automakers in this country. There are now more than a half dozen Japanese owned and operated plants, all of them employing non-union labor.

I look forward to concluding a new agreement in the shortest time possible.

Explaining a New Employee Handbook

THE NATIONAL ASSOCIATION OF FEDERATIONS
14 NORTH 15TH STREET
WESTOVER, MA

June 9, 19—

Dear Association Employees:

Enclosed is the new edition of the NAF Employee Handbook.

As many of you know, we have developed the new handbook over the last six months in the hope it will improve the understanding of all employees about NAF procedures and policies.

The handbook covers many aspects of our work, including job descriptions, working conditions, wage scales, hiring and severance, fringe benefits, sick leave, vacation, and others.

Please take time to look at the table of contents, and I urge you to read carefully those parts of the handbook that interest you the most. File it at your desk and use it as a reference.

I welcome your comments.

Sincerely,

Clyde Baskins
Executive Director

Tips and Comment:

Many business organizations—large and small, profit and non-profit—compile and distribute employee handbooks as part of their management plans. A letter sent with copies of a handbook should point out the importance of the document and urge worker attention to its salient points.

Alternative A:

This is the updated Feltner Company employee handbook. Please examine your copy and keep it for future reference.

Many of the policies in the handbook are new. Although we have addressed these issues several times in staff meetings, this is the official publication of the new policies.

I hope the handbook serves a useful purpose in making work life more pleasant.

Alternative B:

By this time, all of you should have received your copy of the new employee handbook.

This is the first attempt by our company to compile such a handbook, and we hope it makes some aspects of company policy clearer.

Of particular note is the section showing our wage structure. From now on, there should be no secrecy or doubts about pay.

Alternative C:

All workers at Acme deserve open and above-board treatment, so we have decided to issue everyone a copy of the enclosed worker handbook.

Its five chapters cover all aspects of working conditions at Acme.

If you have further questions after reading the handbook, please see your supervisor.

Welcoming a New Employee

K.B. DOLL CORPORATION
346 CARROLL STREET
BROOKLYN, NY

April 5, 19—

Ms. Alice Brown
567 Questor Ave.
Browntown, NH

Dear Ms. Brown:

I want to welcome you to our firm. We are very pleased that you have accepted our offer and we look forward to seeing you at our plant in two weeks, on April 20.

As I discussed on the phone, it is the company policy to pay for our professional staff's moving and travel expenses. The transportation company under contract with us will get in touch with you to move all your household goods. Your personal transportation expenses will be paid when you report for work.

Again, welcome to K.B. Doll Corporation. We are happy you have decided to join our organization, and we are confident that both you and the firm will benefit.

Sincerely,

James F. Doll
Vice President

Tips and Comment:

It is usually a pleasant assignment to write a letter welcoming a newly hired employee to the company fold. It is also a good opportunity to get terms down in writing—things such as moving expenses and date of beginning work. In other cases, it is simply a good initiative in establishing positive employee relations.

Alternative A:

I was very pleased to get your phone call accepting the offer from K.B. Doll to serve as our new comptroller. I am genuinely looking forward to working with you and especially to hearing more of your ideas for the accounting department.

We will have the changes made in your office space before you arrive for your first day on May 15.

Please feel free to call me if you have any questions.

Alternative B:

This is to confirm your acceptance of our offer of employment and to welcome you to the company.

Those who have been with K.B. Doll for several years (I started almost two decades ago on the plant floor) think we have one of the best operations in the country.

I know you will add a great deal to the company, and I look forward to meeting you in person.

Alternative C:

Welcome aboard!

I am very, very pleased that you accepted our offer, and I know that both K.B. Doll and you will look back at this as a great decision.

I have already been thinking over some of what you said at your interview. No doubt you can expand on things when you get here next week.

I hope you have no problems in getting out of your lease, and that your husband finds something in his line here in the New York area. If you need any help, just let me know.

Asking an Employee to Transfer

FROMMELT INDUSTRIES, INC.
2 STATION AVENUE
WILMINGTON, DE

August 6, 19—

Ms. Jane Samuels
Accounting Supervisor
Frommelt Industries, Inc.
234 Turnverein Street
Allentown, PA

Dear Jane:

As you may know, Frommelt is opening a new plant in Tallahassee, Florida. The schedule calls for construction to be complete around October 1 and for operations to begin by November 15.

We are now planning the staff for the new operation, and Curt Claussen, the manager-designate of the Florida plant, has asked me to put together a top-flight team.

Will you consider a transfer to the new plant?

I know you have been happy in Pennsylvania, but I think the new operation will be both a great challenge and a great opportunity. Frommelt could certainly use your experience in setting up the accounting department and seeing it through the first year or two.

We would be able to offer an immediate 10 percent raise in salary as an inducement. And, you could look forward to a light winter in Florida instead of the usual cold and snow of Pennsylvania.

Please give me a call or write.

Yours truly,

Mary H. Travers
Corporate Operations

Tips and Comment:

Large companies with several locations often wish to transfer key employees. A letter broaching the subject might—as does this model—explain the situation and flatter the employee. Do not be fulsome, but do make it clear that the company values the employee's skills and wishes to use them in a new spot. Any added inducements such as salary or fringe benefits (including climate) might be included in the letter. Some business transfers, of course, result from business contraction rather than expansion and require a letter with a slightly different focus.

Alternative A:

Although it has not yet been officially announced, the company will move its headquarters from Louisville to Indianapolis sometime during the next six months.

Naturally, not all of our current employees will go with us, but I hope you will consider a relocation as one of our key people.

This is a decision you will perhaps need to discuss with your family, and I don't want to put you under undue pressure—yet we need to be able to plan for the new staff, so please let me know or ask for a further discussion soon.

Alternative B:

I am sorry to tell you that the Kansas City office will be closed on June 1. The volume of business through the Missouri branch no longer warrants a full office in the state.

We plan to consolidate the regional office in Des Moines, and we can offer you a position in that office similar to your current spot in Kansas City.

Unfortunately, only a few of your fellow workers in Kansas City will have this opportunity.

Alternative C:

Can you move to the New Jersey facility?

As you know we plan to bring the new equipment on line there next month, and we need to beef up the technical staff.

I know we have moved you often in the last year, but this expansion period calls for a lot of flexibility from everyone.

Please give me a call next week when I'll be back in the office.

Company Relocation Policy

GENTECK INTERNATIONAL, INC.
24 RUTHERFORD DRIVE
ORANGE, MO

May 17, 19—

Mr. Paul L. Botts
Assistant Manager
Genteck International, Inc.
333 West Gonders Drive
Oklahoma City, OK

Dear Mr. Botts:

The company policy on relocation and expenses allows up to $1,500 total for company-initiated moves of less than 1,000 miles and up to $2,500 for moves of more than 1,000 miles (or actual costs, whichever is less).

Since you will be relocating to the main plant in Orange, the move will be less than 1,000 miles and you will qualify for the $1,500 maximum.

Please contact the Acme Moving Company branch office in Oklahoma City and ask for an estimate for your move. We have a corporate rate with Acme nationwide.

I'll be happy to answer any further questions.

Yours truly,

Harold Gompers
Manager of Personnel

Tips and Comment:

Policies on company moves are of major concern to employees of large corporations. A clear letter detailing the company policy on paying for relocation expenses will go far toward easing the anxiety of moving for employees. The tone here is formal, which helps reassure the employee by creating an atmosphere of authority.

Alternative A:

We have a company policy of paying 80 percent of actual billed costs for employee moves, if the change has been at the request of the company.

However, since you will be initiating the move to the Florida office, we can pay only 50 percent of the bill.

Please let me know as soon as possible the estimated cost of the move and I will authorize a payment.

Alternative B:

Please rest assured that the company will cover all of your relocation costs, including travel, lodging, and meals in addition to the cost of the moving company.

You need only submit an expense form and a copy of the mover's bill once you arrive in the new location.

If you need it, I'll be happy to write a letter of authorization to the moving company.

Alternative C:

We do not have a firm overall company policy on paying for the cost of an employee's move, but rather we negotiate on a case-by-case basis.

In this instance, I think we can offer a minimum of 80 percent of the mover's bill or $1,700, whichever is less.

Please let me know if you think the estimate will be higher.

Thanks for an Employee Suggestion

BEST MOTOR COMPANY
THE AMERICAN ROAD
DEARBORN, MI

October 2, 19—

Mr. Paul G. Howard
343 W. Linear Ave.
Bottston, MI

Dear Paul:

I'm most pleased to tell you that the Management Proposal Committee has asked me to write you this letter of commendation for the adoption of your proposal to fabricate in-house Part No. 16ZP-738, instead of buying it from outside vendors.

Your suggestion resulted in direct savings to the Company because of the reduced cost of making the part in-house.

We greatly appreciate your initiative and inventiveness, and I hope you will continue to submit ideas to management when they occur to you.

I'm sending a copy of this letter to the Salaried Personnel Section so it can become part of your record.

Truly yours,

George T. Pomppo, Chairman
Management Proposal Committee

Tips and Comment:

It is a nice touch to send a letter to an individual employee's home address when a special pat on the back is called for. This will have more effect than an inter-office memo or a notice through usual channels.

Alternative A:

Your suggestion that the Company consider making Part No. 16ZP-738 ourselves rather than buy it from outside was accepted today by the Management Proposal Committee.

You showed a great deal of insight about our process with your suggestion, and it should save both time and money.

The Committee asked me to thank you formally and wants to encourage you to continue to make suggestions in the future.

I am sending a copy of this letter to become part of your permanent company record.

Alternative B:

Your suggestion that we make upper vector spindles ourselves rather than contracting outside was a great idea. After we looked into it carefully, it became obvious that this was the answer to the problem. We will save money in the long run, and most important, we should eliminate those shortages.

I want to thank you on behalf of the Company, and assure you that your ideas are always welcome.

Make certain you let me know when you are up for a performance review, and I'll make my feelings known.

Alternative C:

The review committee asked me to thank you personally for the fine suggestion you made about switching over to in-house fabrication of upper vector spindles.

This was a super idea, and we are moving immediately to put it into effect. I think it's safe to say it's the best idea we've gotten this year.

If you have more suggestions, please let me know.

Thanks for Special Employee Effort

IMPERIAL SHOPPES
310 OVERVIEW BLVD.
BIG TOWN, OH

To the Store Family:

My heartfelt thanks to each and every one of you for making such a fine effort to be on the job during the three weeks of the transportation strike.

Such loyalty and devotion on the part of our Store Family have been two of the chief reasons for our success over the years.

With the strike now over and with a most impressive sale coming up on this Friday, I hope that all of us regain the momentum we lost and have the best Spring in our history.

Again, thank you.

Harry Jones
President

Tips and Comment:

An extraordinary occasion, such as meeting a crisis, may be a good time for a letter sent directly to each employee. If the situation really calls for it, a "pat-on-the-back" letter is one all workers will be happy to receive.

Alternative A:

Now that we are beginning to get the pieces put back together after the fire, I am writing to thank you as personally as possible for the tremendous load of responsibility you shouldered during the crisis.

Without your energy and resourcefulness, we would never have made it back.

Thanks.

Alternative B:

Well, another edition of the book has now gone to press, and I must tell you how much I appreciate the long hours of professional devotion you put into this year's version.

I know all of our readers will benefit from your expertise, and the company could not exist without you and people like you. We can all be proud of what we have accomplished.

Alternative C:

It sometimes troubles me that the day-to-day efforts of our company employees seem somehow to be overlooked. So, I'm taking time to write you this personal note of thanks.

Without you and your colleagues, the company would not exist and it would certainly not produce well enough to be ranked, as we are, among the top companies in the industry.

Thank you.

Change in Work Schedule

ACME MOTORS, INC.
89 VILLAGE DRIVE
ITHACA, MI

December 3, 19—

Dear Acme Employees:

This is to announce a change in the work schedule that will take effect on January 1.

The main line will begin work at 9:30 A.M. and shut down at 5:00 P.M. with a half hour break for lunch.

We hope to ease the problems we have encountered with the earlier starting time through this change.

Office personnel will also move to a 9:30 A.M. to 5:00 P.M. schedule, but outside salespeople will continue on their previous schedules.

Supervisors and foremen will have more details on the change later in the month.

Sincerely,

John Landers
President

Tips and Comment:

Changes in overall work or plant schedules may be announced effectively through letters. This gives a personal touch to such information and softens the image which the corporation presents to its employees. As in this model, such letters should state the changes directly and, insofar as appropriate, offer an explanation.

Alternative A:

As of November 1, we will change the hours of office operation to 8:00 A.M. to 4:30 P.M.

We are taking this step to make it easier for all of us to get through the morning and evening rush hour traffic. We do not think the change will effect the volume of business, and it should put most of us on the road when there are fewer cars to contend with, especially on the Tri-Boro Bridge.

Let me know if you have any questions.

Alternative B:

I'm happy to announce that, as of next week, we will be moving the second shift to a new starting time, 5:50 P.M.

After the experimentation of the last year, this seems to be clearly the best time for the greatest number of people. The earlier and later hours just don't work as well.

We will review this change after three months, so if you have complaints or comments, please let me know.

Alternative C:

A big change is in sight. Beginning on June 3, we will make a change from a Monday through Friday, 8-hour-a-day week to a Monday through Thursday flextime schedule.

We have been discussing this for some time, so it should come as no surprise.

The details of individual schedules are, of course, complex, but we will make every effort to work out the best combination for everyone concerned.

Announcing Job Description Reviews

GENTECK INTERNATIONAL, INC.
24 EAST RUTHERFORD DRIVE
ORANGE, MO

May 3, 19—

To: All Genteck Employees

As a result of the report submitted by the company's Long-Range Planning Task Force, Genteck will begin a three-month process of job description reviews in June.

All of you will receive a copy of the current job description for your position and a questionnaire about changes you might suggest.

As you can imagine, this will be a big undertaking since we have currently forty-five separate job description categories and nearly 800 employees spread across five locations.

We plan to tabulate the results of the study and look into them closely. No company-wide changes in any of the job descriptions are contemplated until the study and analysis are complete, which will be a year from now at the earliest.

Thanks in advance for your help and cooperation.

Yours truly,

John J. Jefferies
General Manager

Tips and Comment:

Since even the possibility of changes in job responsibilities and job descriptions may cause anxiety among employees, it is a good idea to announce company-wide reviews in a letter that explains the process, the timetable, and the possible result. Such a letter will increase the chances of cooperation and a smooth study.

Alternative A:

During January, we will begin a month-long process of reviewing all job descriptions in order to plan more effectively for the anticipated expansion due to take place later in the year.

I hope all of you will cooperate in the review and let us know your ideas and concerns.

This is a good chance to have an effect on the way we move into the future.

Alternative B:

After conferring with our management consultants, we have discovered that we do not really have an accurate set of descriptions for many of the jobs in the company.

Even though we are a small group and we all tend to know what each other does on the job, it may help us to plan for better productivity if we can get it all down on paper.

Each of you will receive a form later this week, which will ask you to describe your duties. Please fill it out and return it to me by next Tuesday.

Alternative C:

I am asking each of you to review the job descriptions for your divisions and let me have a report within thirty days on any suggested changes.

It has been two years since we looked closely at the designated jobs, and we need fresh insight.

Let me know if you have any questions.

Performance Appraisal Letter

GENTECK INTERNATIONAL, INC.
24 EAST RUTHERFORD DRIVE
ORANGE, MO

January 10, 19—

Ms. Lola McIntyre
Assistant General Manager
Shipping Division
Genteck International, Inc.
24 East Rutherford Drive
Orange, MO

Dear Lola:

As we have discussed, your performance during 19—was rated superior on your annual performance appraisal.

I was especially pleased with the way you made progress in ironing out the problems associated with the changeover to automated bulk handling. This was a complex challenge and one you handled well.

It also appears that you have dispatched the daily business of your office with vigor and efficiency.

There is still some improvement to be made in the productivity of the second shift on the docks, but we have talked over the problem and I think you know the direction to go.

This letter affirms your change in pay status to Step 14, based on this favorable review.

Yours truly,

John J. Jefferies
General Manager

Tips and Comment:

Formal letters of appraisal are usually a follow-up to a face-to-face meeting and provide the opportunity to get the essentials of the appraisal down in writing for the record. The elements of good appraisal letters include a clear statement of opinion of the person's overall performance, citation of specific examples, and indication of suggestions for the future. In many companies, the annual appraisal is also the medium to formally award pay increases or promotions.

Alternative A:

This is the formal notice of appraisal based on your annual review. As I told you yesterday in person, I have rated you as adequate as a manager and superior in technical background.

This is the second year in a row for the "adequate" rating, and I'd like to see marked improvement during the coming months. Please turn your full attention to the areas we discussed.

Pending a mid-year appraisal in six months, I have suggested you remain at your current salary level.

If any of this is unclear, please see me.

Alternative B:

I'm happy to confirm your rating of excellent on the annual work-performance review.

You have taken hold of your responsibilities with vigor and proven to be effective in all the tasks we have asked of you.

I hope you can continue to pile up such a fine record.

Alternative C:

With the major exception of the missed production deadline in the Dallas plant, your work over the past twelve months has been superior.

I trust that you will take the steps necessary to forestall any repetition of the failure, and that next year at this time there will be nothing to blemish your appraisal.

Congratulations on the execution of the Haynes project, which went very well from the company's standpoint.

Prompting Employee Performance

ZENDA, INC.
3101 WEST END AVENUE
SUITE 200
NASHVILLE, TN 37203

October 8, 19—

Mr. John Doe
111 Any Street
Any Town, U.S.A.

Dear John:

I got your report on the affinity group reunion in San Diego, and it looks good. Before I turn anything into Fred, however, I need to get from you right away the taped interview, so I can have it transcribed and edited; your expenses for the entire trip; and an invoice for the stay in San Diego.

Also, as soon as possible, I need the rest of your reports. I've enclosed two documents: a list of the products for the planning stage of the project and a schedule for completing them. This will give you an idea of the real time constraints under which we are operating here.

John, I've been patient and fair, but now I need a clear idea about where you are on these reports and when I can expect them.

Sincerely,

Charles Phillips
President
(Courtesy of Charles Phillips, Nashville, TN)

Tips and Comment:

As this real-life example shows, it is sometimes necessary to prod an employee toward better performance. Unless you are winding up to fire someone, it is probably best to use a relatively gentle touch, demonstrated here by the mild compliment in the first sentence. But, be bold in setting out what needs to be done and what has been left undone so far. As can be seen in this example, it may help to explain the larger picture to the employee.

Alternative A:

Your work on the Higgins account was OK, and we turned in the contract this afternoon.

I'm still in the dark, however, about the extensions to the Jones contract. Can you get this worked up and in my hands as soon as possible?

I'm scheduled to leave on a sales trip next Wednesday, so I need the Jones material before I depart. I think faxing it to me would be best.

Alternative B:

We still seem to have a chronic problem in unit No. 2. Why is it still producing only a 40 percent solution?

I thought you had the difficulty licked when you converted to an alcohol rinse. At least you assured me then it would clear up the problem.

Can you please get on this right away? I want a report by next Friday.

Alternative C:

While I am generally happy with the overall thrust of the Kelvin campaign, I have some doubts about the third phase.

I seems to me that you are relying too much on a consumer-driven approach with little or no data to back it up.

As you well know, this is one of our biggest and best accounts, so we need to be certain we have everything under control.

Let me know your thoughts on this.

4

THE CUSTOMER IS USUALLY RIGHT: LETTERS TO CLIENTS AND CUSTOMERS

There is no single more important group of recipients of executive letters than customers. All letters from business executives to customers must be written with a specific purpose in mind and composed with great attention to tone and detail. The following examples provide time-saving models for a range of customer-related situations. In some cases, the executive must explain policies or technical matters; in other instances, the executive faces the delicate task of saying something negative in a way that will not offend the customer or threaten future business; and one of the most challenging letter-writing tasks is to make an honest apology to a customer. The following sample letters illustrate the techniques of writing such letters effectively.

Explaining a Company Policy

THE VANGUARD GROUP OF INVESTMENT COMPANIES
VANGUARD FINANCIAL CENTER
VALLEY FORGE, PA 19482

April 7, 19—

Mr. Kenneth G. Bancroft
P.O. Box 30
West Bend, MT

Dear Mr. Bancroft:

Thanks very much for your recent note regarding the new minimum purchase requirements on our Vanguard Funds. I appreciate very much your thoughtful and persuasive letter, and most particularly your sending it directly to me.

To begin with, let me say that, largely as a result of discussions with our staff following the receipt of your letter, we have decided to keep the minimum initial investment for Vanguard STAR Fund at $500. I thought that in your letter you made a persuasive case that there should be at least some avenue for investors with modest amounts of money to join Vanguard. STAR seems like an ideal place in that an investor with a minimum investment can actually get the equivalent of something like seven Vanguard Funds "in one."

Having said that, I wanted to take a moment to explain our reasoning in raising the other minimums. Contrary to what you thought, it was not some "young Harvard MBA" who had the idea, but an old non-Harvard MBA, who happens to be Chairman of the Board. I have been concerned about having this place grow too fast, and also concerned about a potential influx of very small investors, for whom the cost of handling an account is disproportionately large relative to the assets involved. Since our costs, of course, are shared by all of the shareholders, we obviously have to be very careful about our average account size.

Page 2

In explanation of the decision that we made, the previous $1,500 minimums had been in place for fifteen years or longer. Mere inflation would have carried this minimum up to $3,000 or so, and it therefore seemed an adjustment would not be inappropriate. With respect to the Vanguard Money Market Reserves, our minimum was $3,000 up until the end of 1982 (when we reduced it to $1,000 to be more competitive with banks, then permitted for the first time to offer money market deposit accounts). So, in a sense, we are just returning to that original minimum, without the inflation adjustment described above.

So, I do not believe what we are doing is irrational. Our mission, we believe, is to make sure that all of our investors in the Funds are served with an extremely low-cost structure, all the while preserving the right of small investors to continue to do business here. I trust that you agree with our decision to retain the $500 minimum in STAR, and I hope that you will become a shareholder.

We have a saying around here that "even one person can make a difference." Obviously, you have made a difference in this case! Thanks again for writing.

Sincerely,

John C. Bogle
Chairman of the Board
(Courtesy of John C. Bogle, The Vanguard Group, Valley Forge, PA)

Tips and Comment:

It is hard to imagine a better customer relations letter than this actual example from the chairman of a financial investment company. It is a personal communication from the top executive of the company in response to a customer who questioned corporate policy. The chairman's reply is warm in tone, and most important, it is obviously a thoughtful response to the customer's concerns. Moreover, the writer's explanation of a relatively complex situation is clear and concise.

Acknowledging a Letter

NATIONWIDE HOTEL CORP.
800 REGENT BOULEVARD
RAMSHEAD, PA

June 27, 19—

Ms. Janice Moss
376 Nicols Drive
Danforth, CT

Dear Ms. Moss:

Thank you for your letter of June 24 to Victor Verdi. Because of the nature of your business, Mr. Verdi forwarded the letter to Diane Foster, Manager of Customer Relations.

Ms. Foster is at a conference in Hawaii until next week, but she will be in touch with you as soon as she returns to the office.

Thanks for your patience.

Sincerely,

Mary Jane Reynolds
Secretary to Diane Foster

Tips and Comment:

Because travel is such a large part of executive business life, incoming letters from customers must sometimes be acknowledged while someone is away from the office. In this case, an extra delay might result because the letter was first referred within the company from the original addressee to another person. Promptness, clarity, and courtesy will forestall any problems with the customer who wrote the original inquiry. The text and tone of an acknowledgment letter can be agreed on ahead of time by the executive and the secretary and become part of standard office operating procedure.

Alternative A:

Mr. Verdi received your letter of June 24, but forwarded it to Ms. Diane Foster, who is in a better position to answer your question.

Unfortunately, Ms. Foster is out of town, so her reply will be delayed. However, I will call your letter to her attention as soon as she returns next week.

You can look forward to an answer within a few days.

Alternative B:

Mr. Verdi has sent your letter to Diane Foster, who handles such matters, but she is gone until next week. She will send you an answer when she returns.

Thanks for the inquiry.

Alternative C:

Please be patient about your letter to Nationwide. Mr. Verdi thought it best to let Ms. Diane Foster handle the problem, but she is gone from the office until next Wednesday.

I'll make certain she sees your letter as soon as she returns.

Aiding Customer Response

INTERNATIONAL WIDGETS, INC.
34 RENDERS STREET
QUESTO, CA

August 4, 19—

Mrs. Jane F. Langers
12 East Summit St.
Tempe, AZ

Dear Mrs. Langers:

I am sorry it took so long to reply to your request for information.

In the future, I suggest that you include your account number on all your correspondence to the Widget Corporation. By doing so, you will speed the process of handling here.

Thanks for your interest.

Yours truly,

Helen Mackey
Customer Service Representative

Tips and Comment:

In many corporations, handling of customer inquiries is keyed to specific references in the company's file or computer system. When a customer wants attention, the inclusion of codes, account numbers, or other such references will speed up processing. A gentle letter to the customer should make this clear without being patronizing.

Alternative A:

Because of the large number of customers we serve it is often necessary for us to refer to account numbers in order to retrieve information.

I realize this seems rather faceless, but it speeds up our response time considerably.

Please include your account number when writing to us.

Alternative B:

If you will include in future letters the mailing label from the front of your catalog, it will allow us to process your requests more rapidly.

Thanks for your interest in our products.

Alternative C:

The world is now ruled by computers, and our ordering system is no exception.

We will be able to process your invoices more rapidly if you are certain to include the code number assigned to your account.

Sorry to put you to this extra effort, but it will mean a faster payment.

Saying "No" to a Customer

JONES MFG., INC.
P.O. BOX 223
DOVER, DE

September 11, 19—

Mr. Fred Garvey
President
Wholesale, Inc.
Lewes, MD

Dear Mr. Garvey:

Tom Kennedy of our sales department has discussed with me your request for a change in the jobbing arrangement with your firm.

I'm sorry to say that after a great deal of thought, I have decided not to approve the change.

It appears to me that Jones Mfg. would be close to a violation of trade customs if we followed the course you requested. I realize this has nothing to do with conditions in Maryland and that you were probably unaware of the difficulty we would face.

I very much want to continue to do business with Wholesale, Inc., and I hope we can continue as in the past.

Yours truly,

Harvey Green
President

Tips and Comment:

Saying "no" to a client is difficult. On such occasions, be polite but be firm. Explain the reasons and circumstances insofar as possible, but do not allow explanations or courtesy to sound equivocal. The goal is to turn down the customer's request but to not cut off further intercourse. This calls for a very firm grasp of communications technique.

Alternative A:

After due consideration, we cannot go along with your request to increase your quota for the coming quarter. As much as we'd like to cooperate, we simply do not have the capacity to meet the request.

In part, this is a problem of dealing with our recent success: we have a demand that far exceeds our ability to supply it.

If this situation changes, I'll let you know.

Alternative B:

It will not be possible to change our billing procedures as you have requested.

As much as we try to keep our customers happy and meet their needs, we simply are unable to change our system to accommodate you on this matter.

Alternative C:

As much as I'd like to say "yes," it is just impossible to do as you ask.

I don't have enough staff to take on such a change just now, and hiring outside help is also not in the cards.

As you must understand, it is painful to turn you down on this one, but I have no choice.

Technical Explanation to a Client

BUSINESS COMPUTER SYSTEMS
1424 TERN AVENUE
ANYTOWN, MN

September 5, 19—

Ms. Jennifer Doe
MIS Manager
Acme Incorporated
Any City, MN

Dear Ms. Doe:

When the host system or its operator sends a console message to the RBT operator, the emulator routes it to the workstation (if one has been allocated) or to the printer.

If the printer is busy, "PENDING CONSOLE MSG" is displayed on the panel at regular intervals.

If the printer is not busy, the emulator prints the message.

After the message is printed, "CONSOLE MSG RECEIVED" is displayed on the panel, and the printer resumes normal printing.

Sincerely yours,

Paul Houston
Systems Coordinator
(Courtesy of Robert S. Burger, Burger Associates, Glen Mills, PA)

Tips and Comment:

Making a technical explanation to a client is one of the most rigorous letter-writing tasks. Be certain you are using a vocabulary that both understand and that you are absolutely clear in your explanation. This example from an actual exercise in letter writing uses a sober, no-nonsense approach. What it lacks in charm it makes up for in clarity.

Alternative A:

In order to respond to your questions about the tensile strength of Model 4 Widgets, I have checked with our technical department.

John Grouper, our senior technician, tells me that the specified strength is 8.2. However, recent experience has shown that if you turn the pressure up to 15 p.s.i., you should reduce the tolerance level to 7.5.

Let me know if you have any further questions.

Alternative B:

To make a stable compound, you must use no more than 4.5 percent gum arabic in the initial mixture. Using a higher concentration will cause a breakdown in the third stage reaction and produces an unusable product.

The alternative is to increase the volume of the batches by at least an additional 40 pounds.

I trust this will take care of the problem.

Alternative C:

I'm sorry to disappoint you, but you cannot take the expenses for the seminar as a business deduction.

This sort of expense comes under Rule 123.89, which clearly eliminates the previous practice of deducting such costs.

Explaining a Point of Law

PLANTERS REALTY CORPORATION
34 WEST FRANCE STREET
LOUISVILLE, KY

May 23, 19—

Mr. James Grant
123 Trotter Drive
Louisville, KY

Dear Mr. Grant:

I will not be able to act on your behalf in negotiating for the Bowers property.

Under the laws that govern the real estate business I am legally responsible to the seller and must act in his interest. This is known as the "rule of agency" and is a basic condition of the business.

Unfortunately, many real estate agents appear to ignore this rule, so you may have received the wrong impression in some of your past transactions.

It is possible to reach a signed agreement with an agent to act for you as the buyer, but this requires a special arrangement and cannot include any property for which we have a current listing.

I'll be happy to discuss this with you further.

Yours truly,

Lawrence Planter
Broker

Tips and Comment:

Many forms of business are regulated by public law—including federal, state, and local statutes—and often customers are unaware of how these laws work. An explanation should be carefully worded to avoid offending the customer, yet be clear in stating the legal conditions under which business must be conducted.

Alternative A:

According to P.L. 1023 we are restricted in our ability to form new processing sites without a full review from the local planning and zoning commission.

This is a long and involved process, involving a pile of applications and forms, so we usually do not undertake it lightly.

The first step is for you to submit a full plan for us to consider.

Alternative B:

Thanks for your letter of May 15 and the ideas for a reorganization. I think they will work just fine, if we can cut through the legal situation here in this state.

We must consult our attorney before we will know for certain, but it appears that we must incorporate anew in this state.

I will be in touch with you as soon as I know something definite.

Alternative C:

I am afraid that the process you suggest is illegal.

It may seem strange, considering the practices in other parts of the country, but in this state we are not allowed to follow your suggestions without violating the law.

Let's try to find another method.

Thanks for a Business Suggestion

MICRO ELECTRONICS CORPORATION
WAYCROSS, GA

August 2, 19—

Ms. Margery Klawitt
324 W. Oak
Sherman Village, KS

Dear Ms. Klawitt:

Thanks so much for your thoughtful letter suggesting that we replace the plain tabs with laminated tabs in our User's Guide for our home computer.

After checking into it, we agree with you completely. Laminated tabs do stand up much better under constant use by our home computer customers.

You will be glad to know that as a result of your letter, our User's Guide will have laminated tabs, beginning with the next printing. To show our appreciation for your suggestion, we will send you the very first new version of the Guide.

Thanks again for writing.

Sincerely yours,

Clara S. Bell
Public Relations Coordinator

Tips and Comment:

Who knows the product better than the user? Often customers have good suggestions for improving or changing a product, and many of them will write with their ideas. An effective reply will not only express gratitude for their interest and the suggestion, but give some details of the company's response.

Alternative A:

Hearing from our customers is something we at Micro Electronics appreciate, and even more so when a customer has a good idea about improving our product.

Your suggestion that we use reinforced, laminated tabs in our home computer User's Guide is a good idea. We have looked into the matter and have decided to make the change.

Thanks for helping us out.

Alternative B:

We were happy to get your suggestion about using laminated tabs in the User's Guide. It sounds like a good idea, and our printing division is looking into the cost of putting your idea to work.

I will let you know if it can be done.

Alternative C:

We certainly appreciate your suggestion that laminated tabs will hold out better than our current plain tabs, and we honestly don't know how we missed this in the first printing. The best ideas are often simple and seem obvious after they have been pointed out.

We're going to make the change as soon as possible, and all of our users from now on will benefit from your good idea.

I'll send you a copy of the improved User's Guide as soon as it's off the press.

Making Adjustment for a Customer

K.B. DOLL CORPORATION
346 CARROLL STREET
BROOKLYN, NY

November 2, 19—

Mrs. Bernice Arthur
455 West Northern Ave.
Hooper, LA

Dear Mrs. Arthur:

Thank you for your letter of October 21, reporting that one of the two dolls your ordered was broken when the package arrived. I cannot blame you at all for being disappointed and frustrated.

I am sorry that you have been put to so much trouble, but a replacement doll is on its way to you today, at no charge. I trust this one will arrive intact.

We have modified our packaging, and I am confident that we have eliminated the reason for the breakage. Again, please accept my apology.

Sincerely yours,

Duane Chalmers
Vice-President

Tips and Comment:

When a customer has a legitimate complaint about a problem that is clearly the company's fault, a polite, concise letter making an adjustment is in order. It is a good idea to be specific about accepting responsibility, what is being done to correct the problem, when action will be taken, and if new costs will be involved.

Alternative A:

I have received your letter about the doll broken in shipping.

I'm sorry this happened, and apparently it was all our fault. We have had some problems in our shipping department, and you were, I'm sorry to say, a victim of shoddy packing.

We will, of course, send you a replacement doll immediately (it should arrive within a few days) at no further charge to you.

If there are any other problems, please let me know.

Alternative B:

I'm sorry to learn that one of the dolls you ordered failed to survive the journey by UPS. From your description it sounds as though we failed to cushion the doll properly, so we will take responsibility.

I'm ordering a new doll for you today, and it should be in your hands by the end of the week.

I hope this clears up the matter.

Alternative C:

It looks like we goofed in packing your doll. I'm truly sorry this happened, and we will correct the problem at our expense.

I'll have a new doll sent out today with special attention to the packing.

We do our best to avoid problems like this, but they still happen occasionally.

Let me know if there are any further problems—I want to keep you as a customer.

Refusing an Adjustment

A.G. ROBERTS & CO.
700 CRESTVIEW AVENUE
DENNIS, IL

March 12, 19—

Mr. Robert Cranford
222 43rd Avenue
Tooperville, NM

Dear Mr. Cranford:

We are sorry that you are having trouble with your six-year-old Perfect Refrigerator, and we are confident that your nearest Perfect Appliances dealer can and will remedy the problem.

I wish we could help, but the warranty on this model extended only for three years from the time of purchase. We cannot accept responsibility for this repair.

Sincerely,

Thomas Carey
Customer Service Representative

Tips and Comment:

Customers with a complaint or a demand for adjustment are not always right, and a firm letter is needed to turn down the request. Again, it is a good idea to be specific as to why the adjustment cannot be made.

Alternative A:

While we regret that your Perfect Refrigerator has broken down, the warranty extended only for 24 months after the purchase. Since your refrigerator is now six years old, the company cannot take any responsibility for paying for the service required.

Please see your nearest dealer for repair.

Alternative B:

Although we are unhappy to learn your refrigerator is causing a problem, it was good to know it provided so many years of service before acting up.

Unfortunately, we warrant these models for only four years (still the best warranty on the market for refrigerators), so we cannot help you in paying for the repairs since you bought the refrigerator six years ago.

The A-1 Appliance Shoppe in Tooperville is our certified dealer, and they will be able to give you service at their usual rates.

Alternative C:

We are sorry to hear that your Perfect Refrigerator is malfunctioning, but you are mistaken in believing the warranty is still in effect. You bought the machine six years ago (we have your registration card on file), and the warranty was good for only five years.

Please call your local dealer.

Apology to a Customer

GLOBAL AIRLINES
622 THIRD AVENUE
NEW YORK, NY

September 4, 19—

Mr. P.J. Tomlin
444 West End
Upper Nyack, DE

Dear Mr. Tomlin:

I regret that we were unable to operate your August 3 flight on time and apologize for the inconvenience it caused you.

We can usually give our customers the dependable service they expect from Global Airlines, but once in a while, there can be unexpected mechanical problems. I am sorry it happened on your flight.

We will do our best to give you better service when you fly with us in the future—I know we can.

Sincerely yours,

John U. Ignazzi
Director of Customer Relations

Tips and Comment:

Facing up to making an apology to a customer is usually difficult. If a customer has received less than top-grade service, however, there is no better course than to admit the mistake frankly and give an assurance of better performance in the future. Most complaints come because the customer feels victimized or frustrated. An honest apology, written with sincerity, will do much to make amends and reestablish a good relationship.

Alternative A:

I'm very sorry that your travel plans were disrupted by a mechanical problem with one of our flights on August 3. We try very hard to avoid cancelling a scheduled flight, but mechanical problems do arise.

Our first concern in these cases is the safety of the flight, so when our crew chief is not satisfied with the condition of the aircraft, we always decide on the side of caution.

I hope you will continue to fly with Global Airlines in the future.

Alternative B:

Please accept our apology for the cancelled flight on August 4. According to the report given to me, the plane developed mechanical problems that made it unsafe to fly.

Unfortunately, there was no alternative but to cancel the flight. Our policy is to put the safety of our passengers first, even though it causes inconvenience and delay in some cases.

Because we so seldom have to completely cancel a flight, the chances are this will not happen again when you fly with us in the future.

Alternative C:

Despite our first-class mechanical maintenance program at Global Airlines, on occasion problems come up that make it impossible to get a plane off the ground on schedule.

I am sorry this happened to your flight on August 4.

We will make every effort to see that it doesn't happen in the future.

Apology for an Employee

VALUED MORTGAGE COMPANY
PHOENIX, AZ

February 29, 19—

Ms. Lettie Rankin
321 Fourth Avenue
Feltville, MN

Dear Ms. Rankin:

Thank you for your recent letter. We are sorry to learn about the circumstances which made it necessary for you to write us, and we apologize for the incident.

We agree with you: it's one thing for the computer to make a mistake, but it's another thing to be ignored by the data processing personnel responsible.

To insure prompt handling, I am referring your letter to Mr. Landos, our data processing department manager. You will hear from him soon.

You may be sure that we will do our best to resolve any problem promptly and fairly.

Thank you for bringing this to our attention.

Sincerely,

Charles C. Goldman
Customer Relations Manager

Tips and Comment:

It is often the responsibility of an executive or manager to apologize on behalf of the company for the sins of other employees. This is not a personal apology, but should be made in the name of the entire organization and should probably be rather formal. Moreover, the most effective apology is to explain what is being done to correct the problem.

Alternative A:

Please accept our apology for the problems you have experienced. Computers errors are a fact of life, but there is no excuse for ignoring your letters that tried to remedy the situation.

I have handed the matter directly to the head of our data processing department, and he will be in touch with you within the next few days.

I can guarantee we will not let this happen again.

Alternative B:

You have certainly not received the sort of treatment we pride ourselves on giving our customers. I am sorry you were ignored by the data processing department, and I have taken action to remedy the situation.

You will hear from the head of data processing within the coming week, and I trust the problem will be cleared up.

Thank you for taking the extra time to call this to my attention. I want to be able to make things right with a customer like you.

Alternative C:

I apologize for both the original computer error and the fact that your letters and calls were ignored up to now. We try hard to train our people to respond better than this, but obviously we need to redouble our efforts.

I have instructed the head of the data processing department to call you immediately and clear up the difficulty.

Thanks for letting me know rather than just walking away. I assure you it won't happen again.

Personal Apology for Minor Matter

A. G. ROBERTS CO.
700 CRESTVIEW AVENUE
DENNIS, IL

June 22, 19—

Mr. Ferdinand Henderson
Land Unlimited
405 N. Fleetwood
Bates City, IL

Dear Ferdinand:

In returning your Real Estate Investment Reports, I want to express to you both my thanks and my apologies.

I'm afraid the length of time I have kept this material is nothing short of disgraceful. My study of the reports, however, has been interrupted frequently, and I finished reading them only last night.

It was generous of you to make this information available to me, and I do hope you have not been inconvenienced by the delay in their return.

Sincerely yours,

James Johnson
Manager

Tips and Comment:

Since everyone makes minor mistakes, a brief, personal apology may keep the wheels of business turning. It is not necessary to over-apologize, and the tone of the letter will depend on both the circumstances and how well the letter writer knows the person to whom the apology is directed.

Alternative A:

I know I said I'd return these reports right away, but my schedule has looked like spaghetti for the last week. I just finished reading them last night.

Thanks for being patient—this is really good material and I'll think about what I might be able to do in real estate during the next quarter.

Hope you didn't need this sooner.

Alternative B:

Thank you so much for letting me look at the Real Estate Investment Reports. I'm sorry to have taken so long to get them back to you, but I was called out of town unexpectedly and therefore was delayed in my reading.

I thought the reports were a fine example of providing just the right information.

Again, accept my apology for the delay.

Alternative C:

I may be shot for holding on to your reports for several weeks longer than intended, but I couldn't help it. The flu bug got me, and I could hardly hold my head up let alone read about investments.

I'm finally back at full steam, and I finished looking through the material last night.

I'll let you know if any ideas spring to mind.

5

MAKING THE DEAL: SALES AND MARKETING LETTERS

At the heart of most businesses are sales—a fact that all high-level executives recognize and must deal with continuously. Without good sales letters, a business will cease to prosper. The following examples show how executives keep the concept of fostering sales in the foreground of all such letters. The content and situation may vary from letter to letter, but the intent of the letter-writing executive is constant: to make the sale or to set the stage for a sale in the future. Some of these sales letters may seem indirect and low key, such as a relatively routine greeting or letter of congratulation. There are, however, no routine sales letters; each one must be crafted carefully to achieve its intended goal.

General Sales Letter

YOU'RE ON
Access to Television and Radio
19 MADISON AVENUE
BEVERLY, MA 01915

October 13, 19—

Mr. John D. Doe
Principal
John D. Doe & Associates
P.O. Box 1342
Wildomar, CA

Dear Mr. Doe:

Thank you for your interest in our products and services concerning your reference 540-US/JH/N.

Our principal product is an album of three audio cassettes entitled "The Success System for Getting Television Coverage." Corporations, trade associations, government agencies, hospitals, universities, and not-for-profit groups across the United States and Canada are using these tapes to obtain positive electronic media exposure for their products, services, and ideas. A partial users list, order form, and promotional brochure are enclosed.

We would be happy to work with you on a drop-shipment arrangement. You send us a check for 60 percent of the cost of each album along with the customer's name and address. The remaining 40 percent goes to you.

I would also like to tell you about a new subsidiary of our company called Writing For Success. We conduct half-day or full-day workshops on-site to help people at all levels improve their writing skills. We can also custom design training materials for individual organizations. For more information feel free to call me at the number listed above.

Sincerely,

Richard M. Goldberg
President, YOU'RE ON
(Courtesy of Richard M. Goldberg, YOU'RE ON, Beverly, MA)

Tips and Comment:

This actual sales letter is a real-life example of a routine but important communication. The writer hopes to establish a new marketing outlet for his company, and he employs a combination of sales pitch, explanation of the product, and details of the financial arrangement. This is all packed into one letter that will serve, therefore, several purposes. The key point, however, is convincing the recipient. One of the good techniques used here is to draw attention to the previous success and wide distribution of the product.

Alternative A:

I'm happy to offer you the chance to get in on the ground floor of our new distribution system. We are launching our product in the tri-state area after great success in the Illinois region.

To date, we have sold 2 million units through dealers such as you. The products seem to leap off the shelf and into customers' hands. In fact, our biggest problem has been to keep up with current demand while planning for this new expansion of our distribution area.

We will supply you with an initial stock and point-of-purchase display units. The retail price per unit is $4.69, with a discount to you of 45 percent.

Alternative B:

Thank you for the letter of inquiry about our services.

Amalgamated is a full-service company, offering pre-production processing. We have been in business since 1975 and enjoy a great reputation among our more than 40 clients in the field (a list is attached).

As you can see, we work with the top companies, all of whom would be happy to supply references for our work.

I'll call you next week to discuss things in more detail.

Alternative C:

Your letter just reached my desk, and I'm happy to reply.

We can, indeed, supply you with artwork for your forthcoming display at the series of conferences. Our staff will be able to schedule your work at your convenience.

I am enclosing a set of sample of work we have done for other clients.

Let me know when we can get together.

Follow-Up Sales Letter

NUMERICA PRODUCTS GROUP
A DIVISION OF NUMERICA, INC.
P.O. BOX 2892
PRINCETON, NY

February 2, 19—

Mr. James Harvey
MIS Division
Hopper, Inc.
Riverdale, KS

Dear Mr. Harvey,

I'm sorry you weren't able to join us at our recent RAMIS II sales seminar. Since you indicated an interest in RAMIS II by registering for the seminar, I thought you would like more information on our system.

RAMIS II is a proven, easy-to-use computer language with comprehensive capabilities for database management, report preparation, and information retrieval. It was created for the UNIX operating system and designed for use with the latest in work stations.

Since its origin, RAMIS II has been expanded continually to include new features and benefits. These improvements have helped users such as financial planners, market analysts, personnel administrators, and management information systems specialists who are among the 2,000 current clients with RAMIS II.

The enclosed material gives a detailed overview of the RAMIS II system. I think it will be worth your time to look it over closely.

A RAMIS II representative will phone you within the next few days to answer any questions.

Sincerely yours,

Jane Babbit
Vice-President
U.S. Operations

Tips and Comment:

Follow-ups are crucial to sales and marketing, and letters are often the best tools for continuing to work towards a sale. A letter is hard to ignore, and it gives the opportunity for both promotion and passing on additional information that may make the sale. The most effective follow-up letters build on previous contacts, add new reasons to buy, and specifically establish another contact in the future.

Alternative A:

It was a pleasure to talk to you yesterday and learn more about your growing company.

I think that the RAMIS II system is just what you need to solve the problems we discussed.

RAMIS II is a comprehensive package of software that we designed especially for the medium-sized user, and it takes into account both the limits and the potential of situations like yours.

Best of all, it's not as expensive as some of the competing software systems, because we have been in the marketplace for so many years and have already absorbed the cost of developing the system.

I'm enclosing some detailed technical information, and I'll call you again next week to discuss setting up a demo.

Alternative B:

Thanks for stopping by our booth at the trade association fair and for signing one of our cards.

I'm enclosing a brochure that shows our full line of products, including the new RAMIS II system.

I'll call you in the next few days for an appointment.

Alternative C:

It was good to talk to you on the phone today. As promised, I'm sending you a sample of RAMIS II by express courier.

Try it out on your own system over the next couple of days, and I'll call you for an appointment on Wednesday.

Let me know if there are any other things we should discuss.

Reminder Sales Letter

TOM ACKERMAN
MASSACHUSETTS MUTUAL LIFE INSURANCE COMPANY
2365 HARRODSBURG ROAD
LEXINGTON, KY 40503

June 23, 19—

Ms. Lisa K. Boone
Route 2
Prescott Road
Paris, KY

Dear Lisa:

Time has passed since our last meeting, and since your age changes for insurance purposes in about six weeks, I think we should review your program. Now is the sensible time to check any change in your status or intentions.

Of course, I would be happy to meet with you at any place that is convenient, but I suggest that we can probably accomplish more by meeting here at our offices where we have the computers and files immediately at our disposal.

I'll ask my administrative assistant to call and set up a time with you to meet me, and she has the ability to make the appointment wherever and whenever you say.

I think you may be pleasantly surprised at how well your program has done and the kinds of flexibility that are available to you. I'll look forward to getting together with you.

Yours truly,

Tom Ackerman
(Courtesy of Tom Ackerman, Lexington, KY)

Tips and Comment:

Sales-based businesses (such as insurance in this real-life example) are smart to review periodically the status of clients. By setting up standard reminder letters as part of a "tickler" system, little new effort is needed to stay in touch with clients and jog their memories. The tone of individual letters may vary depending on the business relationship. Better known and more important clients should get a letter with a personal tone; less personal clients may be addressed more formally.

Alternative A:

This letter is just to let you know that in about six weeks you will be changing age for insurance purposes. If any circumstances have changed which cause you to want to discuss additional coverage, it would be wise to do so before that date.

I don't want to create any unnecessary hassles for you in this regard, so I'll wait for your phone call rather than calling you, if indeed you'd like to get together and review your program.

Alternative B:

A life insurance policy is a "living document" and needs to be tended from time to time to make sure it's doing what the policyholder wishes.

You have a contract with Allied Mutual, and it would seem to me beneficial from your point of view to review where it is and what it is doing in light of your circumstances.

This is a particularly good time to do so because, for insurance purposes, you are about to change age. Anything you might choose to do to alter your insurance program would best be done before you become a year older and the rates go up.

I've included a reply form that you can stick in the mail, and we'll call to set up an appointment.

I look forward to hearing from you.

Alternative C:

Our files show that you are about to change ages for insurance purposes, and that this is the time to review any changes that might be needed.

Please let me know when we can meet to discuss this.

Direct Mail Sales Letter

FIRST NATIONAL BANK
P.O. BOX 1000
HANOVER, MA

August 30, 19—

Dear Quick Cash Invitee:

I sincerely hope you'll share my enthusiasm for this new program.

The banking industry has had to make many changes in recent years to accommodate the changing needs of its customers. But surprisingly, the loan process has remained for the most part unchanged—too inflexible, often impersonal, and generally unsympathetic to the needs and lifestyles of the bank's customers.

Now, that's all changed with Quick Cash. But this program is available only to a select few by invitation. I urge you to take advantage of this opportunity by simply completing the enclosed reply card and mailing it today.

Taking the frustration, formality, and rigidity out of personal loans is an important step for our industry. Quick Cash is an important step for you.

John D. Mills
Vice-President

Tips and Comment:

A lot rides on the persuasive appeal of direct mail letters, so they should be crafted carefully. Sending letters (usually with other materials in the same envelope) to a large number of names selected by special demographic or interest category may be effective, but it is also usually very expensive. Therefore, the text of the letter must be hard-hitting, targeted precisely for the potential buyers. When direct mail letters are successful, they are like owning a goldmine, but the better the focus of the message, the better the result.

Alternative A:

Here is your chance to take advantage of a special offer that we make just once a year.

Until May 1, you can receive 10 percent off on all bulk purchases of thermo-widgets from the Tele-Tik Corporation.

As a previous customer, you know the high quality and superb satisfaction that our thermo-widgets provide. There's no need to sell you on our product.

However, the competition is fierce and price selection is a crucial factor in your purchasing decision.

That's why we make this offer for a limited time. You can stock up on thermo-widgets at a great price and still know you're getting the best.

Fill out the enclosed reply order form, and mail it today!

Alternative B:

You may be able to repair a damaged heart valve with your eyes closed, but how well do you cope with worker unemployment compensation or managing office cash flow?

There is more to the modern practice of medicine than healing. The complex details of the business side of medicine present a challenge that you must meet.

We're now offering a way to stay on top of your day-to-day medical business through a subscription to *The Business Side of Medicine*—an easy-to-understand, monthly newsletter aimed specifically at helping you to solve your problems.

We're making a special offer of only $50 per year for first time subscribers like you.

Look over the enclosed sample and send in the subscription reply form today.

Alternative C:

A free watch? There must be a catch, you say.

Of course there is...but it's an easy catch to live with.

Just call us for an appointment to see our new cleaning and polishing line in action. Not only will you learn how to take care of your cleaning problems at low cost, but we'll give you a new watch, absolutely free.

Call now!

Answering an Information Request

**PRECISE INSTRUMENTS
INCORPORATED**
DALLAS, TX

August 23, 19—

Ms. Amelia V. Blake
Associated Electronics Corp.
430 Tournier Blvd.
Allentown, ME

Dear Ms. Blake:

Thank you for your interest in Precise Instruments products. It's our pleasure to enclose the information you requested.

Precise Instruments has developed and produced literally hundreds of products for the electronics industry. We sincerely believe that our broad experience, technical know-how, and extensive production capabilities can serve you, both now and in the years ahead.

Please let me know if I can be of further assistance.

Sincerely

Philip S. Conductor,
Sales Division

Tips and Comment:

When a potential client requests information, the relationship is a long way down the road toward a sale. The follow-up cover letter should keep the interaction alive and get in a sales pitch. If the customer's request gives a clue as to their interest, try to focus the sales message as tightly as possible by providing specific information. If this is not possible, just include a general message about the company.

Alternative A:

I'm happy to pass on the enclosed information on our product line. I think you will be particularly interested in the material on pages 4 and 5.

We think we have the best line at the lowest cost on the market, and the testimony of our current customers backs up this belief.

I'll plan to speak with you again.

Alternative B:

I'm sending all of the specifications you requested in another package (it will take a couple of days to reach you).

Please give me a call when you have looked over the material. I think there is no doubt we can help solve your current problems, and I'll be happy to go over all this in more detail.

Perhaps I'll ask one of our technical engineers to come along on my next visit.

Alternative C:

Since you weren't certain when you called about exactly what you might need from our line, I'm enclosing our general brochure. We have more specific and detailed information that you may want to look over after you have narrowed the field.

I'll be happy to assist in any way I can.

Please give me a call when you are ready to discuss an order in more detail.

Turning Down an Information Request

PRINCE PUBLISHING COMPANY, INC.
VILLAGE CIRCLE BUILDING
WEST NYACK, NY

May 3, 19—

Mr. Kenneth O'Brien
879 Overview Dr.
Upper Falls, AL

Dear Mr. O'Brien:

Thank you for your letter of April 14, and for your kind comments about our company.

We would like to send you a copy of the pamphlet you requested, but the supply has been exhausted completely by a unexpected recent demand.

We are planning to reprint the material immediately, however, and I will see that you get a copy as soon as it is off the press.

If we can be of service to you in any other way, please let me know.

Sincerely yours,

James K. Parker

Tips and Comment:

It is frustrating, perhaps even embarrassing, to admit that a request for information cannot be met, but it is sometimes unavoidable. The letter to the interested party (who is also a potential client) should stress the soundness of the reasons why the information is not available and explain if the request can be filled in the future. Try to keep the sales contact alive.

Alternative A:

I'm sorry to report that we cannot send you the pamphlet you requested right now. There has been so much demand since the article appeared in the *New York Times* that our modest supply ran out rapidly.

If requests continue to come in, we will probably reprint the pamphlet. If we do, I'll put your name on the list to receive a copy.

Please let me know if we can do anything else to help.

Alternative B:

I wish I could send you the material you asked for, but we have discontinued that line of equipment during the last six months.

Instead, we have put on the market an entirely new series that we think far surpasses our old line. Although it does cost more, it also has about twice the capacity.

I'm taking the liberty of sending you a brochure on the new series.

Please feel free to call me if you are interested.

Alternative C:

The booklet you requested is unavailable at the moment, due to a devastating fire in our New Jersey warehouse.

I'm sorry to say that we lost most of our backlist in the blaze.

We are just now making plans for replacing this stock, and I'll let you know if we decide to go ahead with a reprint of the booklet.

Invitation to an Open House

PRENTICE HALL
ENGLEWOOD CLIFFS, NJ

May 1, 19—

Mr. B. Traverny
347 North Broadway
Glickville, NY

Dear Mr. Traverny,

You are cordially invited to attend our annual Spring Art Festival. The showing will take place in the Prentice Hall cafeteria from 5:00 P.M. to 7:00 P.M. on Monday, May 28. Refreshments will be served.

It has long been our practice to sponsor a continuing program of art appreciation for the enjoyment of our employees and visitors. Now for the first time our employees will have the opportunity to display their creative talents along with our art collection.

During the past several years, the Prentice Hall art collection has grown to include examples from many different schools of painting from many countries. In addition, through the courtesy of various individual art collectors, artists, and galleries, many works have been loaned to us for the exhibition.

We believe you will enjoy yourself, and we are looking forward to your visit.

Cordially,

J. Alfred Persons
R.S.V.P.

Tips and Comment:

Firms make a common practice of sponsoring semi-social or cultural events with no overt business purpose (of course, a major underlying motivation is to promote good customer and public relations). An invitation to such an affair need not be overly formal and may take the form of a standard-text letter, stating time, place, and purpose.

Alternative A:

I'm writing to invite you to our annual Open House and Art Festival to be held on May 28 from 5:00 P.M. to 7:00 P.M. A light buffet will be served in the cafeteria, which is also the site of the art show.

Our corporate art collection is one of the best in the area, and we take great pride in the comments it has drawn in years past. During the last twelve months, we've added some fascinating art to the collection, which will all be on display.

Let me know if you will be able to attend.

Alternative B:

We are holding our annual Paper Show on May 28, from 5:00 P.M. to 7:00 P.M. in the ball room of the Hilton.

This is your invitation to attend.

On display will be samples from over 50 paper companies and allied printing industries. It should be a good chance to see what is happening at the forefront of the business.

As usual, we will be serving our famous buffet (with an open bar).

We hope you will be there.

Alternative C:

This is my personal invitation to you to attend our Open House on May 28 from 5:00 P.M. to 7:00 P.M.

We want all our customers to see the new equipment we just installed, and we want to say thank you for your patronage during the past year.

Please let me know if you will attend.

Publicizing an Award

FITZHUGH SERVICE, INC.
78 UPPER STREET
OVERLOOK HEIGHTS, UT

January 12, 19—

Terminal Hotels Corp.
One West Plaza
Metroville, UT

Gentlemen:

Fitzhugh Service, Inc. is proud to announce that we will be this year's recipient of the Four-Star Service Award from the ASSA.

As you know, this is the highest award given in the hotel service industry and is voted on by a blue-ribbon selection committee.

The actual presentation ceremony will be at the annual ASSA convention in Tulsa next month, but we wanted you to know of the award ahead of time.

We look forward to working with customers like you in the future. Your help and inspiration have given us the opportunity to become a four-star firm.

Truly,

Greg Hancher
President

Tips and Comment

Awards are nice; using them to improve the sales climate is even better. If a business wins an award there is no reason to be unduly modest, and a letter to clients announcing the good news may be an effective tool in cementing a relationship. The tone of such letters is a delicate matter, since the line between justifiable pride and off-putting boastfulness may be a thin one. However, a heartfelt expression of genuine pleasure (plus a thanks for the client's role in providing business opportunities) is never amiss.

Alternative A:

This is to let you know the good news that we have been selected as the Small Business of the Year by the Chamber of Commerce.

We are, of course, very pleased to receive this award, and we realize that it was made possible only through the steady patronage of customers like you.

We intend to continue to offer the same quality of service in the future and look forward to working with you.

Thanks for your help.

Alternative B:

I am pleased to tell you that I have been designated as Realty Agent of the Year by the state Realty Association. The award was made at our recent state meeting in Titustown.

While this is a special honor that only a handful of realty agents ever attain, I know that most of the credit is due to those who have been my clients over the years, so please accept my thanks.

If you have the occasion to think of selling property in the future, I hope you will call me.

Alternative C:

We have just learned that our new building has won the annual design competition for office complexes. This is an exciting event and confirms what we have believed since we moved in: this is the finest facility in the state.

If you haven't been in the complex, please call me and I'll arrange a tour. It is really a state-of-the-art building with many features I think you will find interesting.

Contacting an Inactive Account

AGRO MANUFACTURING COMPANY
CORN AND SOYBEAN PRODUCTS
DECATUR, IL

April 4, 19—

Reliance Milling Products
34 Western Road
Maizeville, IA

Gentlemen:

We have missed you!

In fact, we are concerned when an excellent account such as yours fails to return for more business.

We try to handle our accounts with efficiency, courtesy, and understanding, so we wonder why you have stopped placing orders with us.

Please use the enclosed form and self-addressed, stamped envelope to let us know, frankly, what has happened.

Sincerely,

Jim Hatcher
Sales Manager

Tips and Comment:

A certain percentage of successful sales amounts to nothing more than keeping a close eye on regular customers and following up when sales slacken. This kind of letter should be built into the standard procedures of a sales office, employing a form letter and a tickler file. It may yield large dividends.

Alternative A:

In looking over our order book for the last couple of months, I noticed that you don't appear.

We've had a steady stream of orders from you previously for more than a year, so I am distressed that you seem to have dropped out.

Is there some problem that we don't know about? If so, please call my attention to it, and I will do everything possible to clear things up.

I really want to continue to supply your needs. Give me a call.

Alternative B:

Something is missing—your regular monthly order.

It has just come to my attention that you have not placed an order with us for some time, after many months of activity.

If your needs have changed or you have been unhappy in any way with our product or service, please let me know immediately.

I want you back as a customer.

Alternative C:

It's now been eight months since we heard from you with an order, and I want to follow up, since you have long been one of our most valuable accounts.

If there are any complaints, I'd like to hear about them first hand and be able to correct the problem.

Please use the enclosed to drop me a line. I'll respond immediately.

Introducing a New Salesperson

AMERICAN VISCOSE CORPORATION
LOS ANGELES, CA

February 9, 19—

Film Division

To Our Business Friends:

It is a pleasure to announce that Mr. E.R. "Mike" Smith of our Technical Service Department will now work out of the Los Angeles office to give you prompt assistance with your packaging needs.

Mike, a specialist with cellophane for 25 years, has broad experience in production, quality control, technical service, film evaluation, and development. He is exceptionally well qualified to find solutions to your problems and to answer questions involving cellophane and packaging machinery, laminating, adhesives, and ink.

Now that Mike is with us, you will get even better service from Avisco on the West Coast.

Sincerely,

M.G. O'Connor
West Coast District Manager

Tips and Comment:

A formal letter to customers announcing the appointment or transfer of key sales people not only introduces the new contact, but reinforces the presence of your company in the market. A good introductory letter will explain the background and extol the abilities of the salesperson and make it clear the parent company has confidence in the new appointment.

Alternative A:

This is to let you know that Mike Smith is now taking over the local region for Avisco, and he will be calling on you during the next few days to see about meeting your service requirements.

Mike is a ten-year veteran of the packaging business. Until recently, he worked in Tennessee with several of the large printing and publishing companies there.

We were thrilled to be able to add Mike to our team. I know he'll give you great service.

Alternative B:

Let me introduce Mike Smith, our newest sales representative.

Mike has been around the printing industry for more than fifteen years, and he knows printing operations from the ground up. He began as a press assistant and worked his way up to an account rep.

Mike is especially good at helping customers like you, who have special requirements.

He will stop by your plant soon.

Alternative C:

We have recently expanded our sales force, and I'm happy to tell you that Mike Smith will be your salesperson from now on.

Mike is new to the business, but he has already shown a lot of energy and willingness to work hard on behalf of his accounts.

Please spend a few moments getting to know Mike when he calls on you next week.

Welcoming a Potential Client to Town

FIRST NATIONAL BANK
WAYCROSS, GA

April 1, 19—

Mr. Thomas Jett
Micro Electronics Corporation
Industrial Park
Waycross, GA

Dear Mr. Jett:

I would like to take this opportunity to welcome you and the Micro Electronics Corporation to Waycross and to extend to you a warm and cordial invitation to do your banking with the First National Bank.

Our bank is equipped and staffed to provide the most modern banking services:

- computer payroll services
- interactive, on-line video terminals connecting our main database with all teller and customer service stations
- a telecommunication system for banking anywhere in the world
- fifteen automatic, 24-hour tellers around the city
- safety deposit boxes equipped to handle mainframe computer backup tapes
- a full-time representative for your accounts.

We would appreciate the opportunity of serving you and your operation. Please call me.

Cordially yours,

Frank Como
President

Tips and Comment:

Any company that offers goods or services to the local market will reap benefits from keeping a close eye on the newspaper or local business publications for notices of new businesses moving to town. A letter of welcome that also includes a mild sales pitch is an easy and inexpensive way to make a first contact. A form letter can be written ahead of time and kept on file. It need only be tailored quickly for the specific situation. Getting such a letter out fast may be the difference between winning the business or losing to the competition.

Alternative A:

I was delighted to see that Micro Electronics will open the new plant next month. All of us in the Waycross business community are looking forward it.

As president of the largest and oldest bank in the city, I want to offer our services. We have made special efforts over the last decade to keep our people and equipment at the forefront of banking practices, and I can say without fear of contradiction that we are the only bank in the region which can offer full computer services and full international banking.

I know you do a good deal of trade overseas, so our international capabilities should fit your needs. Please give me a call and we can discuss this.

Again, welcome to Waycross.

Alternative B:

Welcome to Waycross—I know you'll like living and doing business here.

If you haven't yet selected a local bank, I want to offer the services of First National. We have the biggest and most advanced computer banking system in the region and we'd be happy to discuss your needs.

Please call me at your first opportunity.

Alternative C:

It is a pleasure to welcome you personally to Waycross. I enjoyed meeting you last month at the business club luncheon, and I'm excited about the prospects of what Micro Electronics will add to our city.

I'd also like to follow up on our conversation about your banking requirements. As I said at the time, First National is about to put a new and fully up-to-date computer system on line that should be able to handle your special needs in payroll.

I'll give you a call next week to set up an appointment. In the meantime, you might like to look over the enclosed.

Greeting a New Customer

**THE ASSOCIATED LIFE ASSURANCE
SOCIETY OF THE UNITED STATES**
1355 AVENUE OF THE AMERICAS
NEW YORK, NY

December 3, 19—

Mr. and Mrs. Glenn Jenkins
144 Grenoble Parkway
Frankfort, TN

Dear Mr. and Mrs. Jenkins:

One of the business duties that I enjoy most is the privilege of welcoming new Associated policyholders. I want you to know that you now can call on a large group of individuals who are dedicated to serving the needs of each one of our millions of policyholders efficiently, courteously, and promptly, while safeguarding the future for all.

Our Agency and Cashiers' offices throughout the country are staffed by trained, capable men and women whose first concern is to serve you well. They maintain complete policy records on confidential computer files and help you and your Associated agent keep your insurance coverage adequate and economical. They will assist you, for example, in beneficiary changes, policy loans, or other matters that may arise because of a change in your family or your economic status.

You can be assured that the Associated investment organization safeguards your savings as a sacred trust and prudently invests the policyholders' funds in safe and diverse investments.

Since it is impossible for me to meet all of our policyholders, I hope you will accept this note as a personal and cordial greeting.

Sincerely yours,

Leonard Hilts
President

Tips and Comment:

A letter from the head of the company to a new client or customer may help to solidify the business relationship. If the company is a large one and the number of total customers high, there should be no pretense of a personal letter (although computer files are capable of creating this appearance). Nonetheless, the idea of a letter from the company's chief officer is effective. In smaller companies, an individual letter may be possible and may go far toward stimulating more sales.

Alternative A:

Welcome to the Associated family. Although we are one of the largest insurance companies in the country, we have never ceased to look on our policyholders as part of an extended family.

It's our job to see that you receive first-rate service and that your investment is fully protected while earning the highest possible returns. Our record speaks for itself.

If there are ever any questions about your policy records or if you need a policy loan or other services, please let your local agent know, and we'll see to your needs.

Thanks again for joining the family.

Alternative B (small company):

It was a pleasure to see your name appear as a new client this month. Let me assure you that we will do everything we can to keep you happy and satisfied with our service.

If you have any special needs that our representative, Ms. Dawson, can't handle on her own, please give me a call. We have a full team of specialists ready to back her up.

I'm looking forward to a long and fruitful relationship.

Alternative C:

It was really good to sign the contract with you yesterday. I know that we will be able to do good things together over the coming months and raise your volume of sales with a solid program of advertising.

I've already put the preliminary plan down on paper, and I'll stop by to discuss it next week when you get back from your road trip.

I'm really looking forward to working with you.

Anniversary of Doing Business

SECOND MANUFACTURERS TRUST COMPANY
330 EAST AVENUE
NEW YORK, NY

September 1, 19—

Josiah Littleton, President
ABC Company
Dobb's Ferry, NY

Dear Mr. Brown:

More than a generation ago—thirty-five years to be exact—the ABC Company first opened an account with us. We wish to mark this important anniversary by telling you how much this long-standing relationship has meant to us.

Second Manufacturers Trust was then a small bank. The growth we have enjoyed since then has been due in large measure to the confidence and loyalty of friends like you.

We are happy to include you among our best and longest-standing customers, and we hope as the years go by we can continue to make our services even more useful to you and your company.

Sincerely,

Leonard K. Crump
President

Tips and Comment:

A simple letter to customers on the anniversary of beginning business with them is an effective and efficient sales tool. All it takes is a tickler file and a form letter. Both large and small companies can plug into the benefits of such a letter. The letter should remind the client of the long and happy association and emphasize the mutual successes of the past.

Alternative A:

It's hard to believe that you first opened an account with Manufacturers Bank thirty-five years ago today—and even harder to believe the changes that have taken place since then.

We were just a small bank then, and you were a young company just beginning to find a market. We've both grown and prospered together. What a pleasure to note this significant anniversary. Let's hope for many more to come.

Alternative B:

It was a year ago that I walked into your office, and you decided to place your first order with me. Since then, we've done more than $30,000 of business, and I am extremely pleased to be able to mark the anniversary.

Having you as a client has meant a good deal to the success of my company. And, I have personally enjoyed working with you. You are the sort of client who makes this business fun and not work.

I hope we can celebrate many more such "birthdays" together.

Alternative C:

You may not have realized it, but today marks the twenty-fifth anniversary of our business relationship. I think it is a testament to both of us that we have been together so long. Not many things in modern business endure so well as we have.

Oddly enough, we have never met, but I hope someday we will and I can tell you face-to-face how much I have enjoyed the partnership.

Congratulations on a Client's Anniversary

ACME/ZENITH CORPORATION
222 OVERLOOK PARKWAY
WORCESTER HEIGHTS, ND

June 4, 19—

Mrs. Geraldine Gabbard, President
Gabbard Products, Inc.
345 Testament St.
Worcester Heights, ND

Dear Mrs. Gabbard:

Congratulations on the twenty-fifth anniversary of your firm. I know this is a proud day for you, your family, and all of your employees and customers over the years.

There are very few enterprises in our community (or any community) which can lay claim to so many years of success. You must be proud of your accomplishment.

At Acme/Zenith, we are also proud to have been part of your quarter century of business, and we look forward to a long association in the future.

Yours truly,

Bernard T. Keeler
President

Tips and Comment:

Another simple sales device is a letter of congratulations to a client on a significant anniversary of their own business. It may be more or less personal, depending on the circumstances, but it always gives an opportunity to point out shared pride in accomplishment and to look toward more business in the future.

Alternative A:

If our records are correct, today marks the end of your first year in operation, and I want to pass on my congratulations for a successful start up.

I have admired your determination and energy, and I've been especially pleased to be part of your ongoing plans.

It's been a genuine pleasure to do business with you, and I look forward to many more years to come.

Alternative B:

I had to pinch myself when I was reminded that you began your corporation five years ago this month. The time has flown by, and it seems as though each quarter we have done more and more together.

It is a good feeling to know you have been successful and that we have had some hand in all of it.

Here's to many more years!

Alternative C:

I was just sitting here, remembering that day ten years ago when you called me with the news you were going ahead with organizing the company. I recall how many conversations we shared then and in the years since.

It has been a pleasure to see you prosper and grow.

Congratulations on a job well done.

6

MONEY MATTERS: LETTERS ABOUT FINANCE

Top executives are expected to understand finance, and they should be able to deal with the complexities of finance in letters about all aspects of the subject. The following model letters illustrate the range of communications on financial matters, from giving advice to asking for financial participation in a new venture. As the letters show, it is important to avoid the technical jargon of finance in most letters; yet at the same time, an effective executive will not patronize the reader. This balance is sometimes difficult to achieve, but the sample letters provide good models. The selection of an appropriate vocabulary is crucial in financial matters that border on the technical.

Analysis of a Financial Statement

FINANCIAL MANAGEMENT SERVICES, INC.
P.O. BOX 56
UPPER FOREST, MA

March 5, 19—

Ms. Karen Langworthy
President and CEO
Overbrook Enterprises
34 Dover Avenue
Dover Bay, MA

Dear Ms. Langworthy:

We have reviewed your financial statement for calendar 19—, and have the following comments, which you may wish to consider for planning.

The overall picture is healthy, with a satisfactory net income figure. Your sales continue to hold steady in the face of an industry-wide shake-out, and your expenses stayed within an acceptable range.

We do notice, however, that your cash situation remains tight, especially during the third quarter. If you had more cash on hand, you could take more advantage of 30-day cash discounts when ordering, and this would have a very positive overall effect on your net.

We suggest you consider establishing a short-term line of credit with your local bank, which would allow you to draw on a cash reserve during the third-quarter crunch.

Yours truly,

James K. Polders
Vice President

Tips and Comment:

As in most explanatory letters, an analysis of a company's financial statement must be crystal clear. The greatest pitfall is to slip into financial or accounting jargon that the customer may not understand fully. Be orderly and precise, and be certain to use direct language when explaining your analysis.

Alternative A:

Your most recent financial statement looks considerably better than the last one. You have improved the ratio of capital to income, and you have improved your overall cash position.

If the trends continue, we think you will be able to consider the sale of public shares within the next two years, but—as we discussed previously—you should be cautious in taking this step.

Alternative B:

The report of yearly expenses on your most recent financial statement causes some concern.

This has been creeping up for the last two years, and the ratios now appear to be in a state of continual decay.

Perhaps we should discuss this further in light of the sales projection figures.

Alternative C:

If we interpret your most recent statement correctly, you are now assigning the costs of the Weatherby contract to the general overhead account.

While this gives you a rosier view of the contract in the short term, the overall effect is to obscure your actual return.

We suggest a new system of accounts for this contract.

Proposal for Financing a New Business

LAWRENCE C. PLOCK
567 OVERLOOK ROAD
WEST CHESTER, AL

October 5, 19—

Mr. George T. Plano
Venture Associates, Inc.
45 The Lane
Birmingham, AL

Dear. Mr. Plano:

Thank you for the opportunity to follow up our earlier conversation.

Our initial capital needs for the proposed new company will be in the range of $300,000. We have raised thus far $175,000 through a combination of personal investment from the three partners and a loan from our existing corporation.

We seek the balance of $125,000 from you in exchange for a 49 percent equity position in the new company.

As noted in our prospectus, we project a return on capital investment of 19 percent over the first three years of the enterprise.

Based on our extensive analysis of the business projects, we feel the risk is reasonable and the prospects very good. All of our advisors agree. The niche for a small-business industrial cleaning service clearly exists.

I would welcome the chance to discuss this in more detail.

Truly yours,

Lawrence C. Plock

Tips and Comment:

The writer of this letter has chosen the direct, no-nonsense approach as a follow-up to an earlier presentation. This is the hard pitch, asking specifically for an investor's money for a new venture. The letter sets forth the need, the amount desired from the investor, the bare bones of the conditions, and a mild sales message. Depending on the situation, such proposal letters might be more or less detailed and have more or less sales content.

Alternative A:

My partners and I, organized as Fullerton, Inc., wish to discuss with the bank the possibility of establishing a line of credit for a new enterprise.

We have researched and planned the launch of a local company to service the large number of widget manufacturers in the tri-county area.

Enclosed is a copy of our business plan for your examination.

As you will see from the plan, we need only a reasonable line of credit to finance our new venture.

Alternative B:

Power cleaning is the wave of the future in the widget industry, and we intend to take the wave at its crest.

The enclosed prospectus gives you the details of our plan. Please read it carefully.

I'll call you in a few days to discuss the plan and how you can help us with the financial aspects.

Alternative C:

Our conversation a few weeks ago at the hotel set me to thinking seriously about the possibilities of organizing a new company to move into the power cleaning field.

I've talked this over with John, and we agree that it has a very strong potential. In fact, we are ready to move.

Are you interested in taking an equity position with us?

Give me a call.

Funding Approval

PERMIAN BANK
40 DANVERS STREET
MIDLAND, TX

February 2, 19—

Mrs. Helen McIntyre
President
Groves, Inc.
35 West Floral Street
Midland, TX

Dear Mrs. McIntyre:

I am happy to notify you officially that your application for a commercial loan has been approved, subject to the following conditions.

The funds will be available to you on execution of a loan document. The money may be paid directly into your account at the bank or in any other form you require.

The total amount will be $75,000.

The term of the loan will be 36 months with payment due in a lump sum when the note matures.

Interest will accrue on the amount of the loan at the rate of 18 percent per annum and will be due at the maturity of the note.

If you have any questions, please feel free to call me at the bank.

Truly yours,

Glenn Marsh
Vice President

Tips and Comment:

A letter granting commercial funding should spell out the details of the transaction, including the date, the amount, the interest terms, and the repayment requirements. While the essential purpose of such a letter is to make all the information available to the borrower, it does not hurt to keep the tone friendly.

Alternative A:

We are pleased to grant you the loan you applied for last week.

The terms will be as we discussed then: a term of one year with monthly payments beginning May 30; an interest rate on the unpaid balance of 15 percent; and an option to roll over the loan at the end of the year.

Please call me if you have questions.

Alternative B:

Your loan has been approved on the terms set forth on the loan application form.

Please stop by my office at your convenience to sign the required documents.

We look forward to working with you on this project.

Alternative C:

Nothing makes us happier than to be able to supply the financial needs of our community clients.

I'm happy to let you know that your loan application has been approved.

As soon as you execute the documents, we will make $25,000 available to your account. The life of the loan will be 90 days, and we will charge 19 percent interest on the full amount, payable at the end of the note.

Explaining a Finance Charge

FIRST BANK OF WYOMING
P.O. BOX 3
LARAMIE, WY

September 5, 19—

Mr. Patrick N. Butler
President
Butler Enterprises
2121 Lookout Mountain Drive
Laramie, WY

Dear Mr. Butler:

We are happy to add Butler Enterprises as a bank customer and hope you will call on us for all needed financial services.

The bank will collect a finance charge on your new open-end account, which will be calculated by figuring an "average daily balance." We take the beginning balance of your account each day and subtract payments or credits, but we do not add any new advances. This tells us the daily balance.

We add all the daily balances for the billing cycle together and divide that number by the total number of days in the billing cycle to arrive at the "average daily balance."

We charge 18 percent on this balance.

Please call the bank if you have any questions.

Sincerely,

Harold F. Grodsky
Vice-President

Tips and Comment:

Lending institutions are required by law to disclose the rates and method of computing finance charges. In the case of a new business client, a personal letter makes a good vehicle for the disclosure and gives a bank executive an opportunity to make a personal contact. The form of such disclosures is dictated by regulation, and the foregoing letter follows the requirements for explaining the average daily balance method, excluding current transactions. The alternative version is appropriate for disclosure of the average daily balance method, including current transactions.

Alternative A:

The bank will compute charges on your open-end account using the average daily balance method.

We charge 18 percent on your "average daily balance." The average daily balance is calculated by taking the beginning balance of your account each day, adding new loans, and subtracting payments or credits. We add the daily balances for the entire billing period and divide by the total number of days in order to come up with the average daily balance.

Let me know if you have questions.

Recommending Brokerage Services

DONALD Q. PARSONS
FINANCIAL ADVISOR
12 TRENT BUILDING
PAXSON, NJ

November 30, 19—

Ms. Phyllis K. Landers
23 West 5th Street
Paxson, NJ

Dear Ms. Landers:

The best opportunities in purchasing stock will come in the next three months, and I think you could use the services of a discount brokerage.

Although a discount house does not offer the research and advisory service of a regular broker, there are several advantages from your point of view.

First of all, the commission rate will be significantly lower than a regular broker, as much as 8 to 15 percent in some cases. This will make a big difference in your potential profit.

The second big advantage is the speed and convenience of transactions. You can call in your orders and they will be executed with no further action on your part. This will let you keep on top of your buying plan.

I'd be happy to recommend a couple of these discount brokerage firms for you to check into.

Yours truly,

Donald Q. Parsons

Tips and Comment:

Many investors—those with a firm grasp of how the market works and who know what they want to trade—may benefit from use of a discount brokerage rather than a full-service house. This letter details the advantages in the form of advice to a financial client. The important factors are laid out for the client to consider.

Alternative A:

I think you should consider a discount broker even though this will deprive you of the research some full-service brokers provide.

The reason for my suggestion is the speed and convenience of the transaction process with a discount broker. You can call in your orders from anywhere at any time.

This should fit your needs since you are on the road so much.

Alternative B:

Discount brokerages offer high rates of interest on idle funds, just as do bank brokerages or traditional full-service brokers.

You need only to open a money-market account with the broker, placing whatever minimum they demand in the account.

Then, released funds from your trading account are placed directly into the money-market account on a daily basis.

Alternative C:

I believe you should look into establishing a trading account through the brokerage department of your bank.

This department, set up since deregulation, operates much like an independent discount broker, but has the advantage of tying in your trading account to your regular checking or interest-bearing accounts.

Let me know if you want the details.

Inquiry About Trust Management

DONALD Q. PARSONS
FINANCIAL ADVISOR
12 TRENT BUILDING
PAXSON, NJ

February 12, 19—

Mr. James S. Sanborn
Trust Officer
First Federal Bank
First Federal Building
New Bern, NJ

Dear Mr. Sanborn:

I have a client with a significant amount of capital who is looking for a new trust manager, and I wish to outline for you the requirements so you might prepare a sales presentation.

The client is not interested in bond portfolios or short-term cash management, but wishes to concentrate instead on equity growth.

As a rule of thumb, the trust portfolio should maintain a 15 percent to 25 percent cash position in order to take advantage of rapidly developing opportunities. The remainder should be divided about evenly between stocks and bonds.

As to risk, the client seems to lean slightly toward the adventuresome.

Please give me a call if you have further questions.

Yours truly,

Donald Q. Parsons

Tips and Comment:

A letter of inquiry about trust management should outline the general approach desired and be as specific as possible about the goals of the trust. However, at this stage of negotiation, too many details might harm the deal. Keep some information back (such as the size of the trust) until the seller has made an initial presentation. As in most cases when dealing with large amounts of money, the tone is relatively formal. No one gets cute about finance.

Alternative A:

I am seeking a trust manager for a new trust about to result from an estate settlement.

The basic requirements are prudence with the initial fund and steady, certain growth.

I assume this means a larger than usual investment in either bonds or blue chip stocks and a smaller than usual cash float.

Please call me to discuss your services.

Alternative B:

Having recently assumed responsibility for the educational trust of my nephews, I am looking for an institution to manage the money.

The long-term goal of the trust will be to reach maximum value in ten years, with—one hopes—a steady growth of principal during the interval.

Please contact me.

Alternative C:

Since I will soon move to Washington, D.C. to take a position in the federal government, I must place most of my assets in a blind trust.

I will, of course, want the trust managers to move actively whenever the financial markets show an opportunity.

Please call for an appointment in the next few days to discuss this.

Portfolio Management Evaluation

HAWKEYE FIRST BANK
P.O. BOX 34
GILMORE, IA

June 16, 19—

Mr. Samuel L. Wentworth
34 Main Street
Gilmore, IA

Dear Sam:

You have asked for a report on your portfolio for the past fiscal year. A full record of the account as handled by our trust department is enclosed.

The best way to measure the bank's performance is to compare the rate of return of common stocks in your portfolio against the performance of Standard & Poor's 500.

Last year, Standard & Poor's rate of return was 7.89 percent. The common stocks in your portfolio returned 8.13 percent for the same period.

I think you will agree that beating the S & P is a good indication that you are doing well.

Let me know personally if you have any questions about the report.

Sincerely,

Lewis J. Morse
Vice-President

Tips and Comment:

Clients naturally like to know how a financial manager is handling their money. This letter reports to a client on behalf of a financial institution and makes a favorable comparison by giving the industry standard side-by-side with the performance of the client's account. While there are other measures of success, such as safety of investments, the rate of return usually catches the eyes of most clients first.

Alternative A:

While in our hands, your portfolio has continued to produce a healthy rate of annual return.

Last year the rate on all your stocks was 6.23 percent, which is 8 percent higher than the performance of S & P's 500.

We continue to put you into growth purchases whenever it seems prudent.

Alternative B:

Enclosed is a detailed report on the activity in your portfolio over the past six months.

You will note a cumulative return of 9 percent on your account, which is considerably above the market averages as reported in the *Wall Street Journal* (see the enclosed clipping).

At the same time, we think the investments have been cautious and well within the range of risk you have outlined.

Alternative C:

You are correct in stating that your portfolio has returned at a rate only slightly higher than the S & P for the same period.

However, given the restrictions on risk you made clear when opening the trust account, we think we have performed well.

There are no instances of significant losses anywhere in your trust holdings.

Lease Financing

HARROW ENTERPRISES, INCORPORATED
123 FINSTER DRIVE
OGLETHORPE, SD

June 6, 19—

Mr. Donald C. Venturi, Vice President
SD Bancorp
Oglethorpe, SD

Dear Don:

Harrow Enterprises is changing the focus of its current operations, and we have decided to lease some of our equipment. The lease market is strong at the moment, and we have a surplus of machinery.

We would like to set up an equipment lease finance program with the bank, which would allow us to maintain control over the leasing but shift the administration and financing to you.

In return for a fee, you would run the program in our name, provide the funds, and check the credit risks.

As I understand it, this sort of program is part of the services you offer corporate customers.

Please contact me soon.

Truly yours,

George F. Harrow
President

Tips and Comment:

It sometimes makes sense for a company to lease out some of its equipment, and a simple way of handling the operation is to turn everything over to a financial institution. The sample letter outlines the services required from the bank. It is a straightforward explanation of what the company wants to do and assumes a long-term relationship with the financial institution.

Alternative A:

Does the bank operate a lease financing and administration program for customers?

We have excess equipment to lease, but we are not set up to handle the paperwork and we do not want to get into accepting credit risks on our own behalf.

I assume that the bank would require a significant fee for taking on this service.

Please let me know.

Alternative B:

We have been leasing some of our equipment to other companies, but the whole process is causing a lot of headaches. Can you take over this part of the operation?

We no longer want to hassle with checking out credit risks and then riding herd on payments.

We'd appreciate a chat about this.

Alternative C:

I understand from Fred that you have taken over his leasing operations and run them from the bank, still leaving him as the leasor of record.

We have been considering such an operation, but we hesitate to take on the financial risks and the added administrative burden.

We would need to keep our name on the papers, however.

Giving Specific Advice

ROGERS & ASSOCIATES
3 ROPER AVENUE
MEGALOPOLIS, MD

April 7, 19—

Mr. Ben Yakima
222 West 56th Street
Bigtown, MD

Dear Ben:

You asked me for basic information about T-bills and how they might fit into your investment portfolio.

To start with, the U.S. Treasury issues more than just bills (usually called "T-bills"). It also deals in notes and bonds. The T-bills are short term, with maturities of 13, 26, and 52 weeks.

Notes run from two to 10 years. Bonds are written for maturities of 10 to 30 years.

Given the amount of capital you wish to invest and the long-term plan for your income, I'd suggest a purchase of Treasury notes with a maturity of ten years.

You can purchase these directly from a Federal Reserve Bank or branch, or I can handle the transaction for you as your broker.

Please let me know what you wish to do.

Sincerely,

Kevin Rogers

Tips and Comment:

Giving specific financial advice calls for just the right touch in letter writing. The advisor must establish knowledge and authority, but not appear to patronize the client. A clear, concise explanation is usually called for with an offer to assist the client through to the end of the transaction.

Alternative A:

You will not be taxed for the interest on your T-bills on your return for this year. The IRS will not expect you to report the income until the investment matures in another year, so you are safe in making a purchase now.

I'll be happy to explain this in more detail and assist in the purchase. Please give me a call.

Alternative B:

In looking over your investment moves during the last six months, it occurs to me that you are now slightly too heavy in utility bonds.

While these are certainly sound in most cases, the return is not as high as you have indicated a preference for.

I believe you should consider cashing in a portion of the utilities now and reinvesting in short-term zero-coupons.

Call me if you agree.

Alternative C:

I think we should dump the stock and put all of our excess cash into something that will provide some long-term security for us.

We have been fortunate over the last two years to have a good cash flow through the business, but we both know this is unlikely to continue much longer.

Think about this strategy, and let's discuss it at lunch on Thursday.

Advice on a Special Investment

PARTNERSHIP OPPORTUNITIES, INC.
404 WEST FOURTH STREET
GOLDEN, CO

August 8, 19—

Mr. Gerry Johnson
123 Reston Boulevard
Denver, CO

Dear Mr. Johnson:

The secondary market in limited partnerships allows investors to buy a partnership that has a track record, which makes it possible to evaluate the worth of the assets in question. The secondary market we handle deals primarily in real estate and equipment leasing.

Over the past two years of brokering limited partnerships, we have found that even if a buyer pays the full price of the assets, this is still considerably less than the 20 or 30 percent commission and fees premium typical of buying into a new partnership.

Our commissions are steady at 8 percent, which is lower than many other secondary market brokers.

Some of the leased equipment partnerships typically pay annual income of around 8 percent, and the real estate partnerships are better for long-term capital gains.

The biggest advantage, however, is the chance to look at actual performance numbers before you buy, rather than relying on projections.

I'll be happy to discuss a specific opportunity in more detail.

Sincerely yours,

Bill Hamilton
President

Tips and Comment:

Even if one can assume a certain level of sophistication on the part of the recipient, explaining complex financial matters calls for an exceptional clarity of expression. Be certain that the special terms used are part of a commonly understood language, and do not assume too much. Discussions in the area of finance can easily slip into jargon, which may obscure meaning. Avoiding this pitfall calls for a careful calculation of just what the letter's recipient may be expected to know.

Alternative A:

The secondary limited partnership market deals in buying and selling partnerships in established companies. The value of the partnership can therefore be established by looking at the past performance of the company.

This form of investment may be attractive for you especially since you are seeking a steady source of annual income with only a moderate degree of risk.

In short, you would know with a reasonable degree of certainty what you could expect from your investment, based on the figures from previous years.

Alternative B:

While purchasing a previously established limited partnership on the secondary market has its attractions, you should be aware that the initial buy-in price is usually high—$20,000 to $50,000 at the minimum—and that liquidity is often a problem.

In addition, the lifetime of the partnership is usually long. We find that the average is at least ten years.

Before you decide on this matter, please investigate the disadvantages thoroughly.

Alternative C:

The best opportunity for buying a limited partnership on the secondary market is to work through one of the listing services.

These firms provide a central exchange that posts asking and bidding prices, usually by means of either "green sheets" or computer modem.

With patience, you can probably find exactly what you want, although you will still need to actually buy through a licensed broker.

Personal Financial Advice

JAMES T. KEITH
FINANCIAL PLANNING SERVICES
890 EAST ROAD
BUTTONTOWN, NJ

April 13, 19—

Mrs. Phyllis Franks
677 South Lane
Buttontown, NJ

Dear Phyllis:

After reviewing your financial status, I strongly advise that you not take out the home equity loan that you have been considering.

Your overall cash situation is not too bad, and I believe it will only improve over the next twelve months, if nothing disastrous happens to call for a large emergency expense.

The problem with the home equity loan is the danger it represents for the long term. Such loans are really a form of second mortgage on your house, and they are sometimes difficult to control. If you use such a loan for regular expenses or even minor emergencies, the balance can build up very quickly. Without realizing it, you might put ownership of your home in jeopardy.

I think a safer course for you would be to borrow against your paid-up life insurance policy. This would provide adequate cash for your immediate needs and present less risk.

If you agree, then let's meet and I'll begin the necessary paperwork for you.

Call me if you have any questions.

Sincerely,

James T. Keith

Tips and Comment:

If possible, the complexities should be explained simply and directly when offering advice to clients (or friends) on matters of personal finance. This example reassures the client that a solution can be found, but lays out the pitfalls of an open-ended line of home equity credit and suggests a better alternative. To be successful, such letters of advice should be calm and display a command of the situation.

Alternative A:

Your proposed plan for restructuring your personal debt load has some very positive aspects. It would cut your monthly fixed costs considerably and free cash for the tuition payments you face next year.

However, you should also consider the long-term costs. The overall increase will be in the neighborhood of $4,000, which seems high.

Before you make a decision, I'd like to do an analysis of your current bond holdings and see if a better long-term solution is possible.

Alternative B:

I agree that you should move $45,000 from the money market fund into zero coupons.

At your current rate of income, this will help your overall tax situation without causing damage to your cash position.

I am enclosing a detailed analysis.

Alternative C:

I have had John run an analysis of your projected needs for the next five years.

It appears to us that your best course would be to invest in some form of limited partnership, even with the new restrictions.

If we can find just the right opportunity, your tax burden would be reduced by around 20 percent.

I'll have John get on the research right away.

7

THE OWNERS: LETTERS TO STOCKHOLDERS

Letters to stockholders (or board members) fall into a special category. They are written to peers, and they must communicate facts and hard information while projecting a tone of confidence and control. In some cases, letters to stockholders must also meet the corporation's legal requirements. All of these factors conspire to ask the executive letter writer to exercise great skill in constructing even the most casual or routine letters to stockholders. The following examples, covering matters both mundane and essential, demonstrate the appropriate technique and approach to these important communications. At the heart of all letters to stockholders is vital information about their property and how it is managed, and therefore, the letters will be read with considerable attention.

Annual Meeting Announcement

STEEL PRODUCTS CORP.
PITTSBURGH, PA
Notice of Annual Meeting

To Our Shareholders:

You are cordially invited to attend the annual meeting of shareholders to be held June 12, 19—, at 10:00 A.M. in the Conference Room of the Corporate Building.

The agenda for the meeting includes election of the Directors and some corporate changes that are under consideration by the Board.

If you are unable to attend this meeting, please date and sign the enclosed proxy and return it promptly. Unless otherwise instructed, your proxy will be voted in accordance with the judgment of the proxy holders named by you in the proxy.

Thank you.

Yours truly,

John Trevnick
President

Tips and Comment:

Letters announcing an annual meeting of stockholders are important documents in the life of a corporation and are appropriately formal and to the point. They are not the place for idle chit-chat. The letter must state the particulars of the meeting, and it is best to announce the subject matter of any unusual business that may come before the meeting. The letter may also double as a proxy request.

Alternative A:

The annual meeting of the Corporation will take place at 10:00 A.M. on June 12, 19—, in the Conference Room at corporate headquarters in Pittsburgh.

The agenda includes a review of the company's performance over the last 12 months and reelection of the Directors and Officers of the Corporation.

If you will not be able to attend in person, please fill out and mail in the enclosed proxy documents.

Alternative B:

As directed by the By-Laws of the Corporation, I hereby call the regular annual meeting of the shareholders to be held on Wednesday, June 6, 19—, at 10:00 A.M., at the principal office of the Corporation, 444 West Bend Street, City of Pittsburgh, Commonwealth of Pennsylvania, for the following purposes:

(1) to elect the board of directors for the ensuing year;

(2) to consider and vote approval of all contracts, elections, and appointments.

Alternative C:

On Tuesday, May 10, 19—, we will convene the regular annual meeting of shareholders of the corporation at the company headquarters in Pittsburgh. The meeting is scheduled for 10:00 A.M. with a buffet luncheon to follow.

As far as the officers and directors can see, there will be nothing unusual on the agenda.

Please let us know if you will attend by returning the enclosed card.

Thank you.

Proxy Letter With Follow-Up

STEEL PRODUCTS CORP.
PITTSBURGH, PA
Request for Shareholder's Proxy

Steel Products Corporation

Shareholder's Proxy No. _____

Number of Shares _____

This proxy is solicited by order of the Board of Directors, John W. Doe, Chairman, Jane Q. Doe, Vice-Chairman, and Herbert F. Doe, Secretary. Any one of them is hereby appointed the proxy of the undersigned with full power of substitution to vote and otherwise act for the undersigned at any annual or special meeting of the shareholders of the Steel Products Corporation or any adjournments thereof, for the election of Directors and for the transaction of other business that may come before the meeting.

Signed _____
Date _____

Tips and Comment:

As is obvious by the language, a proxy letter is a legal document and should conform carefully to the requirements of the charter and by-laws of the corporation and the statutes of the state in which the company is incorporated. While this sample is typical of proxy letters, legal counsel should be consulted before settling on a final text. It is also usually necessary to have a follow-up letter, since many stockholders typically fail to respond to the first request.

Follow-Up:

We have not yet received the proxy form sent to you with the annual report. In order to have a quorum that will allow us to proceed with business at the upcoming annual meeting, we must have a sufficient number of proxies. Many of our shareholders live too far away to attend in person. This emphasizes the importance of receiving proxies before the scheduled meeting.

We hope you can attend this year's meeting, but if you cannot, please sign and mail the proxy. A second copy of the form with an addressed, stamped envelope is enclosed for your convenience.

Announcing a Meeting and Stock Split

SANDERS CONSTRUCTION COMPANY
JACKSONVILLE, FL

To the Shareholders:

This is to announce that the Board of Directors and the Officers of the Company have agreed on a two-for-one split of common stock.

Therefore, a meeting of stockholders is called for 10:00 A.M. on January 19, 19—, at the Company headquarters in Jacksonville. The conditions of the split of stock will be discussed and voted on at that time.

This is a very important meeting for all stockholders. If you will not be able to attend in person to vote your shares, please sign and return the enclosed proxy statement.

Sincerely,

Ron S. Diamond
President

Tips and Comment

A letter calling a shareholders' meeting may deal with more than one topic, especially if a significant event in the life of the company is about to take place. The letter should leave no doubt as to the nature of the business to be considered. Be clear and precise when passing on such information to shareholders.

Alternative A:

After long deliberation with our financial advisors, the Board of Directors of Sanders Construction Company voted on December 20 to split all shares of common stock two-for-one.

In order to do so, we must convene a meeting of shareholders to consider and approve this action.

The meeting will be held at 12:00 noon on January 15, 19—, at the company offices.

Enclosed is a full explanation of the proposed action and what it is likely to mean to each shareholder. If you have questions, please call me.

If you cannot attend in person, please sign the enclosed proxy and send it in immediately.

Alternative B:

Recent market conditions and the superior performance of the company have caused the Board of Directors to vote in favor of a split of common stock on a two-for-one basis.

This will likely result in a considerable gain in the value of the holdings of current owners of stock.

Formal action will be taken at a shareholders meeting at 12:00 noon on January 15, 19—, at the office conference room in Jacksonville.

If you cannot attend, please send in the enclosed proxy form.

Announcing a Board Meeting

SPX CORPORATION
100 TERRACE PLAZA
MUSKEGON, MI 49443

April 14, 19—

Mr. Frederick C. Latner
2919 Gulf Shore Boulevard
Inland, FL

Dear Fred:

As earlier signaled, the next regularly scheduled Board Meeting is Wednesday, April 26, to be held at the corporate offices at 100 Terrace Plaza.

There are two committee meetings to be held on Tuesday late afternoon, and no committee meetings scheduled for Wednesday.

Our dinner guests will be Messrs. Robert Lancaster, Architect; Fred Upton, Developer; and Bill Hardesty, SPX, who will bring us up to date on the Terrace Point Project.

The overall agenda is as follows:

April 25 (Tuesday)

        3:00 P.M. Retirement Funds Committee—6th Floor Conference Room

        4:30 P.M. Ad Hoc Committee—6th Floor Conference Room

        6:30 P.M. Reception and Dinner—Century Club

April 26 (Wednesday)

        8:00 A.M. Board of Directors Meeting—Board Room

Responding to time commitments, we are going to try to conclude the board meeting by 11:00 A.M.

We will help with transportation where possible. Attached is a summary of travel arrangements made for this meeting. We trust you will advise if we can be otherwise helpful.

Kindest regards,

Robert D. Tuttle
Chairman and Chief Executive Officer
(Courtesy of Robert D. Tuttle, Muskegon, Michigan)

Tips and Comments:

Corporate executives must keep members of their board fully informed about meetings and upcoming agenda items. A letter to all board members can serve as a formal announcement of the time and place of a board meeting, and it can include the important matters to be taken up at the meeting. The foremost requirements of such letters are clarity of format and information. Try to anticipate questions and answer them ahead of time in the announcement letter.

Alternative A:

The next meeting of the full Board will take place at the Holiday Inn West, 200 U.S. Highway 28, at 11:00 A.M. on Thursday, October 15.

Most of the agenda (see attached) will be taken up by reports from the special committee on compensation, which was appointed at our last meeting.

We expect the meeting to end by 2:00 P.M.

A buffet lunch will be served at noon, although we plan to work through the meal.

Please let me know if you have anything else to add to the agenda.

Alternative B:

This is to let you know that the chairman has called a special meeting of the Board for next Wednesday, January 10, at 10:00 A.M. to take up the matter of selecting a new Chief Executive Officer.

The meeting will be, as usual, at the headquarters building. Please be prompt and be prepared to spend the balance of the day in the meeting.

Alternative C:

We need to have a formal meeting of the Board before the end of the year in order to satisfy the legal requirements of incorporation. Therefore, I'm calling a meeting for 12:00 noon on December 20 at the Holiday Room of the Royal Arms Hotel.

We really have little business to consider, so please come prepared to enjoy some holiday cheer and conviviality with your fellow Board members.

Announcing Changes to Board

ABC CORPORATION
45 CORPORATE DRIVE
OLD TOWN, MA

July 6, 19—

Dear Shareholders:

At the meeting of the Board on July 1, the following slate of officers was selected:

John C. Colridge III, Chairman
Angela V. Benson, Vice Chairman
George T. Colridge, Secretary/Treasurer

John C. Colridge, Jr., who has served as Chairman of the Board since 19—, relinquished that office at his request due to health and advancing age. He will, however, continue to sit on the Board of Directors.

The Board also affirmed the appointment of John C. Colridge IV as President and Chief Operating Officer of the company.

Truly yours,

John C. Colridge III
Chairman

Tips and Comments:

The directors of publicly held corporations are obliged to keep shareholders informed of changes in board membership, especially the makeup of the company's officers. A simple letter announcing changes will suffice with whatever additional information as needed.

Alternative A:

We are pleased to announce the election of Ms. Evelyn J. Peters to the Board of Directors and her appointment as Treasurer.

Ms. Peters has served as Comptroller of the company since 19—, and is intimately familiar with all facets of the financial operation.

She replaces John Hughes who retires from active service this year.

Alternative B:

In accordance with the by-laws, a new set of corporation officers was elected at the recent meeting of the Board of Directors:

James Manson—Chairman

Kenneth Green—Vice Chairman

Henry Jenkins—Treasurer

Lawrence Brown—Secretary

Their terms of office will run for three years, until 19—.

Alternative C:

Samuel J. Grant has been elected as Chairman and Chief Operating Officer of the corporation.

Mr. Grant joined the Board originally three years ago and has since taken an active interest in the affairs of the company.

John Foster, previous CEO, will leave the company in May.

Announcing New Management

ALL-AMERICAN INDUSTRIES
12 EVEREST STREET
MT. OLIVET, CA

February 12, 19—

Dear Stockholders:

The Board of Directors is happy to announce that James L. Johnson has been appointed President and CEO of All-American Industries, effective immediately.

Mr. Johnson has been president of Larremont Enterprises, Inc. in Arizona and was previously U. S. Undersecretary of Housing and Urban Development during the last presidential administration.

His experience and management expertise promise to add much to the leadership of All-American Industries.

Bruce Hamilton, who has served as President since 19—, will leave the company to pursue other interests.

I know you will join me in giving our full support to Mr. Johnson and his new management team.

A notice of the changes will be made to the news media on February 17.

Yours truly,

George T. Yount
Chairman

Tips and Comment:

Changes in top corporation management should be announced to stockholders as soon as possible, and a letter from the chairman or the board is a good vehicle. If possible, the letter should be sent in advance of giving the news media notice of the change. In this example, the letter is silent about reasons for the change in management and leaves potentially touchy or embarrassing issues about the previous president unexamined— a common tactic in order to save face for both the corporation and the individuals involved. The tone is formal and official.

Alternative A:

We are pleased to announce today the election of Kenneth Hasborn as the new president of the corporation. He will take office on June 15.

Kenneth has been CEO of the Omni Corporation as well as Executive Vice-President of Willard Industries. Since 19—, he has operated his own consulting firm.

We anticipate that Kenneth will lead the company into the next five years with a renewed sense of purpose.

Alternative B:

This is to announce to all shareholders of the company that President Alan Scott will retire from active management in June after 13 years as chief executive officer. He will retain his seat on the board, and we will continue to benefit from his counsel.

Following a national search, the board has appointed Harold Tolerud as the new president.

Harold has been Executive Vice-President since 19—, and has served in various capacities in the company for nearly 20 years, beginning as an account executive in 19—.

We have every confidence in Harold and look forward to his tenure.

Alternative C:

James Durrance has announced his resignation from the position of CEO, effective immediately.

While the Board of Trustees has accepted his decision reluctantly, we and all shareholders wish him well in his new enterprise.

John H. Langworthy will serve as acting CEO during the process of an executive search.

Annual Report Letter

PRUDENCE MANUFACTURING CORPORATION
DREEDTON, MO

To Our Shareholders:

It is a pleasant duty to report to you that we have had a most satisfactory year. As the detailed figures in the enclosed annual report show, the company has not only held onto the considerable gains of the previous fiscal year, but we have moved ahead in both market share and profitability.

Most of this upward movement is due to finally realizing the full value of the recapitalization and investment in new equipment which we undertook three years ago. During the first two years following those changes our annual profits, as I am certain you remember, were much lower than desired.

However, we had faith that in the long run we would come out ahead, and indeed, this year's financial statement shows that we were correct.

The management of the company has also worked hard over the last 12 months to put in place a new set of labor policies. To some degree these have been successful, but there are still several unresolved issues between the company and the union. If these can be brought to a conclusion in the months ahead, we should anticipate an extremely good report a year from now.

I look forward to greeting as many of you as possible at the annual meeting. If you have specific questions, please feel free to write to me.

Sincerely,

William Nussbaum
Chief Executive Officer

Tips and Comment:

A letter that accompanies the annual report should be more than a covering document. This is a special opportunity to address the investors, and the letter's tone can be less formal than the published annual report text. In general, assessments of performance tend to succeed if they are honest and frank. Ignoring problems that will be obvious to a sharp shareholder can only degrade the company's credibility. On the other hand, reporting the good news is the overall goal of such a letter.

Alternative A:

It is certainly a pleasure to forward to you the enclosed annual report and to write to you for the first time as president of the company.

Since I took office nine months ago, the direction of the sales chart has been upward. This is due in part to the restructuring of our sales territories, but also to a greater degree to the high energy displayed by the sales staff. I'm gratified at their performance.

Meanwhile, the manufacturing division maintained a steady pace and delivered on time and with the quality desired.

In short, it has been a good year, and we should look forward to more progress to come.

Alternative B:

As will be seen by the financial summary in the enclosed annual report, profits per share have declined over the final quarter of the year, following a promising beginning.

There is no doubt that the increased competition for customers on the East Coast is a major reason for the downturn.

We are now in the process of developing a plan to counteract the effects of this development, and we are confident that a turnaround is in sight during the first half of the coming year.

Even with the poor showing of the final quarter, our stock maintained its overall value for the year.

Alternative C:

In sending you this annual report, I must draw your attention to the major decisions that appear to be on the horizon and that will be discussed at our annual meeting.

Over the past few weeks, the Board of Directors has considered the advisability of closing the subsidiary plant in Illinois and relocating the sales and management staff to the home office.

This is mostly a question of effecting an economy of organization and reducing expense without sacrificing overall production capacity. The figures in the report will, I think, buttress the Board's tentative decision to go ahead with the closing.

Quarterly Report Letter

JAMES-HILLIARD, INC.
1444 23RD STREET, NW
DOVER, DE

November 1, 19—

Dear Stockholders:

I am pleased to report that the figures for the third quarter of this year continue the upward trend of the first six months.

Gross sales increased .05 percent during the third quarter, and costs remained steady. These are, of course, promising signs since they come on the heels of a large net gain during the second quarter.

All indications show that the final quarter of the year, when we traditionally experience a drop in revenues due to the holidays, may hold steadier than in recent years. If so, you can look forward to a significant increase in the profits per share for the year.

Yours truly,

Quentin L. Manchester
President

Tips and Comment:

Some companies like to send letters to shareholders after each quarter, reporting on business trends. If the news is good, as in this sample, then such letters are a good stockholder relations tool. Optimism should be cautious, however, and tempered with a realistic view of the future.

Alternative A:

The company revenues for the last quarter held steady, despite the overall decrease in the industry nationwide.

We are pleased that our market share held during what we perceive as a minor shakeout, and we attribute this positive development to the increased marketing program initiated during the beginning of the year.

We will keep you informed of developments.

Alternative B:

The trade industry journals report a slowdown in activity since the beginning of the year, but our first-quarter earnings show a slight increase over the same period a year ago.

We take this as a healthy sign for the coming months.

Alternative C:

During the third quarter of the year, we opened two new branch offices in the Southeast, and as a result, the overall balance sheet for the quarter shows a slight decrease from a year ago.

We are confident, however, that the expansion will pay off in the long run. Already we can see increased sales activity in Georgia and South Carolina.

General Economic Report Letter

GLOBAL DISTRIBUTION, INC.
P.O. BOX 345
NEW YORK, NY

June 1, 19—

Dear Shareholders:

The financial press and the trade papers agree that the coming year will be one of opportunity in international trade. We hope to take advantage of the new economic structure emerging in Europe as well as the chance to penetrate some of the Pacific Rim markets.

Our own in-house research points to Eastern Europe as the place of greatest potential. For obvious reasons, the manufacturing sector of the former Communist nations will remain in turmoil for several years to come. Therefore, a system of distribution from the United States and from the industrial nations of Western Europe will be a matter of some urgency.

The biggest obstacle will likely be the currency exchange system, which is still in a state of flux due to the continued political disorientation of former Eastern Bloc nations.

We will keep you informed as conditions develop.

Yours truly,

Frederick N. Morris
President

Tips and Comment:

A general letter reporting on economic and trade prospects is a good shareholder relations tool. The management of a corporation is usually in a good position to comment on conditions, and even if the news is relatively general, such letters will keep shareholders interested in the company's activities.

Alternative A:

As many of you may have noticed, the trend this year in widgets has been toward a constriction of the general market. Overall, demand for durable widgets has fallen close to 12 percent since January.

Naturally, we have been concerned, especially in light of tightening credit nationwide.

So far, these trends are not yet to be seen in our sales figures, but we anticipate it is only a matter of time.

Alternative B:

The change in the interest rates have resulted in an unusually hot money market, with the added effect of boosting our sales activity over the past few months.

As usual, our business is especially sensitive to interest rate changes, and we monitor the general situation closely.

We will continue to keep all of you informed as to our view of the immediate trends.

Alternative C:

The recent upturn in the growth figures for the Gross National Product has been reflected almost exactly in our sales for the past few months.

We are happy to be able to take advantage of this growth curve, which came as a surprise to most economic forecasters.

As we move into the next quarter of the year, we believe the trend will continue.

Explaining Effects of Government Action

ALL-AMERICAN INDUSTRIES
12 EVEREST STREET
MT. OLIVET, CA

June 5, 19—

Dear Stockholders:

As many of you may know from reports in the news media over the last several months, the Congress of the United States recently passed a bill that deregulates the widget industry.

The law goes into effect on July 13, 19—.

In accordance with the provisions of the new law, All-American Industries will begin to operate on a new basis during the second half of the year and into the foreseeable future.

We will no longer be bound by the pricing formulas imposed by the Federal Commerce Commission, and so we will begin a process of gradual price increases throughout our selling area.

The strategy will be to find the proper market level for pricing on a region-by-region basis.

We anticipate a major change in net income as a result of deregulation, and we will keep you informed well in advance of the end of the year.

Please feel free to comment to me directly on this or any other policy issue.

Sincerely,

James L. Johnson
President and CEO

Tips and Comment:

Top corporate management may need to inform shareholders of the effects of actions taken by government regulatory or law-making bodies, since such actions may touch off significant changes in the value of company stock. This example announces the policy response of the company and cautiously points to the possible effects on the company's balance sheet.

Alternative A:

The Supreme Court of the Commonwealth of Virginia handed down a decision recently that will affect the sale of widgets in the state.

Consequently, we are withdrawing our products from the market in Virginia.

We hope that we can expand our market in neighboring states to compensate, but we anticipate a slight decrease in total sales during the transition.

Alternative B:

Under the terms of the new regulations for the widget brokerage industry, we will now be able to offer a full range of brokerage services to customers.

This good news clears the way for an expansion of our offices in New England, and we intend to move vigorously during the next six months to take advantage of this opportunity.

The result should be a temporary slowing of profits during the expansion phase, but we are confident that ultimately the balance sheet will show a marked increase as a result of the widening of our sales areas.

Alternate C:

The Federal Drug Administration has today granted us approval to market HDF-123.

This is a signal occasion for the company, and we anticipate a successful launching of this new product.

We will keep you informed of its progress.

Welcome to New Stockholder

BROWN, KING & WOOD, INC.
NASHVILLE, TN

October 3, 19—

Ms. Dorothy L. Sader
678 Indian Ave., NW
Gooderville, TN

Dear Ms. Sader:

I want to welcome you as a shareholder of Brown, King & Wood, Inc. You can be certain that we will do our best to fulfill our obligation to you as an investor.

A service organization is only as good as its people, and we firmly believe that our efficient, high-quality team will continue to show increasing sales and profits throughout our wide operations.

Enclosed is our latest annual report and quarterly financial report. I welcome any comments, suggestions, or questions.

I look forward to a long and pleasant association.

Truly yours,

Frederick J. Wood

Tips and Comment:

Since attracting and keeping investors is one of the primary duties of successful management, a letter to new shareholders is potentially a good management tool. The approach and purpose are very close to a good sales letter. The formality of the wording may vary according to the size of the company, but the point is to establish a relationship.

Alternative A:

I am pleased to learn that you have recently purchased shares in our company.

Our performance in the marketplace during recent years has been steady, and we have every reason to believe it will continue into the foreseeable future.

If you have any questions or suggestions, I'd be delighted to hear them.

Thank you for investing in the future of the corporation.

Alternative B:

It's always a pleasure to welcome a new investor. I think your decision to purchase shares in our company was a wise one, and believe you will be pleased with our performance.

I'm enclosing some of our most recent reports, which give a good picture of how we have positioned ourselves in the competitive market-place—and how we have obtained a healthy 23 percent share of the total.

Please feel free to comment or ask questions at any time.

Alternative C:

I'm delighted that you decided to buy a fourth of the company. I don't think you will regret the investment. In fact, as I have told you many times, I think we are poised on the edge of a real takeoff.

Since you are now one of the major owners, I'll send you memos and documents on a regular basis so you can stay abreast of how things are going.

Give me a call at any time.

Letter to a Former Shareholder

NATIONAL EASTERN OIL CORPORATION
AVENUE OF THE AMERICAS
NEW YORK, NY

August 8, 19—

Mr. Horace T. Green
425 Terrace Park Road
Utley, RI

Dear Mr. Green:

It has recently come to my attention that your name no longer appears on our books as a shareholder. While I understand that many reasons may force a shareholder to sell long-held stock, it is a transaction I regret to see.

If your decision to dispose of your NEO stock was related to any aspect of our policies or operations, I would appreciate knowing about it. We value your opinion, even though you are no longer one of our investors.

If you would like to continue to receive our annual and quarterly reports, please let me know. I will be glad to arrange to have your name kept on our mailing list.

Yours truly,

Keith Donaldson
President and Chief Executive Officer

Tips and Comment:

Keeping in touch with former shareholders may bring them, eventually, back into the fold. The message is not complex: we're sorry you left, let us know if you were dissatisfied with something specific, and please keep in touch. It might be a good idea to make such a letter standard procedure when receiving notice of a sale of stock.

Alternative A:

I was distressed to learn that you recently sold your shares in our company. I hope it was in no way an indication of displeasure with the management of our business affairs.

If you have any comments or suggestions, I'd be more than happy to hear them.

Please let me know if you would like us to keep you on the mailing list.

Alternative B:

Your investment in our company was greatly appreciated, and we regret that you have found it necessary to sell your shares.

Please let me know if there is any information you might find useful in the future.

I hope at some stage you may decide to reinvest in our enterprise.

Alternative C:

I'm sorry you have decided to sell your part of the ownership of the company. I have appreciated and enjoyed your support over the years, yet I understand your need to liquidate now.

Rest assured I'll stay in touch because I still want to be able to ask your advice.

It's been a pleasure to work with you.

8

CHANGING CORPORATE CONTROL: LETTERS CONCERNING MERGERS AND ACQUISITIONS

It is a fact of modern business and corporate life that ownership changes hands at a higher rate than in the more placid past. Letters about the vital issues surrounding mergers and acquisitions are central elements in the circumstances of changing corporate control. As the following examples illustrate, all letters about mergers or acquisitions are important and must be constructed with clarity and force. The models cover such topics as analysis, announcing changes, and dealing with public and stockholder opinion. All of these issues require focused attention from executive letter writers. Calm confidence is the appropriate tone, backed by good information and understanding.

Analysis of a Target Company

GOODWIN ASSOCIATES
4 TRACE ROAD
TERRACEVILLE, NJ

January 6, 19—

Ms. Janice Kline
Gigot Industries, Inc.
222 Everest Avenue
Notting Hill, NJ

Dear Ms. Kline:

The key point of analysis in considering a tender offer for the outstanding shares of Widget International is the annual cash flow of the company over the last five years.

Our research shows that WI has generated only a moderate amount of cash during the most recent three years, although the picture had been much brighter during the previous two.

We believe the cash situation to be marginal at best, since the buy-out plan would call for at least $1.5 million per year in debt service. Unless Gigot is willing to pump considerable amounts of its own cash into the acquisition over the coming decade, the purchase would most likely be a significant burden.

We recommend a further search for more suitable possibilities.

Truly yours,

Shawn Dunstable
Executive Vice-President

Tips and Comment:

A letter isolating the important factors in an acquisition and making a recommendation should state the facts of the case and make a definite statement for or against action. Such letters might be backed up with more detailed financial analysis and reports, but the letter is the primary medium of communicating a specific opinion. Those who receive such letters will appreciate candor and decisiveness. The letter must be clear in isolating the crucial factors.

Alternative A:

We have examined the performance of Widgets International for the past ten years and conclude that the company is an ideal candidate for acquisition.

Widgets International's stock is currently undervalued, probably because the company has shown little or no GAAP earnings for the past several years.

However, the cash flow is good, and it appears that the company could generate sufficient income to finance the acquisition over a reasonably short period.

Alternative B:

Widgets International presents a complex picture.

The annual net income as reported is slight—only $150,000 last fiscal year—but the volume of sales is high.

It appears likely that the main plant in Gerryville will require retooling within six months if the company is to continue to hold its market share.

If the retooling moves the company beyond its closest competitors, however, there appears to be a good opportunity to increase earnings.

Alternative C:

Widgets International is ripe for acquisition, and we can probably get it with an offer of no more than $20 per share.

The reasons are simple: the company has not generated a positive income for three years running, yet a relatively minor change in the market approach would boost earnings with no capital infusion.

This is exactly the situation we have been looking for.

Evaluating "Goodwill" Assets

THE YETTER COMPANY
567 LOUDON AVENUE
PLEASANT, CA

February 17, 19—

Mr. Patrick Ordway
The Yetter Company
Anaheim Divisional Office
Anaheim, CA

Dear Pat:

Looking over the books on Theatrical Productions, Inc. shows that we would be forced to write a big portion of "goodwill" into the transaction.

Under the current GAAP rules, it would take almost four years to account for the goodwill factor in the evaluation.

If your analysis shows that this is feasible, then we should continue to think of making an offer for the president's stock, but this should be a matter for the investment committee.

Let me know your thoughts on this.

Truly yours,

Samuel Y. Pless
Manager

Tips and Comment:

Few parts of modern business are more complex than making the decision to attempt an acquisition. Often, there are important factors other than strict financial history that come into play, including the concept of "goodwill," which can change the potential value of a target company. A sharp executive will understand such intangibles and be able to explain them accurately to other decision makers.

Alternative A:

It appears that the Great Western Savings and Loan acquisition will require a large write-off to "goodwill" if we intend to pursue the purchase.

Assets of Great Western are $100 million and liabilities are $93 million, which would normally put it in range under our current criteria.

However, we have discovered that $1.5 million of the assets are really "goodwill." The actual figure should be reduced to $98.5 million.

Alternative B:

Here is the final break-down on the purchase price for XYZ Widgets:

1. The purchase price is $1 million
2. Tangible assets include $500,000 for the factory and land; $250,000 for widget-making equipment; and $150,000 for patents held by the company
3. The $100,000 balance is accounted as goodwill.

Alternative C:

You are entirely correct that the figure included in Widget Manufacturing's assets as "goodwill" can be carried as an asset on our books after the acquisition.

However, unlike the machinery and buildings, we cannot depreciate the goodwill on our tax returns. In fact, the yearly write-off will work only to depress our earnings.

Ending a Takeover Bid

FOUR-LEAF CORPORATION
1 FOUR-LEAF DRIVE
WILMINGTON, DE

March 23, 19—

Mr. Paul Prentiss
Chief Operations Officer
Value Products, Inc.
Summit, NJ

Dear Mr. Prentiss:

In accord with the agreement reached in principle yesterday, the Four-Leaf Corporation will withdraw its offer to purchase the stock of Value Products, Inc. and will desist from further efforts.

Likewise, Four-Leaf Corporation will end the pending litigation in the Delaware courts that has arisen from our offer.

We will offer the 2,500 shares of stock in Value Products which we acquired over the last six months to the company itself at the price of $5.00 per share, payment to be in cash.

Yours truly,

John McNee
President

Tips and Comment:

Letters ending a takeover bid should be definite in setting forth the actions and intentions of the parties involved. Since takeover situations often bruise feelings, a neutral tone is best.

Alternative A:

This is to inform you that the board of directors of Four-Leaf Corporation voted today to suspend our efforts to purchase control of Value Products.

The protests and action in the courts have made it clear that the effort to acquire Value Products will not be in our best interests.

Alternative B:

The Four-Leaf Corporation withdraws as of today the offer to purchase ownership of Value Products, Inc.

The recent downturn in the industry in conjunction with the objections of some of your board members has prompted our withdrawal.

Alternative C:

The tender offer of $5.75 per share of stock for 5,000 shares of Value Products will terminate at 4:30 P.M. tomorrow.

If the offer has not been accepted by then, Four-Leaf Corporation will make no further offers.

Majority Owner Merging Companies

MAGNA PRODUCTS, INC.
UPPERVILLE, MN

July 23, 19—

To the Stockholders:

The managers of the company have determined that considerable adminis-trative savings and tax advantages will result from the merger of Magna Products, Inc. into a new company, All Products, Inc.

Mr. James B. James, who holds 97 percent of the stock in Magna Products, Inc., is the sole owner of All Products, Inc. and will assume control of all the assets of Magna Products after the merger.

Each of you, as minority stockholders in Magna Products, will receive $500 in cash for each of your shares.

The merger will take place on July 30, 19—.

Kindest regards,

James B. James, Jr.
President

Tips and Comment:

It is not uncommon for a majority owner to take over complete control of a company by merging it with a newly-created entity. The announcement of such a plan is usually only a formal statement that follows previous communications, but it should be exact and correct in setting forth the details of the deal.

Alternative A:

Mr. Jones, who holds 98 percent of the stock in our company, has indicated his desire to merge this corporation with a newly-formed company called Omni, Inc.

He intends to vote for this action at a meeting next Wednesday, June 25, at our offices.

All minority stock will be purchased at $4 a share in order to facilitate the new merger.

If there are questions, please contact me immediately.

Alternative B:

I have decided that it will be best to liquidate the outstanding shares in Magna Inc. and merge the old company into Omni, Inc.

I am therefore calling in all the shares of minority stockholders immediately.

I will be happy to discuss the price to be paid for outstanding shares. Please contact me at my office.

Alternative C:

Our accountant tells me that the only prudent course in order to avoid a huge tax loss is to absorb the company into Omni.

Since we have all agreed to this course, I'll call a meeting for next week and we can vote the formalities.

The buy-out will be on the terms I indicated in my last phone conversation with you.

Call me if there are questions.

Announcing Sale of Company

SANDERS CONSTRUCTION COMPANY
JACKSONVILLE, FL

To the Shareholders:

After many months of discussions, your Company has entered into an agreement to sell substantially all of the Company's assets to Plymouth Construction, Ltd. of England for $35 million cash.

This will represent a price of $42 a share, which is considerably higher than the current market value of $37 a share.

By the terms of the agreement, the management of the Company will remain intact, with the exception of the President, who will retire.

The actual sale is scheduled for completion in six months. Before then, we will hold a full meeting of the shareholders to discuss the action and vote approval. A notice will be in the mail about that meeting.

Sincerely,

James I. Dermott
Chairman of the Board

Tips and Comment:

It is the duty of a board of directors not only to make decisions in the best interests of the shareholders, but also to inform them of all significant changes as soon as possible. The sale of a company is the most significant event of all and should be communicated with dispatch. Of course, details of the sale and its financial significance for the shareholders are musts in such a letter.

Alternative A:

As you must all be aware from the reports in the daily press, Plymouth Construction, Ltd. of Great Britain has made an offer for the Company of $35 million in cash.

After due consideration, the Board of Directors has decided that it is in the interests of all parties to accept the offer, and an agreement in principle to that effect was signed today.

The tender means that each outstanding share of stock will realize $52 through the sale and liquidation.

I will keep you informed as the final agreements go forth.

Alternative B:

Although we at first were surprised by the tender, the Board of Directors today voted to accept the offer of Plymouth Ltd. to purchase all the assets of the company for $2 million.

Our declining share of the local market over the past two years seems irreversible, and Plymouth will be in a position to invest new capital into the plant, thereby putting the company back into a competitive posture.

Those of you who are shareholders will, of course, be interested in the effect on the value of your holdings. A detailed analysis is enclosed.

Alternative C:

After talking to you on the phone today, Charles and I agree that the best course for all of us is to accept Omni, Inc.'s offer to buy us out.

We will miss the excitement of the last few years, but the time seems right, and we can hardly pass up the chance to realize the substantial gains that the sale means.

I'll call you later in the week as things move ahead.

Announcing Merger to Customers

SUPERIOR BAKING CO.
12 FUNNEL DRIVE
MINNEAPOLIS, MN

May 25, 19—

Dear Superior Customers:

The Superior Baking Co. is proud to announce to all its customers throughout the Midwest that we have purchased Metropolitan Amalgamated, Inc. and will be adding all of Metropolitan's facilities to our operations.

The new company will be known as Superior-Metropolitan.

Superior-Metropolitan will continue to offer the same high-quality, low-price baked goods and snack products to which our customers and the retail trade are accustomed.

Effective immediately, all orders, billing, and correspondence for former Metropolitan accounts should be directed to our headquarters in Minneapolis. All Metropolitan contracts will be honored as written.

We look forward to serving you in the future under our new organization.

Yours truly,

David Bronski
President

Tips and Comments:

Mergers affect customers as much as they do shareholders, so a letter to key clients after a merger can form part of a campaign to educate customers about the new identity. Such a letter may also serve to reassure customers that service or existing financial arrangements will not be disturbed by the merger. Change is unsettling to most people, so a bit of hand-holding is in order after a merger.

Alternative A:

This is to let all of you know that we have purchased all the accounts of Barton & Barton and will incorporate B&B's business into our own, effective immediately.

All of the B&B staff will join our firm, with the exception of Bill Barton, who is retiring.

Please rest assured that we will be able to offer the same services as has B&B in the past, and with the same staff.

Alternative B:

General Widgets announces the acquisition of Mini-Widgets, Inc.

As of the first of the month, all former Mini-Widget customers will be served by route salespeople from General Widgets. We feel confident that the level of satisfaction will remain the same.

Please call on us here at our main office if you have comments or questions.

Alternative C:

I am happy to tell all my customers that my company, which has served you for the last ten years, has been sold to Allied, Inc., and will operate from now on as a division of that company.

My staff and I will continue with the new company, and in fact, you will hardly notice much change.

We intend to continue to offer the same products on the same basis as in the past.

Divesting Part of Acquired Company

MAGNA CORPORATION
667 MAGNA DRIVE
NEW YORK, NY

May 23, 19—

Dear Stockholders:

The management of Magna Corporation has sold the corporation's holdings in Metropolitan Amalgamated, Inc. to the Superior Baking Co. for a total of $5.6 million.

This is a move on the part of Magna Corporation to realize a capital gain after the purchase of Metropolitan Holding Company last year.

The sale will strengthen our position and streamline our operations.

You may expect a significant increase in the value of Magna Corporation shares as a result of this sale.

Truly yours,

John J. Grant
Chief Corporate Officer

Tips and Comments:

Divesting part of a newly acquired company is a common business decision. A letter designed to announce such a move might also explain the reasons or policy that prompted the divestiture. The simplest and perhaps the most common reason is to realize a financial gain from the sale, but some parts of an acquired company may just not fit with the new owner's plans or operations.

Alternative A:

In an attempt to streamline the position of Magna Corporation and consolidate our situation in the food and drink industry, the company has moved to sell the insurance division of the recently acquired Lettson Services, Inc.

We received a fair price for the division, and we believe this will allow Magna to concentrate on the lines of business we know best.

Alternative B:

One of the pleasant surprises to emerge from our recent acquisition of Lexington Industries was the discovery that the smelting plant in Wilmore was far more valuable than our initial analysis indicated.

Consequently, we have received several offers to buy the plant from companies who want to expand their smelting capacities.

We are considering the offers now, and intend to make a sale within the next month.

Alternative C:

This is to announce the sale of the Litton Division of Transfer Industries, a company recently acquired by Magna Corporation.

The sale was a straightforward exchange of stock for cash, which increases our current cash position by 23 percent.

We plan more sales within the next six months.

Stockholder Comment

JOHN L. OPPENHEIMER
998 WESTBROOK STREET
OKLAHOMA CITY, OK

March 24, 19—

Mr. Robert H. Links
Chairman of the Board
Mesquite Corporation
456 Davis Drive
San Antonio, TX

Dear Mr. Links:

The recent restructuring of the Mesquite Corporation is an outrage to the company's shareholders.

Your actions are little more than a thinly disguised attempt to protect the jobs of the high-level management at the expense of the owners of stock.

Not only were the shareholders denied an opportunity to realize a significant profit on stock, but the new financing now both burdens the company with a massive debt load and lowers the value of Mesquite shares on the open market.

Attorneys acting on my behalf have today filed a suit in the Court of Common Pleas, asking that the restructuring plan be reversed and that the current board and executive officers be removed.

Sincerely,

John L. Oppenheimer

Tips and Comment:

Stockholders are technically the owners but often have little control over management decisions arising from mergers or acquisitions. Letters commenting on such business situations may take many forms, but they are often contentious and written in protest. While it is best to remain civil, criticism should not be sugar-coated. Make your position clear and use forceful language, since a great deal may be at stake.

Alternative A:

In response to your recent announcement of the impending sale of Mesquite Corporation to Magna Industries, I must protest.

The offer of $15.50 per share seems too low. If Mesquite remains patient and courts other buyers, I believe we can come closer to $20 per share.

Please consider a delay in making the deal final until other parties can be heard from.

It is your duty to act in the best interests of the shareholders, not to cave in to the first corporate suitor who comes along.

Alternative B:

Why have you announced the intention to bid on Mesquite Corporation stock?

Such a precipitous announcement can only drive the price of shares up and cost Magna dearly.

I have no objection to an aggressive policy of expansion, especially in light of our comfortable cash position after last year's good performance. Nevertheless, you and the rest of the management committee need to examine your tactics.

Alternative C:

This is to let you know that I intend to support those members of the shareholders' meeting who will vote to sell the company.

I know you object to the sale and want to hold on in the hope of reviving sales during the next quarter, and in the past I have deferred to your judgement.

However, the time has come to face realities. All of us who hold significant amounts of stock need to withdraw our capital and turn to other affairs.

9

CREDIT AND COLLECTIONS: LETTERS ABOUT LOANS, ACCOUNTS, AND OVERDUES

Few letters are trickier to write than those dealing with credit and collections. They all share the common goal of trying to get the recipient to act, yet they usually must not be too threatening and they may never be abusive. The executive who can master the task of writing collection and credit letters will quickly gain the upper hand in business life. The following series of letters illustrates the recommended approach in a variety of situations. In all cases, applied psychology is at the heart of writing such letters. The successful executive letter writer will know when to be subtle and when to turn up the pressure. The true test will be in the payoff.

Charge Account Collection Series

THE BLUM STORE
NEW YORK, NY

Letter 1

Mr. James T. Farrell
444 West Deadbeat St.
Aurora, NY

Dear Mr. Farrell:

I wish to call your attention to your past due account. If your payment has already been sent, please disregard this notice.
Your cooperation as well as your patronage is appreciated.

Truly yours,

THE BLUM STORE
NEW YORK, NY

Letter 2

Mr. James T. Farrell
444 West Deadbeat St.
Aurora, NY

A review of your account shows a balance now past due more than 45 days.
Please send in the required amount so we can continue to serve you.

Truly yours,

THE BLUM STORE
NEW YORK, NY

Letter 3

Mr. James T. Farrell
444 West Deadbeat St.
Aurora, NY

Your outstanding balance is now 60 days past due. Please send us a check for the amount immediately.

Truly yours,

THE BLUM STORE
NEW YORK, NY

Letter 4

Mr. James T. Farrell
444 West Deadbeat St.
Aurora, NY

You have not responded to our previous notices that your account is past due. You are now more than two months behind in payment.

Please send us the amount you owe by return mail.

Truly yours,

THE BLUM STORE
NEW YORK, NY

Letter 5

Mr. James T. Farrell
444 West Deadbeat St.
Aurora, NY

Your account with us is now more than 90 days overdue. We cannot extend credit any longer and must have the payment in full within the next ten business days.

Truly yours,

THE BLUM STORE
NEW YORK, NY

Letter 6
FINAL NOTICE

Mr. James T. Farrell
444 West Deadbeat St.
Aurora, NY

We have been patient in asking for the amount you owe us, but our patience has run out. Your account is now more than three months over-due, yet you still have failed to make payment.

Unless we receive payment within five days, we will be forced to turn the account over to a collection agency, which will result in a loss to us and a great deal of unpleasantness for you—including damage to your credit rating.

Truly yours,

Tips and Comment:

Collecting on a past due account is a delicate procedure. The recommended approach is to use a series of standard letters, each scheduled to go out as time goes by with no payment. The first letters in the series should be low key—they should balance the desire to continue business with the need to collect what is due. As the bill becomes more and more delinquent, however, the letters escalate in tone and pressure, ending with the final notice.

Collection Letter to Valued Customer

OK JUICE COMPANY
ORLANDO, FL

Mr. Hervey Allen
Whole Sale Foods
67 Indiana Avenue
Westover Heights, SC

Dear Mr. Allen:

We have been doing business together for a long time and have a sound relationship. Consequently, I know you will understand that my motive is entirely friendly in writing this letter about something that has caused me concern.

Our Accounts Receivable records show that your payments are reaching us increasingly late. We have always appreciated your promptness in the past. It is, however, important to you and to us that we continue receiving payments according to our standard terms.

If you are confronted with business problems, please let me know and perhaps we can help. If, on the other hand, somebody in your office has been careless, please see that our account is given closer attention in the future.

Meanwhile, please send us a check for the amount now past due.

Sincerely,

John Smith
Credit Manager

Tips and Comment:

When a long-time, valued customer begins to fall behind in payments, most companies will allow some slack. When the lagging account becomes too much of a problem, however, a gentle reminder and inquiry may clear up the problem. An overbearing letter is not called for, yet neither should the letter mince words. The future value of the account must be balanced against the need to collect money due.

Alternative A:

The head of our accounting department has just asked me again if I know why your account—which has never been any trouble in the past—is now growing more and more delinquent as the weeks go on.

I had to confess that I didn't understand it. You have been one of our better customers for a long time, and this is the first instance of having to worry about past due payments.

If you are experiencing special problems at the moment, I'd be happy to hear the story and try to accommodate any short-term needs.

Otherwise, it grows more important each day that we get payment on your account.

Alternative B:

It is distressing to note that your account with us is now 60 days overdue. In the past, you have always paid promptly as the bills came due.

If you need special terms for some good reason, I'd be happy to discuss it, but we do not like to have even long-time customers get so far behind.

Please give me a call about this matter.

Alternative C:

Hardly a day goes by when I don't thank the stars for clients like you over the last five years. You have been steady and reliable, and one of those who form the bedrock of our business.

However, I have noticed with concern that you seem to be slipping behind in making payment on our monthly bills.

Since this is such a departure from your usual practice and causes us considerable problems in cash flow, I'd like to talk to you about it.

Please call me soon.

Debt Collection Letter

JAMES COLLECTIONS, INC.
444 23RD AVENUE
AURORA, NE

May 1, 19—

Ms. C. Robbins
222 Ends Avenue
Aurora, NE

Reference: Your check No. 224 for $1400.00 payable to Robert Franken, Jeweler dated March 18, 19—

Dear Ms. Robbins:

Mr. Franken has placed the matter of this check in my hands. The check was returned from Chase National Bank in New York City with the notation "Refer to Maker."

In matters such as this, we first contact the writer of the check to learn the circumstances from your point of view.

Please call me for an appointment to discuss the matter.

Yours truly,

Fred C. Jones
President

Tips and Comment:

The purpose of this letter is first and foremost to collect the debt owed. It must pull no punches, yet it should not be overly threatening at this stage: there may be an adequate explanation and there may be more business to transact in the future. However, the goal is to collect, so don't be too subtle.

Alternative A:

I have been asked by my client to take over the matter of your debt to him in the amount of $12,000.00. He has placed in my hands the documents in the case.

It appears that you are now seriously in default. I must ask you to make full payment immediately, or I will be forced to seek a stronger remedy.

Please deliver a certified check to my office by the close of business on Wednesday, May 5.

Alternative B:

It has been six months since I received a payment on the note still outstanding between us. I have been extremely patient in this matter, since I understand the difficulties you have had since June.

However, I must have the balance of the amount due immediately. Please send a check by return mail.

Alternative C:

The matter of your interest payment has now become serious.

You are more than two months overdue in making the interest payments on your loan, and we cannot extend the grace period any longer.

As you know, you are obligated to make these payments on time or the property in question will revert to us.

I hope you will deliver a check by the end of this month, or I will be forced to turn the matter over to our legal department.

Please let me hear from you.

Apology for Erroneous Collection Letter

MARS CORPORATION
1592 DOWNS AVENUE
PHILADELPHIA, PA

March 23, 19—

Ms. Wanda Hickey
567 Upper Touchstone
Hammond, WI

Dear Ms. Hickey:

Please accept our sincere apology for the notice you received recently about your account. We made an error, and your account is in perfect order.

We make every effort to avoid such mistakes, but they do occur once in a great while.

I am sorry if our error inconvenienced you.

Sincerely,

Jay Burst
Collection Department

Tips and Comment:

The situation is obvious: someone in the company made an error in billing, and this letter must be dispatched to clear it up and apologize for the embarrassing event. Directness and sincerity are much prized in this situation and will probably defuse hostility from the wronged customer.

Alternative A:

I am very sorry that you received a second collection notice about your account. You are entirely correct—you paid with cash at the time of purchase.

Our data processing department erred in recording the payment.

The error in our records has now been corrected, and your account is clear.

Thank you for your patience and understanding.

Alternative B:

We are red-faced.

We sent you a collection notice by mistake, and in fact, your account is fully paid up to date. For some reason, our billing department failed to make the proper entry.

Please accept my sincere apology. I'd like you to take a 1 percent discount on your next order to make up for the inconvenience we have caused this time.

Thanks for understanding.

Alternative C:

I'm embarrassed that Joan sent you that collection notice by mistake. You are, of course, fully paid.

This was a silly and careless mistake, and I hope you will overlook it.

Let me know if there is anything more I can do to correct the situation.

Credit Extension Request

TRUE BUILT HOMES, INC.
BRACKTON, CO

March 23, 19—

Mr. Kenneth L. Leyendecker
Brackton Savings and Loan
West Mall
Brackton, CO

Dear Mr. Leyendecker:

This is to inform you officially that we will be unable to make the interest payment due this month.

We are in this embarrassing position due to the recent changes in government regulations on financing condominium developments (a change you are all too aware of). The unexpected ruling has delayed sale of all of our current market units.

However, we expect that the new procedures will be functioning within a few days, and we will then be able to resume sales.

We plan to make our regular payment next month as well as the skipped payment for this month and late fees.

Thank you.

Sincerely,

Tom J. Thompson
President

Tips and Comment:

All except the most cash-rich businesses may, on occasion, find themselves unable to meet all monthly obligations, and it becomes necessary to write a letter to creditors, explaining the need to delay or reduce payments due. Such a letter should be phrased directly and clearly. If there is a sound reason for the temporary shortfall, it might be wise to explain, but too much complaining is unlikely to be effective. The goals are to satisfy the creditor for the time being and keep lines of communication open.

Alternative A:

As we discussed yesterday, we request an extension of our outstanding note held by your institution. By rolling over the note for another six months, you will allow us to complete the additions to our plant and put the new line into production.

We will make all required monthly interest payments, but no further payments to reduce the principal during the six-month extension.

Thank you for your help.

Alternative B:

After looking at our accounts for the past month and noting a reduction in sales due to seasonal fluctuations in trade, I wish to request an extension of further credit on our outstanding balance with you.

I know that we agreed to pay off the balance of our account at the end of 30 days, but we will not be able to do so this month.

We are confident that the coming weeks will see a resurgence of sales, and the results will allow us to meet our obligations on schedule in the future.

Alternative C:

This is to inquire if it will be possible to delay payment to you for a few more days.

The exchange of funds we had planned with our Leipzig office has been delayed, and we will not have the money in our local account until at least the 23rd.

If this causes a difficulty, please call me at once.

Credit Application Letter

WIDGET DISTRIBUTING, INC.
34 EAST FIFTH STREET
OGLETHORPE, AR

August 23, 19—

Mr. Charles W. Reed
Credit Manager
Worldwide Widgets, Inc.
Tonner's Ford, TX

Dear Mr. Reed:

My company began operations 18 months ago as a regional distributor of widgets in the Arkansas and Missouri area. For the past six months we have purchased supplies of widgets from Worldwide on a C.O.D. basis.

I would like now to establish a wholesale trade credit account with you, allowing us to order shipments as needed and to pay once a month for all goods received during the previous thirty days.

Please let me know what I need to do to set up the credit account. I can supply credit references in the two-state area, and my accountant will be happy to provide copies of recent balance sheets.

A credit account will make bookkeeping much easier for me, and it will probably concentrate my wholesale buying in your hands.

Thank you.

Truly yours,

John B. Carruthers
President

Tips and Comment:

Establishing credit in many industries is essential, especially for a new company. This sample letter of application describes the pertinent background, makes the case for granting credit, and hints at an increase in sales if the credit is granted. It wisely uses a confident tone that implies the applicant is a serious business with a long-term future.

Alternative A:

After doing business with you for three months on a cash basis, I would like to set up a credit account.

We anticipate that we will be increasing our purchases over the coming months, and a credit mechanism will make this easier and more efficient.

Please let me know what paperwork will be required.

Alternative B:

Your company supplies HD-34 semi-widgets in bulk lots of 500, which we use in the manufacture of electronic controls.

Over the past year we have purchased 2,000 of these semi-widget units on a cash and carry basis.

Would it be possible to set up a credit account, whereby we can simply order the shipments and pay when billed?

Alternative C:

I would like to set up a charge account for office supplies in the name of my real estate company.

We find that we are making regular purchases of supplies from you, and a credit account would make this simpler and easier to control.

Please let me know if I need to fill out an application.

Application for Credit Increase

ALLIED CHEMICALS CORPORATION
P.O. BOX 45
PROVO, UT

January 18, 19—

Ms. Joan Kerns
Sales Manager
Universal Products, Inc.
112 Delavan Drive
Sacramento, CA

Dear Ms. Kerns:

We would like to increase our credit line for orders.

We currently have a limit of $20,000 per month, and we have been pushing that hard over the past few months, due to an increase in our production.

It appears that we will continue to increase our need for supplies, so an increase in purchasing is inevitable.

Please let me know when we can discuss details.

Sincerely,

George T. Yount
Production and Plant Manager

Tips and Comment:

When asking for an increase in credit limits, it is a good idea for the letter to make a sound case for the change. The best persuaders are to point to increased business and a good payment record. As in most letters dealing with financial matters, it is best to keep the tone sober and the facts clear. Matters of personality or emotion seldom figure in such communications.

Alternative A:

After reviewing our purchasing activity for the past several weeks, it appears that we will begin to reach our credit limit with you within the next quarter.

Therefore, we would like to request a further extension of credit from you on our orders.

We have paid all outstanding bills when due.

Alternative B:

Can we bump up our credit line?

We have been coming pretty close to the limit recently, and it would certainly make life easier if we extended the amount to include large orders that come in late in the quarter.

Let me know if we need to do anything formal.

Alternative C:

This is to formally request an increase of $4,000 in our line of credit.

While our sales continue to show a slow but healthy increase, the recent expansion of our staff has put considerable pressure on our cash position each month.

This increase would allow us to operate much more comfortably.

Credit Investigation

A. G. ROBERTS COMPANY
700 CRESTVIEW AVENUE
DENNIS, IL

February 24, 19—

Ace Credit Reporting
345 Towanda Drive
Kilver, IL

Dear Sir or Madame:

Because we anticipate a large order from Simco, Inc. of San Diego, California, we would like a credit profile of this company.

We understand that you do not make recommendations or comments about the firms you report on; however, a credit history of Simco will be sufficient for us.

Thank you for your cooperation.

Yours truly,

Liz Tratteria
Credit Manager

Tips and Comment:

It is an important function to check the credit of a customer who wishes to begin business. The letters typically go to credit agencies and the references provided by the potential customer. Care should be taken to protect the confidentiality of the information.

Alternative A:

The Simco company has placed a large order with our firm and given your name as a reference.

We would appreciate learning any information you can supply about Simco's reputation and general standing in the business community, especially in meeting financial obligations.

Of course, we will keep all such information in confidence.

Alternative B:

We would like to know more about Simco, Inc., which has just given us indication that it wishes to place a series of orders with our firm.

We understand you have done business with Simco for several years and should be in a position to comment.

We are particularly interested in how they meet accounts receivable.

You may be assured that any comments will be kept in confidence.

Alternative C:

We operate on a credit basis with most of our customers, so it is important that we screen new clients carefully.

Simco, Inc. has recently joined our list of buyers, so if you have any pertinent information about the company's credit worthiness, we'd like to have it.

If you are unable to supply information, perhaps you could give us suggestions of who else to ask.

Granting Credit

K. B. DOLL CORPORATION
346 CARROLL STREET
BROOKLYN, NY

October 4, 19—

Mr. Richard Pener
Toys and Collectibles, Inc.
West Bend, DE

Dear Mr. Pener:

The credit references you provided have reported with highest satisfaction.

It is our pleasure to extend credit terms to you, and we can assure you of our cooperation at all times.

Thank you for choosing us as a supplier. We have no doubt that our future business relationship will be a source of satisfaction to both of us.

Yours truly,

David Gains
Credit Manager

Tips and Comment:

It is a mutually happy occasion to grant credit to a new client after a good report from credit sources. Everyone is pleased and can look forward to getting down to business. Use the letter as an opportunity to begin to cultivate a long-term business relationship.

Alternative A:

It is a pleasure to tell you that your line of credit has been approved and you may place orders with us immediately.

All of your references reported favorably on your credit history, and we are certain we will be able to do the same in the future.

Your account number is 2223. Please use it as a reference on all orders and correspondence.

If I can do anything else, please let me know.

Alternative B:

After checking with the names you gave us, I'm happy to report that you qualify for extended credit terms. We will allow a line of purchase up to a $100,000 outstanding balance.

We will bill you for each order and send a cumulative statement at the end of each month.

Please send orders directly to Mr. Thomas' department.

I'll be happy to help at any time.

Alternative C:

Your credit report came back today, and I'm relieved to be able to grant you charge privileges immediately.

This should make our bookkeeping much simpler, and I hope, increase the volume of business you are able to do with us.

Let me know if there are any problems with the new arrangement.

Turning Down a Credit Application

WESTMAN PHOTOGRAPHY COMPANY
WESTMAN DRIVE
ROCHESTER, NY

November 23, 19—

Mr. Theodore Glasser
Photo World
East Side Mall
Georgetown, KY

Dear Mr. Glasser:

Thank you for your patience while we looked into your credit standing.

Unfortunately, the information we received does not allow us to extend credit to you at this time. We shall, of course, be happy to review your account later, if you wish, and we hope that credit terms could be extended then.

In the meantime, please enclose a check for payment with all orders.

Sincerely,

Wanda Trench
Credit Manager

Tips and Comment:

Turning down a credit application is unpleasant, but sometimes necessary in the course of duty. The letter must be unequivocal, yet if there is legitimate cause for reviewing the application later, this message may soften the blow and allow continued sales on a cash basis.

Alternative A:

I'm sorry to report that your references were not good enough to allow us to extend the credit line you requested.

If you wish to reapply for a line with a lower ceiling, we may be able to help you.

Please let me know.

Alternative B:

It appears from the credit report we just received that you have not been in business long enough to have established a full credit record.

Therefore, we will not be able to advance terms of credit to you this quarter.

If you think your status will improve, please let us know and we will check again.

Alternative C:

After reviewing all the information on your credit application, I must tell you that the committee decided to not grant the requested line of credit.

It is a standing company policy to refuse credit to any applicant who has filed for bankruptcy within the last five years.

Thank you for your interest.

Change in Credit Status

MARKMAN STORES
ONE PARK PLACE
PHILADELPHIA, PA

September 5, 19—

Ms. Cynthia Williams
290 Upper Turnover
West Rewston, MS

Dear Ms. Williams:

In reviewing our records, we find that your account often exceeds our terms of sale and now has a past due balance of $1,855.00. It may be that our regular 30-day revolving credit plan is not best suited to you.

If you think a different kind of account would be better for you, we will be happy to discuss the matter at your convenience.

Cordially yours,

Blanche D. Wood
Credit Manager

Tips and Comment:

Chronic problems by a customer in meeting their payment schedule may indicate the need for a change. It is a headache for everyone if the credit terms do not fill the customer's ability to pay. A simple suggestion of discussing options may benefit both parties. A similar situation may show prompt payment but a constant overdraft, which calls for a suggestion of increasing the credit limit. It is important to strike just the right tone of voice in such a letter—concerned and helpful, but with a responsible amount of caution.

Alternative A:

In looking over your account records for the last year, I notice that you have frequently exceeded your assigned credit limit, yet pay off the balance due within 30 days.

Since going over your limit means we must assess an extra fee, I suggest that you make an application to increase the ceiling on your account.

If you would like to do so, please fill out and send in the enclosed application form.

Thank you.

Alternative B:

The accounting department has called to my attention that your account is technically in default almost every month. It appears that your date for making routine payments is five days after the grace period on your credit account expires.

If this is simply a matter of timing, then I suggest we change your account to better fit your office and bookkeeping procedures.

Please call me about this change.

Alternative C:

Based on the record of your account, you have a difficult time meeting the monthly payments. This is a matter of considerable concern, and I would like to take action to correct the problem.

Please make an appointment to see me and discuss the matter.

Denying an Unearned Discount

OK JUICE COMPANY
ORLANDO, FL

October 12, 19—

Mr. Thomas Hardie
Lagniappe Grocers
333 Wendover
Titusville, FL

Dear Mr. Hardie:

The premium of 2 percent cash discount allowed customers is for prompt payment. Since we did not receive your check for our invoice No. 12576 until 30 days after the discount period expired, we cannot allow your deduction.

We would appreciate your check for $702.50 representing payment in full of the invoice.

Our discount policy was adopted as a way to treat all our accounts equitably. To forgive one oversight and not others would be unfair to the majority of our customers.

Thank you.

Sincerely,

John Smith
Credit Manager

Tips and Comment:

On occasion, a customer may take an unearned cash discount when paying a bill, either through oversight or in an attempt to cut a sharp corner. The letter denying the discount must be firm but tactful. Laying out the details and quoting precise numbers should leave little doubt about the situation.

Alternative A:

We have received your payment for Invoice No. 4029, but the amount is short by $456.00. You deducted 2 percent for a cash discount; however, the time limit for this discount is thirty days and your check was dated forty-five days after the initial billing.

Therefore, the discount cannot be allowed.

We are happy to extend a cash discount to our regular customers, but all the conditions of time must be met.

Please send in a check for the additional amount.

We look forward to doing business with you as usual in the future.

Alternative B:

I'm sorry to inform you that I cannot allow the customary 2 percent discount for "prompt payment" on your last bill.

Our company policy is to grant the discount if payment is made within 15 days of billing, which saves us considerable time and money. If the payment is later than 15 days, we must have the full amount of the billing.

Your check was issued on June 30, more than 25 days after the invoice.

Please send me a check for the difference.

Alternative C:

There must have been a mistake in your office when you paid our invoice for May.

We allow a 3 percent discount for immediate cash payment, but the offer expires after ten days.

Your check was not sent to us until fifteen days had passed, so the discount did not apply.

Please let me have a payment for the difference.

10

BUYING GOODS AND SERVICES: LETTERS FOR PURCHASING

The field of purchasing is somewhat specialized, and many of the letters connected with buying goods and services border on the technical. Nonetheless, even top-level management executives will be called on to write such letters on occasion, and they should be prepared. The following examples provide a guide to writing purchasing or procurement letters. Most of them have a formality that must be observed in order to maintain good purchasing policies. These model letters should save time for executives who must deal with this set of issues.

Request for Proposal

AMERICAN STEEL COMPANY
ALLENTOWN, GA

July 2, 19—

To: Prospective Contractors
From: Department of Purchasing
Subject: Request for Proposal for an Employee Health Insurance Program

Purpose: The American Steel Company wishes to contract with an independent firm to process and pay claims for the Company's comprehensive Employee Health Insurance Program. The proposed system to process, validate, verify, and pay the claims is expected to be a highly efficient and cost-beneficial computer system.

Time: The sealed cost and technical proposals under separate cover and subject to conditions in the attached RFP will be received until 2:00 p.m., August 30, 19—.

Note: Indicate the firm's name and address and the words "Cost Proposal" or "Technical Proposal" on the front of each sealed envelope, along with the date.

Tips and Comment:

Requests for Proposal (RFPs) are formal, technical documents, and the cover letter sent with them to vendors is usually similar in tone. The cover letter may set forth additional conditions surrounding the submission of the RFP. Again, the same letter should go to all potential vendors.

Alternative A:

Attached is Drawing No. 40322, showing a walkway from the precipitator to the stack. Please quote in triplicate the cost of furnishing this walkway, ready for erection, but not erected, including one coat of shop paint.

If you have any questions concerning this project, please contact Mr. L. Crinic, Plant Engineer.

Proposals are to be addressed to Mr. Joseph G. Smith, Vice-President, Purchases and Raw Materials.

Alternative B:

We are pleased to invite you to submit a proposal for landscaping services around the Corporate Headquarters building.

The details are outlined in the attached document and site plan.

The Company currently has a contract with a firm to provide these services, but it expires next month.

It is anticipated that a contractor will be selected no later than September 10 to provide us with complete landscaping services for the next three years. Consequently, all proposals will have to be on Mr. Smith's desk no later than noon, September 1.

Alternate C:

Enclosed in an RFP for a feasibility study for the expansion of the current marketing program.

We invite you to respond by May 1.

If there are further questions, please contact me at the address and number listed above.

We anticipate awarding a contract by May 15 and beginning work on the study by June 1.

Purchase Recommendation Letter

WIDELY MANUFACTURING
222 FRONT STREET
ANYTOWN, U.S.A.

June 4, 19—

Ms. Jane Doe
Plant Supervisor
Widely Manufacturing
222 Front Street
Anytown, USA

Dear Jane:

The best way to improve our housekeeping is to hire a sanitation consultant. John Silver of Anchor Janitorial Services and I toured the plant and discussed housekeeping problems and possible remedies. He seems competent and knowledgeable. For example, he said the white spots on the carpets are caused by commercial "ice melt" products that contain bleach.

He suggests we:

- Sweep the excess off sidewalks to avoid tracking, and use a bleach-free calcium-chloride product.

Anchor offers two basic programs:

- A one-time consultation service that includes a complete housekeeping survey. They will recommend frequency of cleaning, methods, equipment, chemical products, manpower levels, job duties, and quality-control checklists. This costs $3,000.

- An initial consultation and weekly follow-up visits for six months. They will prepare procedure manuals and train both individual workers and the Sanitation Supervisor. This costs $6,000.

Sincerely,

John Doe,
Corporate Manager
(Courtesy of Robert S. Burger, Burger Associates, Glen Mills, PA)

Tips and Comment:

This actual letter (similar to a memo) delineates the solution to an internal problem by recommending the purchase of outside services. Note that the writer wastes no time in making the recommendation and uses the rest of the letter to make the case and set forth the details and options, including the costs. This is a model of how to precisely state a recommendation: clearly and without qualification.

Alternative A:

After a thorough review, I believe we can best solve the problems connected with the Jones contract by temporarily employing the services of a competent independent analyst.

John Doe Associates has worked for us before on similar projects, and I recommend we hire them again for this project.

They price their services by the day at a rate of $500. I estimate at least five days work.

Let me know if you agree, and I'll contact Doe immediately. They could be on the job by mid-week.

Alternative B:

The Grundik Model 004 will be our best option.

I have run tests on all five of the products now on the market, and the Grundik is superior in five of six categories (see attached data table).

The price of $49,000 is slightly higher than the nearest competitor, but the warranty is six months longer and the local service organization has performed well in the past.

I recommend purchase of a Model 004 within the next two months.

Alternative C:

Charles and I agree that we need help in getting together the data for Jim.

We also agree that Data Path can do the job better, more quickly, and more cost-efficiently than we can in-house.

Let's call Data Path and get them started before the end of the week. We can take this out of the operations budget.

Awarding a Contract

FIRST FEDERAL SAVINGS AND LOAN ASSOCIATION
JOHANTOWN, CA

May 4, 19—

Treadlight Security Company
333 Lower Bend Avenue
Johantown, CA

Gentlemen:

We are happy to once again award you the contract for provision of 24-hour security services at our main office and two branch offices. The price stated in this contract is as you quoted to us in your bid of April 22.

I am enclosing our signed contract in triplicate. Please countersign two copies and return them to me. The third copy is for your files.

We look forward to working with you on a continuing basis.

Yours truly,

Lorraine J. Kenton
Vice-President for Administration

Tips and Comment:

Awarding a contract is another exercise in formality. The letter may well constitute part of the legal contract, so it should be straightforward and specific. Friendliness is fine, but the basics should be covered first. The highest virtues in such a letter are absolute clarity and precision.

Alternative A:

This is to inform you that we have decided to award to your firm the contract detailed in our RFP dated April 1. The contract is now being drafted in final form by our attorney, and it will be in the mail to you within a few days.

The terms of the contract will reflect the provisions of the RFP, with the addition of the change of schedule you outlined in your proposal.

We have no objection to the payment provisions you requested, but we would like to draw your attention to the possible tax advantages for both parties of delaying the final payment until after the close of the fiscal year.

I anticipate a fruitful relationship during the course of this project.

Alternative B:

We have reviewed all of the proposals submitted for the development of a feasibility and plant site study, and I'm pleased to report that you will be awarded the contract, subject to agreement to the following stipulations:

(1) The schedule of site visits should include Jacksonville.
(2) The final report must be submitted no later than September 30, in triplicate.
(3) All expenses connected with paragraph three in the proposal will be borne by you, the contractor.

If these conditions are agreeable, please sign and return the enclosed document.

Please call me if there are further questions.

Alternative C:

It is once again a pleasure to announce that you have won the contract for printing our annual report, based on your quotation of April 25.

I will ask Mr. Lenter to be in touch with you immediately to nail down an exact schedule for each phase of the project.

I know we can look forward to producing yet another prize-winner.

Letter of Agreement for Services

ZENDA, INC.
3101 WEST END AVENUE
SUITE 200
NASHVILLE, TN 37203

Letter of Agreement

Zenda, Inc., whose principal place of business is located at 3101 West End Avenue, Suite 200, Nashville, Tennessee 37203, hereby agrees with John L. Doe that he will serve as Research Director of its XYZ research project. Doe will consult on all aspects of the project and oversee all research at various locations throughout the country, helping to produce narratives of two units of the project, exhibit encapsulations of the units, and various other documents and products as required. He will advise the project director on the administration of the projects, provide information as needed for monthly reports, and assist in all other activities related to the project.

Zenda will compensate Doe for his consultant work at the rate of $xxxx, as billed on the following dates: January 15, February 15, March 15, April 15, May 15, and June 15, or at the successful conclusion of the project, whichever is later. Zenda will reimburse Doe for all reasonable and documented expenses upon receipt of invoices for these expenses.

The signatures below indicate agreement with all the terms detailed herein. This agreement cancels and replaces all previous agreements between the parties in respect to consultant work and is not subject to any other oral or written terms or representations.

_____   _____
On behalf of Zenda, Inc.   Date

_____   _____
John L. Doe   Date

(Courtesy of Charles Phillips, Nashville, TN)

Tips and Comment:

Letters of agreement are useful tools in purchasing services. As a rule, they are formal documents, to be checked by an attorney. They should set forth all the important facts, including duties, schedules, compensation, and payment procedures. Letters such as this example from an actual corporation read almost like contracts, but many are less detailed and have fewer clauses. In some circumstances, letters of agreement may be informal in tone, but in all cases they form a basis for common understanding.

Alternative A:

This is an agreement between James L. Doe Associates and Jane M. Doe for services to be provided between January 12 and February 15.

These services will include a survey of manufacturing methods, a quantitative analysis of the survey results, and preparation of a written report.

The report is due in the offices of James L. Doe Associates no later than February 15.

Upon submission of the report, James L. Doe Associates will pay Jane M. Doe the sum of $xxxx.

Alternative B:

National Inventory Control, Inc. agrees to employ the services of Regional Processing Co. during the month of May.

Regional will perform routine data entry duties as directed by National Inventory Control, Inc. in the Dayton office.

These services will be billed at the rate of $xx.xx per hour and paid at the completion of the agreement upon receipt of invoice.

Alternative C:

Gearing Consultants, Inc. agrees to provide consulting services to Amalgamated Partners in regard to marketing.

Gearing will prepare a market plan after discussion with the principals of Amalgamated Partners and advise Amalgamated on the planning and execution of the resulting plan.

The fee for services will be $xxxxx, plus reasonable expenses. One third of the fee is due on signing of this letter of agreement and the balance at the completion of the project.

Rejecting a Bid

K.B. DOLL CORPORATION
346 CARROLL STREET
BROOKLYN, NY

October 2, 19—

Ms. Deidre Quanter
Consulting Designer
34 West 42nd Street
New York, NY

Dear Ms. Quanter:

Thank you for the time and effort you spent in preparing your proposal of September 2.

We regret to inform you that we are giving this contract to another vendor because of price.

Be assured you will be included in any future invitations to bid.

Sincerely,

Charles B. Doll

Tips and Comment:

A letter turning down a bid is a requirement of doing courteous business, and it assures that more bids will be received on future projects. If possible, it is a good idea to give the unsuccessful bidders some idea of why they did not win the contract, but it is not absolutely necessary.

Alternative A:

I'm sorry to tell you that we have decided to award the contract for the feasibility study to another firm.

Your proposal was competitive and included many good ideas; however, the winning company has more than 15 years experience in exactly this sort of study.

If we entertain bids on similar projects in the future, I will be certain to include you on the list.

Thanks for your effort.

Alternative B:

This is to let all of you know that the Carl Hershorn Co. of Lackawanna has been awarded the contract to rid our buildings of asbestos.

We appreciate your bid, however, and wish you well in the future.

Alternative C:

Please be informed that you were not among the finalists to receive the award of contract for RFP No. 334.

If you would like to be considered for future RFP solicitations, please fill out and mail the enclosed reply card.

Thank you for submitting a proposal.

Declining to Do Business

ALABAMA ATLANTIC CORPORATION
FORESTRY BUILDING
PORTLAND, OR

May 12, 19—

Mr. Leonard Tuchman
Amalgamated Logging, Inc.
Seattle, WA

Dear Mr. Tuchman:

Thank you for bringing your Canadian interests to our attention. We buy a good deal of veneer in Canada now, and also a few logs from time to time. Our use of logs is not extensive and probably will decrease rather than increase due to recent connections made for the purchase of veneer under a contractual arrangement.

No one, of course, knows just how fast our needs may change or how our current supplier's operations will work out. Consequently, it would be our pleasure to talk with you from time to time about the products you have available. However, at present, we are unable to make any definite commitments.

Sincerely,

Max Good
Purchasing Manager

Tips and Comment:

Not only does simple courtesy call for a polite letter of refusal, but it is good business to keep lines of supply open for the future. This is a fine example of how ordinary business etiquette may serve a deeper purpose.

Alternative A:

It was good of you to send me the information on your company, and I have read it with care and attention.

I do not have occasion to use your services at the moment, but I am always happy to learn of the existence of a potential new supplier.

Please keep me informed as to your activities and progress.

Alternative B:

All of our machine service is now under contract to a single vendor, so I am unable to seriously discuss your proposal.

However, one never knows what will develop, and I will be happy to have you stay in touch.

Good luck in starting up your venture.

Alternative C:

As much as I liked the quality of your material as indicated by the samples you left with me, my plant manager tells me that we cannot handle anything with a tensile strength of this magnitude.

If we are ever in a position to do so, I'll be in touch.

Dispute with a Vendor

AMERICAN CORPORATION
100 PLAZA
GARDEN CITY, NY

April 21, 19—

Wendover Corp.
Industrial Park
White Plains, NY

Gentlemen:

We have had a most serious problem in delivery on our order of February 23. The components were due to ship from your plant on April 15 as part of a larger order that was to be forwarded to the Department of Energy. Your schedule obligation as subcontractor was clearly spelled out in the original contract.

Repeated calls to your office have brought no satisfactory response.

There is still time to correct the situation, if you act with dispatch. However, if you continue to lag behind the contracted schedule and continue to fail to discuss the matter, we shall be forced to take stronger action.

We want to avoid any unpleasantness and desire only to make good on the DOE contract.

Please call me immediately with a satisfactory solution to this major problem.

Your truly,

Pat Ceti
Manufacturing Manager

Tips and Comment:

When things go awry with a vendor and informal methods fail to rectify the situation, a formal letter of complaint may break loose a solution, and it may help establish a paper trail of responsibility in case disaster develops. Such letters must be forceful but tactful. Threats should be low-key but firm. It is a good idea to state specifically what has gone wrong and to suggest immediate action.

Alternative A:

We received your shipment of widgets on the 24th; however, on unpacking, our people discovered that 80 percent were damaged in transit, apparently because of faulty packing.

We need an adjustment in the billing, and we will require full replacements as soon as they can be delivered. As you know, we have a contract to meet by the middle of next month.

If you check your order documents, you will find that you bear full responsibility for the condition of material delivered to our dock.

Alternative B:

On inspection of your shipment to us of 100,000 sheets of 20 pound bond, we discovered faulty watermarks.

Please make arrangements immediately to pick up the first shipment and to replace it with properly made paper.

We anticipate a large order for printed letterhead within a few weeks, and we need to have a supply of bond in our warehouse.

Alternative C:

As we discussed on the phone today, your latest delivery failed to meet industry standard when we attempted to put the material into our mixing vats.

We have not yet determined exactly the cause of the failure (our plant chemist is still conducting tests), but the result was a stoppage of our production lines for more than three days.

Since this came at a crucial point in our current run, we have had to cancel a major contract.

We suggest that you will bear full financial responsibility for our losses under industry custom, which as you know has been upheld in court several times.

We will forward a full report when the tests are complete.

Canceling an Order or Contract

PREMIER ELECTRONICS COMPANY
455 GAINSBORO AVENUE
TALUSA, SC

January 4, 19—

Ms. Jeri Ketchum
Wendover Corp.
Industrial Park
White Plains, NY

Dear Ms. Ketchum:

Since you are unable to send us the material listed in our Purchase Order No. 3445, we are forced to cancel our order.

As you know, we needed these items to complete an order for our Australian account. The customer in Sydney informs us that he can no longer wait for the material, so the shipment is being sent without your part.

We are sorry to cancel, but we have no choice.

Sincerely,

Henry Gibbs
Manager

Tips and Comment:

A letter canceling a contract or an order should be concise and clear, with a statement of exactly what is being canceled and why. It should be kept in mind that serious financial or legal ramifications may arise from the cancellation, so careful wording is recommended.

Alternative A:

Due to a recent downturn in sales, we are forced to shut down production on line no. 2 for at least two weeks in order to adjust our inventory.

Consequently, we will not need delivery of our most recent order from you (No. 4567).

This is to formally cancel the order.

When we resume production, we will issue a new order.

Alternative B:

I'm sorry to tell you that we feel we must cancel the contract under which you have been providing services.

The quality of your performance has steadily deteriorated over the last six months, a situation we have discussed several times. You have been given ample opportunity to correct the problem, but no solution is in sight.

The last day for payment of your previous retainer will be the thirtieth of this month.

Please return to our offices all outstanding material in your possession.

Alternative C:

This is to let you know that I will no longer provide service for your company after the first of the month.

I regret having to give up the account, but I have just signed a new contract with a major manufacturer that will take all of my time. I will no longer be in business locally.

I have enjoyed working with you, and I wish you continued success in the future.

Enclosed are all the files of your work to date.

Purchasing Authority Letter

JONES AND ASSOCIATES, INC.
23 ROVER DRIVE
WESTBROOK, ME

September 23, 19—

Dear Vendors:

All purchases on behalf of Jones and Associates, Inc. must be accompanied by a signed and dated purchase order.

Purchases over $500 must be countersigned by me as president. Purchases for less than $500 need only the signature of the office manager.

Please include the Jones and Associates purchase number on your invoice, since this will speed payment.

Thank you for your help.

Truly yours,

Harold K. Jones
President

Tips and Comment:

In many situations it is desirable to let vendors know of your company policy about purchase orders, including who is authorized to place orders and any limitations. This helps protect both the company and the vendor from abuse.

Alternative A:

Please restrict orders from our company to cases in which a completed purchase order is submitted.

It is our company policy to pay charge bills only if a copy of our purchase order is included with the invoice.

We appreciate your cooperation in this matter.

Alternative B:

As of this month, we will require all employees of our company to obtain a completed and signed purchase order before placing orders with you. We would appreciate it if you will include the purchase order number and date on all future invoices.

If you have any questions about this policy, please call our accounting department.

Alternative C:

This is to let you know that Gladys Harris is now the authorized purchasing agent for our company.

Only purchases approved and signed by Gladys will be honored.

Please include the purchase order number on your bills.

Requesting Information from Vendor

TACOMA COMPANY, INC.
BOULDERS, ID

January 22, 19—

Wink Office Equipment Corp.
78 Industrial Blvd.
Lowell, ID

Dear Vendor:

We wish to replace our electronic typewriters with a complete word processing system, and we would be interested in getting detailed information on your "Winkword."

Specifically, we want to know its capabilities, price, maintenance cost, and modularity. Also please let us know about documentation that comes with the Winkword and how much training you provide for the system.

We look forward to your early reply.

Sincerely,

Roger R. Goes
Purchasing Director

Tips and Comment:

Requesting information from potential vendors calls for a basic letter that sets forth the circumstances and lays out the specific information required. At this level of first contact, the letter need not be personal. As in all purchasing situations, it is best to ask all vendors for the same information in the same format.

Alternative A:

We are about to launch a new product onto the market, and we are therefore looking for a new advertising agency in the local area.

We would be happy to entertain discussions and a proposal from your firm.

Specifically, we will want a full media campaign over the next six months, with a unique approach to making our product known to the buying public. We will require full creative services, art and production, and media buying.

Please call me for an appointment to talk about a proposal.

Alternative B:

Please give me a unit price and delivery dates for 10,000 units of No. 4, Grade 2 widgets.

The price should include freight to our manufacturing plant at the above address.

All units must be pretested to Industry Standard 404.

I need your bid in writing no later than March 12.

Alternative C:

We anticipate a large order for letterhead from one of our customers and would like to get a quotation from you on the job.

We will need 100,000 sheets of 24 pound, 25 percent cotton bond, 8½ x 11, printed on one side in three colors. The art will be supplied camera-ready, and delivery must be within two weeks of submission of art. The letterhead must be shrink-wrapped in quantities of 500 each.

Please indicate the discount to us.

Complimenting a Vendor

AMERICAN CORPORATION
100 PLAZA
GARDEN CITY, NY

February 2, 19—

Mr. Herbert Swift
S and W Management Services
450 Towa Drive
Dobb's Crossing, NH

Dear Mr. Swift:

Over the years we have enjoyed a most satisfactory relationship with your company to our mutual benefit.

Every once in a while, however, your ingenious staff does something outstanding that is above the normal call of duty. Such was the case recently when your organization produced an unsolicited prototype database management package for our computer system.

On behalf of all of us, please accept our sincere appreciation.

Sincerely,

James K. Lowe
Vice-President

Tips and Comment:

It is pleasant to hand out compliments to vendors who provide outstanding service or products, and it can bring continued dividends in the future. Keep such letters pitched at the appropriate level, and be certain to keep the lines of communication open.

Alternative A:

Over the past month we have had several demanding situations that required fast action from you.

We would like to thank you and your staff for the excellent service and extra special efforts put forth.

Please convey our particular thanks to your engineering department.

Alternative B:

Your help during our crisis last week was a life-saver. I don't think we could have weathered the storm without your quick and efficient response.

Please thank everyone involved.

Alternative C:

Once again I must compliment you and your people for the fine job. Our client was very pleased with the delivery, thanks in no small part to your help.

We will continue to look to you for the best.

11

DEALING WITH GOVERNMENT: LETTERS TO OFFICIALS

Government and business are inextricably intertwined in the modern world, and letters to government officials are almost a daily occurrence for many business executives. As the following examples show, such letters call for a firm tone of voice, coupled with an informed persuasiveness. Business executives should work hard to cultivate the most effective relations with government, and a letter to an official is one of the primary tools—most governments thrive on paper communications. Using the following model letters will save an immense amount of time and energy in this important endeavor.

Opposing Legislation in Congress

DIRECT MAILERS, INC.
404 WEST TRENTON AVENUE
HUNTINGTON, KS

April 4, 19—

The Honorable John Hooks
Chairman
Committee on the Judiciary
House of Representatives
Washington, DC

Dear Representative Hooks:

Recent news reports indicate that you are considering the introduction of a bill to allow states to levy sales taxes on mail orders from out of state, the so-called "Bellas Hess" situation.

I strongly urge you not to introduce such a bill.

It would be a crippling blow to the multi-million dollar catalog sales industry which has developed into such a strong part of our national retail economy over the last decade. Not only would millions of customers be dissuaded from the purchase of goods through catalogs, but the paperwork and red tape would be terrible burdens to both seller and buyer.

The small amount of tax revenue derived by individual states would in no way compensate for the damage such a move would cause.

I hope you will refrain from further legislative action on this matter.

Yours truly,

John Keeton
President

Tips and Comment:

Timing is important in affecting the course of legislation. Making a position known before the introduction of a bill in Congress is crucial and may head off a problem before it causes actual damage. As in all letters to legislators, the tone should be firm but not aggressive. Leave no doubt as to the course advocated and support the argument with a few reasons or facts.

In this case, the writer hopes to forestall a bill that would have sweeping effects in his industry. Most likely his trade association has alerted its members and urged a mail campaign.

Alternative A:

I understand that you have discussed the introduction of a bill to allow offshore oil drilling near the Point Reyes National Park.

This would be a potentially devastating blow to the efforts of the tourism industry in Northern California, and I ask in the strongest possible terms that you reconsider this bill.

This area currently attracts more than 2 million visitors a year. If the shoreline is disfigured by oil derricks, the flow of visitors would cease and the area would be threatened with significant environmental damage.

Thank you for your consideration.

Alternative B:

I'm writing to ask you not to introduce or to support legislation restricting the ability of domestic companies to include "goodwill" as an asset when evaluating worth.

As I'm certain you know, such a law would severely hamper the acquisition of one American company by another and play directly into the hands of foreign investors.

There are better ways to accomplish your goal than this legislation, and I sincerely hope you will not bring the bill forward.

Alternative C:

This is to protest the movement in Congress to ban automatic toaster ovens.

Despite the hysteria in the news media over the supposed dangers of toaster ovens, our industry has worked long and hard to prove their safety in the home.

I'd be happy to supply more information on this issue.

Letter to Regulatory Body

HOLBROOK ENTERPRISES, INC.
45 NORTH THIRD AVENUE
ANNISTON, OH

February 4, 19—

Mr. Fred Bannerman
Workers Bureau
State Capitol
Columbus, OH

Dear Mr. Bannerman:

I have received your letter of January 30 and the notice that Mr. Herman has filed a complaint against us for age discrimination.

After examining the documents in the matter and interviewing our department supervisor, it appears clear that Mr. Herman was dismissed for incompetence and failure to perform duties, not for his age.

He repeatedly failed to show up for work during his assigned schedule (10 absences in 35 working days) and was regularly rated as "poor" in his work performance. After three months of this, he was dismissed according to our usual procedures for probationary employees.

The case is fully described in documents in our files, which I would be happy to share with you.

Mr. Herman's complaint is completely without basis, and we reject it totally.

Yours truly,

Joseph P. Larkin
Personnel Manager

Tips and Comment:

Dealing with governmental regulatory agencies can be a time-consuming burden, but it is an ever-growing and important function of business executives in many areas of commerce. The above example shows a firm grasp of the situation and sets a steady tone in dealing with a potentially harmful complaint. There is no empty bluster in the letter, but rather a clear rejection of the complaint buttressed by documented facts.

Alternative A:

Thank you for your letter of June 17, regarding our failure to pay withholding taxes for our "employees."

I must point out to you that we have no employees in the legal sense of the term. All those performing work for our company are independent contractors with whom we sign individual contracts on a project-by-project basis.

Thus, we have no payroll and no employees who qualify for withholding.

Alternative B:

Your inquiry about our materials handling practices was forwarded to me as plant manager.

We involve very few hazardous materials in any part of our manufacturing operation; however, a small amount of BBV compound—less than 15 milliliters—passes through our plant annually.

The minimum amount of BBV that we are required under law to report is 20 milliliters per year. Therefore, we are well within the minimum limits and not required to make a formal report.

Alternative C:

Enclosed is a copy of our permit application.

We have included a full environmental impact statement and a report from our consultants on the historical authenticity of the project.

If you have any questions, please contact me immediately.

Complaint About Unfair Government Competition

D & T TELEPHONE COMPANY, INC.
200 GRAND AVENUE
NEW YORK, NY

February 24, 19—

Ms. Jane D. Doe
Director
Federal Communications Commission
Washington, DC

Dear Ms. Doe:

D&T finds itself at an extremely unfair disadvantage in bidding on the new federal phone system, due to your recent ruling in favor of Southeastern Phones.

If you allow Southeastern to propose a system based on traditional land lines while we at D & T have based our price on fiber-optics, there will be a huge advantage to our competitor, and the federal government will be stuck with an antiquated system of dubious value.

Your ruling will, in effect, lock us out of the competition at a time when taxpayers' money needs to be spent as efficiently as possible.

I have spoken to the White House about this issue as well as Senator Cole.

I urge you to reconsider the ruling.

Sincerely,

Arthur Q. Davis
Chief Executive Officer

Tips and Comment:

Corporations may find themselves placed at serious competitive disadvantage by the actions of government agencies. This sample letter deals with big stakes, and it tackles the problem head on. Nothing is to be lost at this stage by a direct and frank statement of the company's position. The thinly veiled threat of applying political pressure is clear.

Alternative A:

We have become increasingly concerned about the way your agency is enforcing the regulations on purchasing.

Over the past six months there have been several instances in which our bids were disqualified for ostensibly failing to respond directly to the RFPs.

We believe this is a result of a faulty understanding by your eastern regional office.

Under the provisions of GR 22.8, we have the right to submit alternate proposals, if we think the specifications warrant a change.

Alternative B:

I wish to call to your attention the action of the FTC in recently ruling against all widget manufacturers in the process of passing regulations for area networking.

Whatever the intention of the Congress in passing PL 345, the result is now to eliminate all domestic widgets from the government marketplace.

The economic and social dislocations resulting from this action may well reverberate for decades to come.

Alternative C:

This is to protest vigorously the proposals before the House to subsidize widget makers.

Currently, domestic widgets account for no more than 6 percent of the widgets sold in this country. This state of affairs has come about entirely because American widget makers declined to retool over the last decade.

Meanwhile, companies such as ours moved into the widget import arena and maintained the supply of widgets to the market.

Now we will be faced with heavy burdens.

Letter to Quasi-Governmental Agency

RIVERTON CORPORATION
P.O. BOX 44
RIVERTON, OH

March 3, 19—

Mr. James Norton
Executive Director
Ohio Valley River Commission
333 West Grand Street
Cincinnati, OH

Dear Mr. Norton:

The recent resolution of the OVRC on filtration systems for coal-fired generating plants is a step forward in the struggle to revive the river. The Riverton Corporation is pleased that you have finally taken such action.

Our independent studies show that the quality of water flowing below Mile 34 has been in a prolonged process of degradation, due, we believe, to the effluvients from the five power plants up stream.

Rest assured that we will support a strong effort to urge all the states to pass enabling legislation during their forthcoming law-making sessions.

Please let me know how we can help.

Truly yours,

Ms. Karen Hatcher
President and CEO

Tips and Comment:

There are a host of interstate or regional bodies that have quasi-governmental status. While such bodies seldom have direct control over the making or enforcing laws affecting commerce, they are sometimes very influential. Letters to such quasi-governmental groups share the characteristics of communications with strictly governmental agencies.

Alternative A:

First and foremost, we want to protest the recent announcement by the Commission of a new policy toward regulation of transformer shipments. This is a short-sighted attempt by narrow-minded people to cripple an entire industry.

It has been shown over and over again that transformer transport under controlled conditions presents no danger to the adjacent communities.

We will be happy to once again share the information at our disposal on this issue.

Alternative B:

Thanks for your letter of last week about the forthcoming legislative session.

I quite agree that it will be necessary to make the Commission's position known to the members of the House and Senate, especially in light of the possible introduction of HB 20.

I will delegate three members of our legislative affairs department to work with you on this issue.

Alternative C:

I will be happy to attend the forthcoming meeting of the Commission's task force on quality control, and I will bring with me several members of my staff to provide informational backup.

Please let me know how much time I will have for the presentation.

Request for Government Bidding Information

TECHNOLOGY CONSULTANTS, INC.
P.O. BOX 4
CLEVELAND, OH

April 3, 19—

Mr. George H. Jenkins
Procurement Officer
Department of Energy
Washington, DC

Dear Mr. Jenkins:

I would like to get the bidding specifications for contract No. DOE2987, as announced in today's *Commerce Business Daily.*

My company has wide experience in analysis and planning for similar projects on the state level. And, we qualify as a minority-owned business.

Please forward the specs to my attention as soon as possible.

Sincerely,

Helen Merger
President

Tips and Comment:

Selling goods or services to governments is a potentially lucrative business, and many alert business people regularly scan such sources of information as the federal *Commerce Business Daily* for opportunities. A brief letter in response to notices should ask for the specifications by number and allude to any special qualifications.

Alternative A:

The notice of a forthcoming contract to be let in connection with rebuilding Highway 28 between Junesville and Cairo is interesting to my firm.

Please send me the full bidding documentation along with any special comments.

I will plan to submit a proposal by the deadline.

Alternative B:

I would like to receive the full specifications for the contract advertised today in the *News*.

My firm has carried out similar contracts with the Department of Environmental Control during the past five years.

We are now expanding into new areas and will appreciate an opportunity to bid.

Alternative C:

Please send me the bidding package for state contract No. 1223, as listed in the "State Projects Forthcoming" computer bulletin board.

My firm is qualified as a state bidder (permit No. 345), and has a record of full compliance in the past.

Thank you.

Seeking Program Information

WEEDON MANUFACTURING, INC.
4 WEEDON DRIVE
WEEDON, PA

July 6, 19—

The Honorable Jane F. Doe
Treasurer of the State
Capital, PA

Dear Ms. Doe:

Having read of the state's new linked-deposit program that is aimed at providing low-interest loans to state businesses which can demonstrate both need and the creation of new jobs, I am interested in learning the specifics.

This company wishes to expand our production facilities and increase our output, which would create approximately 40 new jobs in this corner of the state, but we have been unable to reach a suitable financing arrangement so far.

The linked-deposit program sounds as though it is exactly what we have been looking for.

I'll look forward to learning more.

Sincerely,

Phillip K. Weedon
Chief Executive Officer

Tips and Comment:

Government programs, especially at the state level, often hold promise for private businesses. A letter seeking more information is best directed to the highest-ranking official that can be identified. The letter is likely to be passed on to a subordinate, but in the hierarchy of government, action is gotten by beginning at the top.

Alternative A:

My company is interested in learning more details about the subsidy program announced by the Governor at his press conference yesterday.

The reports on the evening news seemed to indicate that we might be of value in organizing and administering the local aspects of the program, and we would like to discuss this with the Governor.

Please let me know specifics of the plan as soon as possible.

Alternative B:

We have been trying for several weeks to find out who is responsible for the statewide lottery ticket distribution, but so far our inquiries have not produced anything concrete.

We would greatly appreciate your help in this matter. Please let us know who to talk to in order to get the information we need.

Thanks for your help.

Alternative C:

Please send us all the information available on the current comprehensive health care system proposal put forward in the General Assembly last month.

As we understand it, the proposal would affect businesses like ours by increasing the number of units available for funding.

Thank you for your assistance.

Informational Letter to Local Government

ALLIED PRODUCTS HANDLING, INC.
34 DOVER STREET
STEELTOWN, PA

July 17, 19—

Mr. James F. Bannon
Director
Environmental Emergency Response Agency
Steel County
Steeltown, PA

Dear Mr. Bannon:

On Tuesday, July 23, we will load and transport one truckload of potentially hazardous substances from our plant on Dover Street to the receiving yard at Tangier, PA.

This is a formal notice to you of the event, in compliance with the local and state ordinances on transport of hazardous waste.

The wastes will be comprised of liquid heavy metals contained in 55-gallon drums which will be sealed on site. There will be approximately 100 of these drums.

Our permit is number 1122.

Please let me know if you require further information.

Truly yours,

Alan M. Moyers
Materials Manager

Tips and Comment:

Local or state laws may require companies to provide specific information to government authorities, such as for the transport of hazardous wastes in this sample letter. Such messages should be businesslike and conform to the requirements of the law. If the information is routine and must be provided over and over again, a standard form letter may be devised and altered suitably for each occasion.

Alternative A:

This is to inform you that the Allied Company will begin on January 5 to discharge treated effluvients into the river from our main plant.

The discharge will comply with state law PL 12, and we have secured the necessary permits from the state environmental agency.

I would be happy to discuss the procedure with you.

Alternative B:

The Landers Company, Inc. has decided to demolish the old plant building at the corner of Fourth Street and Jefferson. It has been out of use for more than five years and is beginning to present a hazard to the community.

We have secured the necessary permit from the housing authority, but we want to inform your department of the impending action.

Alternative C:

After receiving a permit from the state department of industrial development, we will commence construction of a new smoke stack at our main plant in July.

The construction phase will last approximately three months and entail closing off Grant Street to through traffic for at least half of that period.

We anticipate no other complications during the project.

Special Request to Local Government

THE GRAND HOUSE
MAIN STREET
HARRODSBURG, IL

November 24, 19—

Ms. Jane Frommer
Property Administrator
Harrod County Court House
Harrodsburg, IL

Dear Ms. Frommer

The Grand Holding Corporation, Inc. recently received notice of the reassessment of The Grand House Hotel property on Main Street.

We feel that the evaluation of the property at $4 million is too high, and we wish to appeal the assessment.

The property changed hands in 19—for a sales price of $3.5 million. Since then, the local economy has been in a slump.

We feel that any assessment over and above the $3.5 million sale figure is unfair and based on unwarranted assumptions about a projected increase in value.

Attached are documents in support of our appeal.

Yours truly,

David C. Noyes
President and Chief Executive Officer

Tips and Comment:

Since corporations are the economic lifeblood of most local communities—large or small—special requests may be expected to get full attention. Be specific and direct when making requests, using a confident tone backed by facts and figures, where appropriate. Since such letters may ultimately find their way into the hands of the news media, exercise care in the exact wording, especially if the issue may in any way become controversial.

Alternative A:

Enclosed is a formal application for a zoning change from A-1 to R-3 for the property on Fourth Street.

We plan to convert the building on the site to high-density apartments within the next year, and we understand that this conforms to the overall urban master plan adopted by the Council in 19—.

Please let us know when a hearing on this issue can be held.

Alternative B:

The Allied Co. plans to convert the building at Tenth and Grovers Streets to a storage facility.

In order to do so, we would like to have the alley behind the building declared a private drive. This will make it possible for us to improve access to the rear docks of the building.

Please let me know what steps we can take to apply officially for this change.

Alternative C:

As I understand the provisions of the ordinance passed at the last Council meeting, we now need to apply for a new permit to operate our office in the downtown section of town.

Since we plan to close that office within the next six months, I would like to request an extension of the current permit until the office is terminated.

This will save us the considerable expense and paperwork connected with applying for a new permit.

Please let me know.

Proposal to Local Government

THE DESIGN GROUP
P.O. BOX 34
GROVE CITY, FL

September 5, 19—

Mr. Thomas Gomez
Director
Economic Development Commission
City Hall
Grove City, FL

Dear Tom:

In thinking about the recent discussions on attracting new business to Grove City, we have come up with ideas for a simple but, we believe, effective campaign.

If we were to organize carefully and select exactly the right media and markets along the eastern seaboard, we could expect to get results.

Instead of the usual newspaper campaigns, we think placing simple ads in city magazines would be more effective.

I would be happy to volunteer time and materials to this project if the city is interested.

Please call me for a date to discuss this.

Sincerely,

Wayne Yount
President

Tips and Comment:

Local governments and community-based businesses often act in concert, especially in areas such as local economic development. In putting forth a proposal to local government, it is important to make clear the costs and the scope of the proposal. Volunteering help will usually get a positive response.

Alternative A:

It has occurred to me that the small area between the Winters Building and the corner of Main and Heaton Streets would make a suitable mini-park.

I would be happy to work up a site plan for the park and estimate the cost of plantings and furnishings, if you think the city would entertain the idea.

This seems to me to be the sort of project that we need to keep the flow of pedestrian traffic through the area.

Alternative B:

What do you think the Council would like to do in regard to the forthcoming meeting of the USAG?

This should be a good opportunity to make our city's story known more widely, and I would be willing to donate services and materials for a presentation during the meeting.

Please call me for an appointment to discuss this.

Alternative C:

I have a proposal on my desk from Tom Tinker that relates to the forthcoming Art Campaign.

Tom thinks our firm could play a key role in the campaign and support the efforts of the County Arts Council in ways that would increase the overall result.

Our services would, of course, be donated to the county.

Inquiry About Privatization

HANSON SERVICES, INC.
34 RETREAD AVENUE
AFTON, MO

November 17, 19—

The Honorable Wilma G. Evans
Mayor
Centerville, MO

Dear Mayor:

The Hanson Company has recently expanded its operations in this area, and we now have full capacity to service local governments through the private collection of residential refuse.

We currently work under contract with five other cities in Central Missouri to collect, haul, and dispose of all residential refuse.

Since the City of Centerville now operates its own collection service but is facing an overall financial squeeze (at least according to the reports in the *Telegraph*), it might be worth the city's time to consider privatization.

I believe we can offer expanded services at approximately 80 percent of your current costs.

We would be happy to discuss this with you or the Council and prepare a formal proposal for your consideration.

Sincerely,

John Hanson
President

Tips and Comment:

Privatization of formerly public services has been a powerful recent trend, especially at the local level, where governments have come to realize private business may be able to provide services more efficiently and economically. A proposal or inquiry about taking over a local service should be persuasive but nonthreatening, with an emphasis on the positive financial possibilities. Avoid invidious comparisons, but make your point.

Alternative A:

The city's operation of the welfare support program has proven successful in the past. However, the increased burden of paperwork now threatens the efficiency of the service.

I believe that my company could offer a computerized system of private administration that would not only streamline the city's current work, but prepare for the future.

We have such a system in place in several cities in the Midwest, and I'd be delighted to discuss our success with you.

Alternative B:

After attending the most recent meeting of the County Board of Corrections, I was struck by the need for a change in methods if the county is to meet the challenges of the next five years.

One area in which my company might be of help is the provision of food service for the three county jails. The current system of county-run meals service is nearing the point of overload. My firm has at its disposal all the means needed to not only meet the current need, but to handle expansion.

In addition, I believe we could cut overall costs.

Alternative C:

I wish to propose that the city consider changing over to a private firm to maintain all official vehicles, including the street-clearing equipment.

Such a move would not only save money, but would likely result in a higher percentage of work-ready vehicles on a day-to-day basis.

My company has all the needed personnel and equipment to maintain the city's fleet, and I would be delighted to discuss a proposal in more detail.

Offer of Assistance to Local Government

JENNINGS SOFTWARE, INC.
223 DANFORTH AVENUE
TRENT'S PASS, TN

October 4, 19—

The Honorable James R. Vining
Mayor of Trent's Pass
P.O. 2
Trent's Pass, TN

Dear Mayor Vining:

I have recently become aware that the city is planning to convert the old Leestown High School building into a senior citizen's center, complete with recreational facilities.

If you plan to include—as many senior centers in the nation now do—a computer setup, my company would be happy to provide some of our software packages free of charge.

We have available not only the usual word-processing and data-processing materials, but also several recreational packages that would provide a variety of interesting opportunities for visitors to the center.

If you are interested in discussing this offer, please call me at my office.

Sincerely,

Herb Jennings
President

Tips and Comment:

Businesses may wish to forge a connection with local government, both as a genuine expression of concern for the community and as a potentially valuable business opportunity. One way to get the attention of local government officials is to offer a donation of products or services, as does this letter, with the ultimate goal of making your company known to those in local power.

Alternative A:

As I understand it, the city is attempting to evaluate the future potential of the area in downtown between Main and Fourth Streets.

I would like to suggest that the Council consider the services of my company in this effort. We have wide experience in conducting case studies of urban areas, and we would be happy to donate this study as part of living up to our social responsibilities.

The study could begin as soon as you give approval.

Alternative B:

We would like to donate enough landfill to make the area in Westover near I-35 into a smooth, level arena, ready for development.

The lack of action on this problem has created a serious roadblock in opening the Westover section to development, and it would be in the best interests of the business community and the citizens to get this project moving.

Please let me know if you are interested and if any legal obstacles are in the way.

Alternative C:

As a new corporate resident of the community, we would like to volunteer to staff the forthcoming Fund for the Arts drive.

We can provide three executives for the duration of the drive, to work full-time on fundraising.

Please call me at my office to discuss the details.

12

IN THE NEWS:
LETTERS TO THE MEDIA

Like it or not, business today is under the close scrutiny of the print and electronic news media. The goal of the successful executive is to understand the power of the media and use it to best advantage, and a powerful tool in this quest is a good letter. As the following examples demonstrate, there are a variety of situations in which letters are the proper forms of communication with the news media. In many cases, the object will be to get the media to cooperate; in other situations, a business must get its case across directly to the news-consuming public. Whatever the circumstances, letters from business executives must be both persuasive and make clear the merits of the executive's position. The following model letters show how to go about eliciting a positive media response.

Announcing a Press Conference

JKL ENTERPRISES, INC.
34 WENTWORTH ROAD
HATTON, WV

August 8, 19—

Press Conference Announced

JKL Enterprises, Inc. will hold a press conference at 1:00 P.M. on Tuesday, August 12, in the cafeteria at the JKL building at 34 Wentworth Road.

Harry Jenkins, President of JKL, will make an announcement about the construction of a new plant in Hatton, which will employ 200 people in the manufacture of clothing.

Mr. Jenkins will also be available for interviews after the formal conference.

An informal lunch for the working news media will be served at 11:45 A.M.

Ned Bourroughs
Director of Public Relations

Tips and Comment:

A brief letter or memo to all news media is sufficient to alert them to a press conference. Include all the basic facts of time, location, subject, and who will make the presentation. Providing free food helps to insure coverage. Such messages can be standardized and gotten out quickly, much like a news release.

Alternative A:

What: Press Conference
Where: JKL Building, 34 Wentworth Road
When: 1:00 P.M., Tuesday, August 12
Who: Harry Jenkins, President of JKL
Subject: New plant in Hatton
Lunch will be served to the news media at 11:45 A.M.

Alternative B:

We will hold a press conference on the steps of Old Capitol at 2:00 P.M., Wednesday, October 5.

Chairman of the Board Tom Klein will announce plans for a new capital campaign to raise $2 million over the coming two years.

A news release and interviews will be available.

Alternative C:

All news media are invited to attend a press conference at 1:30 P.M. on Monday, April 13, at the Center for Commerce on Main Street.

The Center's Executive Director, Eve Blandings, will discuss plans for expanding the Center.

Please let us know if you need special setups.

Soliciting Media Coverage

YOU'RE ON
Access to Television and Radio
19 MADISON AVENUE
BEVERLY, MA 01915

April 4, 19—

Mr. Joseph Doe
Executive Producer
Evening Magazine
WWT-TV
1170 Sailors Road
Boston, MA

Dear Mr. Doe:

Just two miles from your office is a small company with a big idea. It's an idea that affects everyone who drives a car or truck, especially since the price of gas has gone up.

The XYZ Corporation is successfully adapting an oil company fuel-saving technology to automobile engines. It's been so successful that the company's president has been interviewed on more than 80 radio and TV programs from coast to coast.

Four years ago, XYZ researchers found that in the presence of very small amounts of a special ingredient, fuel would burn more completely. Major oil refiners have been using a similar method to save millions of dollars when breaking down large quantities of crude oil into gasoline, diesel fuel, jet fuel, etc.

XYZ has found a way to get the ingredient inside the engine where it can do the most good. When you can burn a higher percentage of each gallon of fuel in your tank, fewer gallons are required.

Page 2

A few months ago, the company released results of tests conducted on twenty-six vehicles owned and operated by the Anonymous Corporation. Overall, these vehicles increased their mileage by 20 percent. Test results and background information are enclosed.

This can be a very visual story. Your camera can see how this process works under the hood of any car. If you speak with James Doe, president of XYZ, you'll discover that this is a subject that would make an interesting feature on Evening Magazine.

I'll call you next Tuesday to see what you think. If you want to move on this sooner, I can be reached at 555-6768.

Thank you for your consideration.

Sincerely,

Richard M. Goldberg
President
(Courtesy of Richard M. Goldberg, You're On, Beverly, MA)

Tips and Comment:

The author of this actual business letter attempts to interest a television station in covering his client's story by an adroit mix of enthusiasm and fact. The enthusiasm is necessary to get the station's attention, and the facts are intended to convince the show's producer of the newsworthiness of the story. The first sentence points out the ease of access to the story and the potential wide viewer interest. Such letters address a tough audience—television stations and newspapers receive dozens of such appeals each day—but this example has proven effective.

Alternative A:

On May 10, a celebrity will be in town to boost the annual Environmental Day, and you can have an exclusive interview for the *Times*.

Jane Doe, star of TV's "Last Laugh," will make a private appearance at a reception in the home of Mrs. Janet Doe.

We can arrange for an invitation for one of your reporters and for an interview after the meeting.

This will be a great chance to meet a star and get a good story for the mid-week Features Today section.

Alternative B:

XYZ Corporation will hold a special media interview session at 10:00 A.M. on Tuesday, May 10, at the Civic Center to discuss a major development for downtown.

Enclosed is a press packet with more details.

I will be happy to set up a special interview with our president, so please call me.

Complimenting Coverage

TRAVEL, INC.
TITUS PLAZA
TITUSVILLE, NJ

August 2, 19—

Mr. Harold G. Ender
Managing Editor
Daily News
Titusville, NJ

Dear Mr. Ender:

I want to congratulate you on the excellent job of covering the 19—Trade Fair and Exposition last week.

Your stories in the Sunday edition were complete and accurate, and they gave area readers a fine run-down on what the Exposition has to offer.

Thanks for the professional skill shown by your reporters and editors.

Yours truly,

F. Murray Jacobs
President

Tips and Comment:

When local news media do a good job of reporting on an event important to business, a note of appreciation will go far toward fostering more good coverage in the future. Even though reporters and editors cultivate an image of detachment (which may lapse into professional cynicism), they still like to know when they are admired for their work. Keep such notes simple and avoid overstatement.

Alternative A:

Thank you for the excellent series of stories on local education. Your reporters found just the right examples and used them well to tell the story behind our schools.

We in the business community depend on the local educational system for our workers and therefore have a vital interest in maintaining strong schools.

Series such as yours help foster community support for schools.

Alternative B:

You have my compliments for your strong coverage of the recent mess in city hall.

No one likes to discover that public trust has been misused, but it is best for all of us in the community to understand what is happening in local government—especially when things go wrong.

Keep up the good work.

Alternative C:

Your recent review of the local housing and office building markets in the weekly Business News section was first-rate.

This sort of clear-cut reporting and analysis helps everyone in the business community understand the challenges and opportunities facing us.

Please feel free to call on me at any time for information.

Letter on Behalf of Association

XYZ CORPORATION
P.O. BOX 12
ATTENBURY, VT

April 2, 19—

Ms. Janet Reinhold
Community Affairs Editor
Upper River Gazette
Attenbury, VT

Dear Ms. Reinhold:

A group of manufacturers in the Upper Valley area has recently formed the Upper Valley Manufacturers Association as a nonprofit, public interest association in order to help the community better understand the role and operations of our members.

Over the coming months we will sponsor a series of informational meetings in most of the Upper Valley communities, and we will launch a public information program.

As part of our activities we will be in touch with you.

Please read our materials and plan to cover our meetings.

Thanks for your help.

Truly yours,

Kenneth Francis

Tips and Comment:

Businesses can band together into local associations or join regional or national associations in order to make their voices heard. One major way of gaining public attention is to work with and through the news media. The sample letter on page 299 is an early shot in the war for favorable publicity.

Alternative A:

I want to suggest that the local branch of the National Association of Retailers would make a good story for your ongoing series on community resources.

The NAR has been working both nationally and locally for the last two decades and has developed interesting programs.

I'd be happy to fill you in.

Alternative B:

Women in Business is a group you should know about.

We formed a local chapter six months ago and since have been active in recruiting women business workers into our association.

We think this is a unique and newsworthy organization and would be pleased to talk with you.

Alternative C:

The Association of Retired Teachers is about to launch its third annual membership drive in the local community.

We would appreciate your help in publicizing our group and its goals and activities.

I'll call you soon to discuss this in more detail.

Media Coverage for Public Event

CHAMBER OF COMMERCE
23 MAIN STREET
WATERSBURG, UT

May 23, 19—

To: News Media

This is to let you know that the Chamber of Commerce will sponsor a Memorial Day Parade this year to take place at 10:00 A.M.

The parade route will begin at Fourth and Water Streets and move down Main Street for six blocks.

We have bands, floats, Shriners, and lots of private entries (including a kiddie's division), which should provide colorful sights and sounds as part of the holiday observance.

Please plan to cover this event. If you want more information, call my office at 555-1212.

Thanks for your help.

Truly yours,

Jim Needles
Executive Director

Tips and Comment:

Attracting media coverage for public events is mostly a matter of alerting the local newspapers and radio and television stations. The significance of the event itself will make it attractive to the media. Since there is little need to promote the event as newsworthy, a low-key announcement should suffice. Taking on the duty of alerting the media to such a news event helps a private firm to establish long-term credibility.

Alternative A:

On Sunday, April 12, Golder's Department Store will once again stage the annual Downtown Easter Egg Hunt.

The event will begin at 1:00 P.M. in Main Street Park, across from our store.

We hope you will be able to cover the festivities.

Alternative B:

As part of our community service commitment, we are sponsoring a series of public lectures during 19—.

The next lecture will be by bestselling author Janice Blatt, who will speak on "Family Planning versus Abortion" at 8:00 P.M. in Auditorium B of the Public Library Main Building on Third Avenue.

Ms. Blatt is one of the nation's leading authorities on the abortion and family planning issues and has appeared frequently on television talk shows and news features.

We hope you can cover the event.

Alternative C:

Please plan to cover the forthcoming Charity Auction and Ball to be held at the Reed House Hotel at 8:30 P.M. on Tuesday, February 6.

The event, sponsored by several local businesses, will raise money for the Save the Children Fund.

Please call my office for more information.

Letter to the Editor: Commenting on an Editorial

CALIFORNIA TEACHERS ASSOCIATION
1705 MURCHISON DRIVE
BURLINGAME, CA

Dear Editor:

In a recent commentary, "Disciplining Teachers," your associate editor observed that criticizing schools and complaining about teachers seems to be "increasingly fashionable." He is uncomfortably correct, but it's a myth that our schools are failing.

Today we have more boys and girls finishing high school than ever—over 75 percent of our youth. About half go to college. More blacks and Hispanics, as well as students with physical limitations, are finishing school.

In California our assessment program shows excellent gains, except for the 12th grade. Recently, the National Assessment of Education Progress reported gains in all grades except the latter part of high school. Young blacks were reported substantially better than a decade ago. The problem at the high school level is not with the basics but in the ability of students to reason and think critically, according to the report.

Your associate editor noted in his column "deep frustrations" about public schools are resulting in attempts to discipline teachers. The targets are gains won by teachers over the years, such as due-process evaluation and dismissal, improved salaries and working conditions, and being involved in decisions affecting the classroom through collective bargaining.

This is frightening because it's an emotional response to deep frustrations. Such emotional responses generally result in half-baked solutions or in punishing scapegoats, such as teachers, and usually are off-target.

Yes, the schools have problems. We have too many kids who need special help so they can grapple with space-age academic demands. But our No. 1 problem is not in the classroom. It's this "fashionable" negative criticism of schools and teachers based on myth, not fact. The schools need public support and positive, not punitive, approaches to their problems.

Sincerely,

Ed Foglia
President
(Courtesy of Ed Foglia, California Teachers Association, Burlingame, CA)

Tips and Comment:

Newspapers state their opinions most directly in editorial page articles. Often, it is desirable or even necessary for a businessperson to comment or amplify on an editorial by means of a letter to the editor. Such letters are, of course, intended for publication, so they should be well-written, well-reasoned, and to the point. A comment on an editorial opens a wide door. The paper has broached the subject, and it is the letter-writer's turn to have a say, positive or negative as opinion demands.

Alternative A:

I read your editorial of October 29 with increasing dismay and alarm. To be blunt, you have cast the entire situation in just precisely the reverse of the truth.

Amalgamated Industries did not dump hazardous wastes in northern Fletcher County last year or in any other year.

Amalgamated Industries has always disposed of the small amount of hazardous wastes generated by our plant according to all the state and USEPA regulations.

The private industrial landfill we established in northern Fletcher County has received only nonhazardous wastes, a point we have been trying to make to the general public for the last six months.

Editorial alarmism such as you displayed is a disservice to both Amalgamated Industries and to the reading public.

Alternative B:

How right you are! Your lead editorial of last Sunday on the need to support elementary education in our community was squarely on target.

As a member of the business community, I totally support the efforts of the Citizens' Committee to upgrade the special programs in elementary schools and urge every segment of the city to join the campaign.

Nothing is more important to the future well-being of the city than strong schools.

Alternative C:

The scurrilous cartoon on your editorial page last Wednesday was a disgrace to what has up until now been a fine family newspaper.

There is no place in our daily press for opinions such as expressed in this cartoon.

I hope you fire the artist and refrain in the future from hiring people like her.

Letter to the Editor: Making an Additional Point

CALIFORNIA STATE AUTOMOBILE ASSOCIATION
150 VAN NESS AVENUE
SAN FRANCISCO, CA

Dear Editor:

I read with interest your editorial in yesterday's paper on "The Tax on Gasoline".

The California State Automobile Association suggests another approach which does not involve increasing taxes and fees. That approach is to use the windfall revenues accruing to the general fund from the sales tax on gasoline. This tax should not be confused with the 7 cents per gallon state tax on gasoline.

When the sales tax was imposed on gasoline, it was for the specific purpose of raising revenue for transportation purposes. Since then, the cost of gasoline has increased dramatically, as has revenue from the sales tax.

The net result is some $460 million per year more is being collected from this source than is being allocated for transportation purposes.

If this windfall was used for transportation, no deficit would develop and there would be no need to increase taxes on motorists.

Sincerely,

R. V. Patton
President
(Courtesy of R. V. Patton, California State Automobile Association, San Francisco, CA)

Tips and Comment:

An alert businessperson will watch the paper and take advantage of an editorial to state an opinion in the form of an additional comment on the original editorial. In such a situation, a letter to the editor makes an inexpensive and effective way to reach the reading public.

Alternative A:

Your editorial in the Sunday edition made a good point about the desirability of developing Zuckerman's Point as a public area. What is often overlooked, however, is the additional need to extend the protection of city fire and police departments to that corner of the country.

Currently, neither the police nor firefighters are allowed to answer calls in that area, which creates a dangerous situation for anyone living there or using the area for recreation.

The city should consider at least some form of extended protection, especially if this beautiful part of our county is likely to become more used by the general public.

Alternative B:

Your editorial writer made an excellent point in Tuesday's editorial about general revenue bonds.

All too often the public is led to believe that private enterprise takes advantage of the power of government to raise tax money.

This is almost never the case—in fact, government usually comes begging to the door of private businesses.

Each case should be examined on its own merits, with the clear understanding that private developers and builders are citizens too with a big stake in the community.

Alternative C:

In discussing the cost to citizen taxpayers of closing the downtown bus terminal (the *Herald-Express* for September 5), you state well the case for retaining the central facility.

However, there is also the question of what to do with the satellite terminal in Crossroads Center. This is a little-used facility that was built four years ago to serve the south side.

Does it make sense to close the central terminal and still pour tax money into a facility that is used by only 13 percent of the riders in the system?

A recent study by a public interest group showed that a restructuring of city transportation priorities should take into account the value of selling off the Crossroads terminal and updating transfer facilities downtown.

I hope the Board of Transportation doesn't ignore this recommendation.

Letter to Editor: Supporting Candidate or Legislation

GOODWIN ENTERPRISES, INC.
GOODWIN DRIVE
WEST QUINCY, NM

October 15, 19—

Editor
Sun Valley Times
P.O. Box 34
West Quincy, NM

Dear Sir:

I want to urge voters in the upcoming general election to cast their ballots for Jim Kerns for Mayor.

Jim has served the West Quincy community for the last ten years as a Council member and on a variety of important volunteer commissions and boards.

He is a person of proven ability and will be able to give the office of Mayor the sort of attention it deserves.

Jim's record as a successful merchant in the community demonstrates his good grasp of management and his feel for the public.

He will make a great Mayor.

Yours truly,

Lorraine Goodwin
Executive Vice-President

Tips and Comment:

The Letters to the Editor column provides an effective forum for supporting candidates or legislation. In fact, the letters are really directed toward the general voting public and should be written with this in mind. State the case for the candidate or legislation concisely (space is usually restricted) and be certain to include a firm personal endorsement.

Alternative A:

I urge all members of the Council to support the proposal to make part of the downtown area an enterprise zone in order to attract new businesses to the area.

The enterprise zone idea has been proven in many cities across the nation to be an effective tool for revitalizing the economy.

In the long run, enterprise zones create more tax revenue and bring people into the city as well as providing much-needed jobs.

Alternative B:

I hope voters will call or write to their state representatives and ask them to vote for HB 23 which will establish a State Department of Economic Development.

Our state has lagged far behind others in the region because we have failed to provide for economic development.

Please let our legislators know how important this issue is.

Alternative C:

Please give your support to Jane Hawes for State Senator.

Jane is the sort of person we need looking out for our interests in the state capital.

She understands our community and will make a fine legislator.

Asking Rebuttal to TV Commentary

SPRITZER'S STORES, INC.
67 TROWBRIDGE LANE
REEDVILLE, TN

December 3, 19—

Mr. Frederick K. Lyons
Station Manager
WWWK-TV
Reedville, TN

Dear Mr. Lyons:

I want to take up your standing offer of air time to rebut the "Commentary" you presented at the end of last night's 6:00 P.M. news broadcast.

You alleged that area retail stores have hiked prices during the holiday shopping season, and that we are all out to gouge the consumer.

This is total nonsense.

I can document the fact that we do not raise our prices during any season, and certainly not during the Thanksgiving to Christmas period when we do close to 50 percent of our business for the year.

Please let me know when I can come to the studio to tape the rebuttal commentary.

Sincerely,

Carl Spritzer
President

Tips and Comment:

Local television stations routinely run on-air editorial commentary and just as routinely offer time for rebuttal or opposing opinions. This letter asks the station manager for time to refute such an editorial, making it clear what position the rebuttal will take.

Alternative A:

I totally disagree with your statement on Tuesday's "My Opinion" spot about raising parking fees in the downtown area.

If the city moves to increase the fees it will only further discourage shoppers from the downtown stores that have traditionally formed the commercial heart of our city.

I would like to present an opposing view on the air. Please let me know how this can be arranged.

Alternative B:

Your featured editorial last night during the late news complained of the effect of our plant on the community's health.

This is an unfair and one-sided expression of opinion that I want to correct.

Please schedule a three-minute spot for me before the end of the week.

Alternative C:

The so-called "feature" story on last night's news was completely in error about the activities of the local Chamber of Commerce.

I want to present a counter viewpoint on the air as soon as possible.

In no way does the Chamber represent only the merchants, and I can make this case with facts and figures.

Correcting a News Media Error

REEDS COMPANY
EVANSTOWN, TX

July 7, 19—

Mr. Kent Durden
Executive News Editor
WXYZ-TV
Evanstown, TX

Dear Mr. Durden:

We at Reeds Company are highly disturbed about part of your news broadcast last night in which you stated that the "Executive Vice-President of Reeds Company, Evanstown, James Derek, has been indicted for tax evasion."

Mr. Derek does NOT work for Reeds Company of Evanstown. He works for Reeds Corporation of Chicago. There is NO connection whatsoever between these two firms.

We ask that you correct this misidentification as soon as possible on your regular evening news show.

Yours truly,

William K. Reeds
Executive Vice-President

Tips and Comment:

For whatever reasons, the daily news media is subject to a relatively high volume of error, especially in matters such as misidentifications. If such an error causes a problem for a business, a quick letter should be sent (perhaps by messenger) clearing up the misinformation and asking politely for a public correction or retraction. Most media executives are happy to correct mistakes.

Alternative A:

I must call your attention to the misidentification of the photograph on page 1 of yesterday's business section. The picture is of our new sales manager, Marilyn Henderson, but the caption says it is a photo of Geraldine O'Brien.

We would appreciate it if you could correct the error in the first edition possible.

Thank you.

Alternative B:

In the edition of your magazine for February 20, you say in the article beginning on page 32 that the corporate tax rate on inactive property in the state is 33 percent.

This is no longer true. The passage of the omnibus tax and lottery bill changed the rate on inactive property to 28 percent, with a trade-off for increased use tax on raw materials imported from out of state.

I'd like to see this error cleared up in your next edition, since it may seriously mislead your readers.

Alternative C:

I was very unhappy to see my name mentioned in an article in yesterday's paper in connection with Mr. Gabbard. While I was associated with him in several companies during the last decade, I have not had any connection with Gabbard since January of last year.

This is a matter of some concern, since Gabbard is now engaged in a competing business.

Would you please correct this error?

13

THE INTERNATIONAL MARKETPLACE: LETTERS FOR DOING BUSINESS ABROAD

A large number of executives at the top of American businesses are involved, sooner or later, with the international marketplace and find themselves dealing with foreign business counterparts. Letters in these situations are crucial, since misunderstanding may result in disaster. It will be a definite advantage (and a time saver) to know how to cope with such letters, as demonstrated in the following chapter. The examples range from manufacturing abroad to the financial intricacies of international commerce to understanding cultural differences. All of these factors come into play when writing international letters.

Manufacturing Abroad

PLATINUM RECORDINGS, INC.
33 WEST DRIVE
DETROIT, MI

February 23, 19—

Mr. F. Nakatashi
Nippon-American Company
23 River Street
San Francisco, CA

Dear Mr. Nakatashi:

Platinum Recordings, Inc. has long been a leader in the American sound recording industry, specializing in the production and distribution of vinyl disk records.

We are interested now in moving into the developing market for compact disk recordings. Our research shows that the CD market will likely expand two-fold over the coming two years, and we have a ready-made backlist of potential albums.

Therefore, we are seeking a manufacturer who has the plant capacity to make compact disks from our masters.

We anticipate placing orders for at least 3 million disks within the next six months.

Please let me know if the relationship sounds attractive.

Truly yours,

Kenneth Gladdings
President

Tips and Comment:

A letter feeling out a foreign manufacturer should describe the basic products desired and the volume of anticipated business. While such a letter is merely a preliminary, the tone is important, especially when dealing with a foreign executive. Circumspection is perhaps the best attitude to take at this early stage, leaving precise details for later.

Alternative A:

We are interested in the possibility of a joint venture with Lanterns, Ltd. to produce a new line of lampshades for the domestic American market.

Our current manufacturing capacity is stretched to the limit, yet we believe a new market is about to open in the home decorating field.

The details would take further discussion, but we would appreciate an expression of interest on your part at this stage.

Alternative B:

We have recently learned that Osterreich Gesellshaft has a widget plant in Augenblick that may be able to produce the TDF 109 widget in large numbers.

Our current projections show that we might be able to distribute and sell TDF 109s in this country, if we could be assured of a steady supply.

Please communicate directly with me on this matter.

Alternative C:

As you know, we specialize in the sale of turned wooden widgets to the American trade market.

Within the past year, we have reached full capacity from our current suppliers and are therefore seeking new sources of high-quality turned wooden widgets.

If you are interested in discussing this further, specifically the process of producing and exporting wooden widgets from your facilities in Ontario, please contact me as soon as possible.

New International Markets

NEW WORLD COAL COMPANY
BLACK GOLD ROAD
BECKLEY, WV

August 23, 19—

Mr. Nigel Tompkins
National Power
13 Grosevenor Circle
London AH5 3WS
United Kingdom

Dear Mr. Tompkins:

I wish to draw to your attention the possibility of purchasing imported low-sulphur coal from the United States, especially from the West Virginia fields, where the New World Coal Company has extensive holdings and mining operations.

We can supply at least one-third of your total import requirement, or approximately 1 million tons during 19—.

Moreover, New World Coal Company's leads producers in the United States in mining high-quality, low-sulphur coal.

Our mines are only a day's rail transportation from the Virginia ports, so moving the coal is a simple matter.

I would be happy to discuss price and conditions at your convenience.

Truly yours,

Patrick J. Boone
President

Tips and Comment:

Probing for new business among international markets calls for good research and aggressive sales. In this example, the letter writer is moving quickly to exploit a change in the British power generating industry to private ownership and understands the British interest in his special brand of low-polluting coal. The writer's tone is relatively low key, in keeping with the British approach to business, but he suggests several key advantages of his company.

Alternative A:

With the recent reductions in your government's subsidies for widget production, it may be to your advantage to consider importing widgets from the United States.

Our plant at Secaucus, New Jersey, has produced high-quality widgets since 1966 and is located near shipping facilities.

We believe we can deliver widgets at a price at least slightly below your projected domestic price.

I'd be happy to begin a discussion of details.

Alternative B:

I am pleased to respond to your inquiry of June 15.

Our company could supply three-pronged widgets with integrated circuitry for $4.25 per hundred, delivered to Lisbon.

Shipping times would not exceed three weeks.

Alternative C:

Since it appears likely that your central government will create a new economic structure within the next three months, I want to take the opportunity to suggest the possibility of providing high-tech widgets.

Under the impending trade agreements, the widgets could enter your country at reduced duties, making them very competitive in your domestic market.

Please look at the enclosed figures and reply at your convenience.

Cross-Border Manufacturing

GRANDSTAND INDUSTRIES, INC.
333 DEPFORD STREET
SAN DIEGO, CA

January 5, 19—

Ms. Helen Jones
Widgets International, Inc.
444 Johnston Avenue
Salt Lake City, UT

Dear Ms. Jones:

I am happy to fill you in on our so-called "maquiladoras" operation here in San Diego.

Along with several other manufacturers, Grandstand has established a large industrial processing facility within a half mile of the Mexican-American border.

Products assembled at our Mexican plant, which is located near Tijuana, are trucked to the facility duty-free under Provision 807 of the U.S. Tariff Schedule. We then pack and ship the products to our network of U.S. distributors from San Diego.

We can therefore take advantage of the very low wage rates in Mexico, but still maintain our status as an American manufacturer, including the right to put the "Made in America" label on our products.

Let me know if you would like more details.

Sincerely,

Lewis Lancaster
Vice-President

Tips and Comment:

Many American manufacturers have devised methods to take advantage of the disparity among international production costs by making products abroad but packaging them domestically. Plants located near an international border, in this case the Mexican-American border, are allowed under the law to import finished or nearly finished products with no import duty. The sample letter explains the situation.

Alternative A:

There are now more than thirty American companies taking advantage of the industrial facilities provided by the city near the Mexican border.

Under American law, these companies are allowed to import finished goods from plants they own in Mexico without paying import duties.

The lowering of costs is, of course, significant, since labor is relatively inexpensive and since the city subsidizes the facilities.

Alternative B:

We are happy to welcome your inquiry about the opportunities in our new "maquiladoras" facilities near the Mexican-American border.

The advantages are obvious: lower production costs in Mexico and no import duties.

In addition, we are prepared to offer you greatly reduced rent on as many square feet of space as you require.

Alternative C:

I think we should look further into the possibilities of establishing a processing plant near the border.

As I understand it, we would be allowed to set up a sister plant in Mexico and then import the finished product duty-free. And, so long as we package and ship from the U.S. side, we can still claim to be "made in America."

Payment for Goods or Services

MT. LIGHTER BIBLIOGRAPHIC SERVICES, INC.
45 TWEETER BOULEVARD
MT. LIGHTER, PA

October 4, 19—

Mr. Trevor Chatwick
International Group, Ltd.
4 Catteshall Lane
Guildford
Surrey GU4 2XW
United Kingdom

Dear Mr. Chatwick:

We will be happy to supply your company with the services you requested. The complete report should be sent to you by international express no later than October 23, 19—.

We will submit an invoice with the report, and we request that payment be made in U.S. dollars by check or bank draft on a U.S. bank.

I trust this will present no difficulties. When dealing with British firms in the past, we have on occasion accepted payment in sterling, but this caused considerable delay and loss in collection since we have only limited international banking available to us.

Thank you.

Truly yours,

James P. Looper
Vice-President

Tips and Comment:

Although it is not always possible or even advantageous, many U.S. firms prefer to be paid in dollars when billing a foreign company for goods or services. It is a wise precaution to arrange this ahead of time by letter. One of the disadvantages of dealing abroad is the slowness of mail. International express service can alleviate some of the problem, but it is expensive and is still slow compared to domestic mail.

Alternative A:

This is to confirm your order of October 1, and to request that payment be made on our invoice in U.S. dollars rather than in British currency.

We will assemble the order and forward it by air freight as soon as we have confirmation of payment from you.

The shipment will include a *pro forma* invoice for customs.

I'll look forward to hearing from you.

Alternative B:

We are once again pleased to do business with you and express our appreciation for the order we discussed on the phone yesterday.

As in the past, we will bill you in dollars and expect payment in the same currency through a check on your New York bank.

If you anticipate any change from the earlier procedures, please let me know immediately.

Alternative C:

In order to take advantage of the falling exchange rates, we would prefer that you make payment in U.S. dollars rather than sterling. It is impossible to say how long the current trends will continue, but there is a clear advantage to both companies in the present situation.

Please forward a check for the amount of the invoice as soon as possible and I will issue a receipt.

Thank you.

Currency Exchange Rates

TOLLIVER ASSOCIATES
19 REALTO STREET
GLENDOVER, WI

May 17, 19—

Mr. James T. Pearshall
Nevers-Pearshall, Ltd.
29 Tattes Street
Liverpool UX3 HR2
Great Britain

Dear Mr. Pearshall:

This is to confirm the terms of our deal at the exchange rate of 1 pound sterling to 1.6385 United States dollars.

We will hold to the contract as written, unless there is a 10 percent change in the currency rate before delivery.

If that happens, both sides will renegotiate the price.

The rate quoted is the closing rate for May 16.

Truly yours,

Frederick L. Langguth
President

Tips and Comment:

The rate of currency exchange is a tricky part of international business. Some companies prefer to stipulate the exact range of rates acceptable or to fix a rate for a specific transaction. Letters dealing with this aspect of international business should be explicit about timing, conditions, and exact ratios.

Alternative A:

I want to confirm the rate of exchange on which our agreement to supply 10,000 semiconductor widgets is based.

We mutually agree on the valuation of the franc at $5.65 as quoted on May 16.

Alternative B:

The complexities of this contract mean we must keep a close eye on the exchange rates of three currencies.

As of today, the pound was at $1.63 and the peseta was $.0093.

If there is a major change in the next 30 days, it will alter the profitability of the contract.

Alternative C:

As of today the European Currency Unit stood at 93.45.

We understand that if the ECU evaluation should fall more than 5 percent in the next ten days, the terms of the contract will be altered.

Please keep us informed.

Transfer of Payments

WORLDWIDE PRODUCTS, INC.
231 EAST BENDER AVENUE
DOVER, DE

November 2, 19—

Mr. Enzo Pappas
89 Via Rosa
Milano
Italy

Dear Mr. Pappas:

We will prefer to make payments under our new contract by means of
foreign drafts.

The drafts will be hand-delivered to you at your Milan office within two
days of the issuance of payment here in Dover.

One of the advantages is the ability to send messages and copies of our
invoices at the same time.

Payment by this means is also a great deal simpler for us, since we need
only to deal with a local bank to have the drafts issued.

Please let me know if this method is satisfactory.

Sincerely,

Sewall Jones
Vice-President

Tips and Comment:

In addition to deciding what currency to employ in foreign transactions, it is also necessary to deal with the actual method of transfer. Several options are open, and it is wise to agree ahead of time on the specific mechanism, since there is considerable variation in time and negotiability. A preliminary letter should spell out the method and the reasons for its selection.

Alternative A:

You have suggested payment to you from Consolidated be made in the form of a foreign draft.

We propose a simpler method: sending a certified check (drawn on our local bank) by international express service.

While this is slightly slower, it is a great deal easier for us to handle on a routine basis.

Alternative B:

We agree on the transfer of payment funds by wire from our commercial bank in Dover to your bank in Milan.

We will order the transfer on receipt of goods and an invoice.

Alternative C:

If it is agreeable with you, we propose to make payments by regular bank draft, drawn on the Banco Italiano in Milan where we maintain an account.

This should provide the fastest and most secure form of payment.

Confirming Shipments

INTERGLOBAL, INC.
45 TREADWELL STREET
NEWPORT NEWS, VA

October 8, 19—

Mr. Sean O'Brien
Downey and Co., Ltd.
34 Upper Road
Dublin
Ireland

Dear Mr. O'Brien:

The shipment of your order No. 4567 is scheduled to leave harbor on October 9.

Enclosed are the following:

- copy of the invoice
- copy of an irrevocable letter of credit
- copy of onboard ocean bill of lading
- copy of Import Permit No. 334
- copy of consular invoice.

This letter will serve as your confirmation of the shipment.

Sincerely,

Sheila Burns
Shipping Manager

Tips and Comment:

Shipping goods abroad usually calls for a great deal of paperwork. A letter confirming shipment and enclosing all the necessary financial and legal documents will keep the transaction in order. It should be straight to the point and complete in describing the enclosures.

Alternative A:

Enclosed is a full set of shipping documents for your order of widgets.

The shipment is fully containerized, as you requested.

We will alert you by telex when the plane is due to land at Heathrow.

Alternative B:

The paperwork is finally complete for the shipment of containerized widgets, and I enclose a full set of copies.

Notice especially the changes to the bill of lading.

We will let you know by phone when the shipment leaves our dock.

Alternative C:

Included in this package are copies of the international bill of lading, the customs permit, the consular invoice, and the point of origin statements.

You will need to have these on hand when the shipment of widgets arrives.

Please check with your local office to see if anything else will be needed.

Advice on Cultural Differences

GLOBAL ENTERPRISES, INC.
23 AVENUE OF THE AMERICAS
NEW YORK, NY

April 23, 19—

To: All Foreign Area Representatives

This is a good time to emphasize again the importance of observing carefully the cultural customs of the countries in which you are operating.

Many of these customs are subtle. What is acceptable, casual behavior to you may offend your hosts, so be certain to do your homework on such matters.

A good example is the perception among most Europeans that Americans talk too loudly and are therefore boorish and arrogant. Your messages will come across much better if you can modulate your tone of voice.

Attention to these kinds of subtleties will be repaid in smoother business relationships.

Sincerely,

John M. McIntyre
President

Tips and Comment:

Preparing your staff to work abroad includes instruction in the often delicate matter of cultural differences. Seemingly casual habits—such as crossing the legs to reveal the sole of the shoe—may be perceived as crass in another country. Some forms of behavior are even dangerous, since they may indicate deadly insults in other cultures. Letters of instruction should alert staff to the potential problems and emphasize the care and research needed before traveling abroad for business.

Alternative A:

Following the difficulties encountered by our team in Saudi Arabia last month, let me point out once again that no representatives of this company should attempt a sales trip without doing all the homework about local customs.

The problems could have been avoided if the team members had remembered the proper form for directing a taxi. As illogical as it seems to us, one should never simply give a command to a Saudi taxi driver, but rather make an indirect suggestion of the destination.

Alternative B:

Enclosed is an orientation guide for business travelers in Africa. Please read it carefully and carry it with you on your trips.

We have discovered over the past five years that careful attention to casual conversation will be well repaid.

At all costs, it is necessary to avoid any hint of condescending attitudes. If you are ever perceived as putting on an air of superiority, business comes to an end.

Alternative C:

Don't sneeze in public in Japan.

I know this seems silly to some of you, but it is an example of what you need to know before going to Tokyo next month.

There are certain forms of otherwise casual behavior that your hosts will find offensive. It is your duty to know and avoid all such gaffes.

International Management Differences

THEOBALD MANUFACTURING, INC.
89 RESTON DRIVE
GASTON, TX

June 6, 19—

Mr. Wilhelm Schmidt
Hanseatic Holding
123 Unterreise
Hanover, West Germany

Dear Mr. Schmidt:

We continue to have some friction between the group here in Gaston and the group from Hanover, but I believe we are making progress.

The root of the difficulty seems to be relatively simple: our American managers behave in ways that seem too aggressive to our German team. The Americans are really only following their usual methods, but the Hanseatic Holding managers are not accustomed to some of the techniques.

For example, many of the American divisional managers like to do most of their business discussion and decision making on the phone. The Hanseatic group prefers most business to be conducted by written memo.

This seems like a small matter, but it has proven to be a major stumbling block to effective communications.

I have suggested to both groups that they make some concessions about methods.

Truly yours,

Lawrence B. Nash
Divisional President

Tips and Comment:

Foreign investors have purchased a large (and growing) share of American businesses in recent years, and attempts to meld managerial teams and styles have sometimes run into cultural obstacles. Acute observers on both sides should be able to untangle the difficulties and explain the precise sources of friction. A letter discussing such matters should adopt a careful tone in order to avoid labeling either side with blame.

Alternative A:

It appears that some of the basic rituals of business life are at the root of the recent complaints from our American management group.

The executives involved are accustomed to using the telephone for rapid communication, and they often announce significant decisions in the course of phone conversations.

This apparently grates on the German management team, who prefer to move more deliberately and deal with important matters only by memo.

We should attempt to smooth over this problem.

Alternative B:

The deliberate style of decision making, built on a well-discussed consensus, is second nature to your management team. Our team, on the other hand, has been conditioned to respond very quickly to new market conditions and to make decisions individually with little discussion.

I believe our task is to bring these two styles together.

Alternative C:

I believe that the recent decline in sales revenues can be attributed directly to the change in marketing focus directed by Gustav during the last quarter.

While he certainly understands the process of manufacturing widgets, I believe he overestimated the interest in the American market for mini-widgets.

In part, this can be attributed to his natural viewpoint as a European marketer.

I suggest that we reassess the approach and take into consideration the advice of our American market experts.

Approaching Japanese Businesses

VALUE CORPORATION
45 TRAVERS ROAD
HUTTON, WY

December 5, 19—

Mr. Y. Hamata
Fujika Corporation
Tokyo
Japan

Dear Mr. Hamata:

We welcome your interest with greatest pleasure.

Your company is, of course, well known in our industry, and the people of Value Corporation respect and admire your accomplishments.

We would be happy to entertain a group from Fujika Corporation whenever it would be convenient for you to travel to our plant and headquarters.

We look forward to establishing a relationship of mutual trust.

Truly yours,

David F. Gadsen
Chief Operating Officer

Tips and Comment:

Although it may seem like a cliché, it is important to approach Japanese businessmen with extra measures of polite friendliness. Japanese business culture is based to a large degree on developing what might seem to Americans as overly personal relationships between companies. In general, before serious discussion can take place a feeling of trust must be established. Letters (or any other form of communication) to Japanese businessmen should strive for a warm, friendly tone, laying the foundation for the future.

Alternative A:

It was pleasant to receive your recent letter about our plant and operations in Dallas.

Our company has only the warmest regard for the Fujika Corporation, based on our short relationship.

We would welcome the chance to show you more of how we make and distribute widgets.

Alternative B:

Please accept my personal gratitude for your recent visit to our headquarters.

Our conversations began to establish what I hope will become a long-term relationship, and I was happy to learn more about your interest.

Please call on me at any time for more information.

Alternative C:

I was very pleased to learn that the Fujika Corporation may consider our Denver plant as a source of supply for your new manufacturing facility in Colorado.

Our plant is close enough to meet your requirements for daily delivery, and I believe that our plant managers are dedicated to producing the first-quality products you need.

I hope that further discussions and further mutual knowledge will lead to a beneficial relationship.

Letters to Japanese Businessmen

MONTANE PRODUCTS, INC.
567 PLACER DRIVE
SAN JOSE, CA

February 21, 19—

Mr. H. Kamakura
Nippon Manufacturing
Kyoto
Japan

Dear Mr. Kamakura:

The examples of calendar printing sent by you are beautiful. The quality of the presswork is exquisite and among the best we have ever seen.

We admire the skill of your workers and the dedication of your quality control supervisors.

Our many customers in the United States would surely like the opportunity to purchase similar products.

We will be happy to speak to you further.

Sincerely,

Harold J. Prentiss
Manager

Tips and Comment:

As unusual as it may seem to American executives, their typical direct approach to letter writing should be put aside when addressing a Japanese recipient. The general culture of Japan, Japanese business culture specifically, and even the structure of the Japanese language, prize indirectness—even ambiguity—and a direct approach may be perceived as impolite or offensive. This presents a delicate problem, but one typical of those to be solved when dealing with a foreign culture. Letters should be phrased with great circumspection; objectives should be hinted at rather than baldly stated. Above all, never ask a negative question: it would be impolite for a Japanese to reply in anyway but affirmatively.

Alternative A:

My company manufactures equipment used in the processing of widgets.

We admire the desire of your company to begin a widget-making program and believe that it might be to our mutual benefit to understand each other's goals.

Ours is an old, well-established company—one we hope you may come to know better.

Alternative B:

My company has been in the process of surveying the entire field of widget chip manufacturing, and needless to say, the Nippon Widget Company's products appeared consistently at the top of the list.

We have come particularly to admire the LDC-23 widget chip, which would fit well into a new product we are now developing in our test laboratories.

We hope to make and sell thousands of the new units each month.

Alternative C:

As you know, we have often done business in the past, including your rather large purchase last year of our mini-widgets.

Our work continues to go well, and in fact we have increased the production capacity of our plant by 25 percent during the last six months.

We now can make 34,000 mini-widgets per month and offer them at a price of $.05 per unit.

14

LOCAL RESPONSIBILITIES: LETTERS CONCERNING COMMUNITY AFFAIRS

By definition, businesses are all a part of their individual local communities and usually make strong efforts to participate in community life. Executives should be able to communicate effectively with a variety of community organizations concerning many activities. The most typical keynote in such letters, as illustrated in the examples, is service. Executives must be able to represent themselves and their businesses as responsible members of the local community.

339

Invitation to Community Service

OFFICE OF THE MAYOR
TERRYVILLE, VT

October 15, 19—

Mr. Benjamin K. Powers
President
Apex Development Co.
445 Carriage Hill Road
Terryville, VT

Dear Mr. Powers:

Mayor Jones has asked me to invite you to the first meeting of his campaign to fight juvenile delinquency through affirmative action.

The meeting will be at City Hall on Tuesday, October 28, and will be concerned with initial planning for the project.

This will be a gathering of only a few local citizens and will chart the course for future organization.

Please let me know if you are willing to serve.

Truly yours,

David Frederick
Assistant to the Mayor

Tips and Comment:

Few civic projects go forward without participation by key local businesspeople. This letter is a standard invitation to serve and uses a straightforward approach to recruiting. Presumably the appeal of the cause is obvious. In other cases, more persuasion might be needed.

Alternative A:

The City Council in its meeting last evening nominated you to the zoning board for a three-year term.

I hope you will accept this responsibility, since the zoning board deals with a host of matters that are extremely important to the community.

Please let me know in writing. The first meeting of the new board is on the 23rd, with an official swearing-in ceremony at 6:30 P.M.

Alternative B:

As you know the city is nearing its fiftieth anniversary as a separate incorporated community, and we are now organizing a steering committee to plan an anniversary celebration.

We would like you to serve on the steering committee and help us with preparations. So far, we have twelve people on the committee, with a goal of a total of fifteen.

We hope you can join us.

Alternative C:

This is to tell you that the Mayor has appointed you to the Youth Center board for 19—, as he discussed with you last week.

In addition, he would like you to serve as chair of the fundraising committee. This is a job that will call on your past successful experience in the community.

The first meeting of the new board will be on the 12th.

Accepting Invitation to Community Service

APEX DEVELOPMENT CO.
445 CARRIAGE HILL RD.
TERRYVILLE, VT

October 23, 19—

Mr. David Frederick
Assistant to the Mayor
Terryville, VT

Dear Mr. Frederick:

I'm pleased and honored to join the town's citizens who are participating in the mayor's campaign to fight juvenile delinquency through affirmative action.

I have always been interested in this problem, and I am happy to accept your invitation to work with the mayor. I hope I can make some meaningful contribution to the success of this worthwhile project.

Thank you for inviting me to the first meeting. I will be there. If I can be of any assistance before the meeting, please let me know.

Sincerely,

Benjamin K. Powers
President

Tips and Comment:

Since businesspeople are a prominent part of any local community, they are frequently asked to participate in civic affairs. Such invitations call for a formal letter accepting the position, if such is the inclination. It may also be a good time to indicate willingness to devote time to the project.

Alternative A:

It was a pleasure to receive the invitation to serve on the zoning board for a three-year term, and I am happy to accept the appointment.

There are few matters more important to the orderly development of our city than zoning.

I will be there for the meeting on the 23rd and to be sworn in.

If there are documents I might profitably look at ahead of the meeting, please send them along.

Alternative B:

I am grateful for your invitation to sit on the steering committee for the organization of the fiftieth anniversary celebration.

I will look forward to working with you and the other members of the committee.

Please feel free to call on me at any time.

Alternative C:

I accept the appointment to the Youth Center board, and I will be happy to chair the fundraising committee.

Even though this will involve the commitment of a good deal of time and effort, I think the cause so important that I am happy to make whatever contribution is called for.

I look forward to our first meeting so we can get under way.

Fund Raising Letter for Local Charity

STERLING ENTERPRISES, INC.
12 SOUTH FIFTH AVENUE
PARSIPPANY, PA

September 3, 19—

Mr. Kenneth G. McNee
President
McNee Construction
45 Indian Drive
Parsippany, PA

Dear Mr. McNee:

I am writing to ask your financial help with the Community Fund for 19—.

The Fund is a nonprofit organization that was set up in our community twenty-three years ago by a group of civic-minded businesspeople. Since its founding, the Fund has provided direct financial assistance to a wide range of community projects, including a homeless shelter, summer camp for disadvantaged children, a food bank, and medical care for the elderly.

Hundreds upon hundreds of people have been helped directly by the Fund, and our city is a better place for the efforts of those who have supported the Fund.

Please make a contribution and join the businesses who are working to improve life in our community.

All donations are tax deductible.

Fill out the enclosed card and send in a donation today.

Thank you.

Sincerely,

H. Roger Sterling
President

Tips and Comment:

Fundraising letters are hard to write. They must appeal to another person in a way that risks rejection, and most writers find this a difficult psychological hurdle. The best approach is to be direct and straightforward. Don't beat around the bush, but make it clear immediately that you are soliciting a donation on behalf of a worthy cause. Then, make the case for the charity by pointing out the role it plays in the community and the good it does. Establish the bona fides of the charity and indicate whether a tax deduction is possible. Be bold and confident in tone.

Alternative A:

This is an appeal for a donation to the Save the Children Fund.

As you may know, the SCF has been a fixture in our community for many years and has reached out to help thousands of children. Each year we make almost $200,000 available for projects directed by the Fund.

Your help is needed in order to reach the Fund's goal for this campaign.

I know you will want to join the patrons of this fine cause.

Alternative B:

Once again we are asking local businesspeople to get behind the Fund for Excellence in Local Education.

When we began this effort two years ago, we hoped to raise $100,000 to assist the local schools. We were thrilled to reach that goal immediately and go on last year to collect $175,000.

This year, we are aiming for gifts totalling $200,000.

Please fill out the enclosed donation card and send in your pledge today.

Alternative C:

I'm serving as chairman for the Committee on Aging, and we need your help.

No...I'm not asking for time, only your money.

In order to get the program off the ground this year, we need to raise $100,000 in seed money. I'm asking each business in the community to contribute.

Please send in a donation today to help us begin this vital program to improve life for the elderly in our community.

Contributing to a Charity

TRANSIT FREIGHT CO.
3900 JUNIPER AVENUE
KINGSTON, NY

March 1, 19—

Mr. Thomas Johnson
Greater Buffalo Center
Buffalo, NY

Dear Mr. Johnson:

We found your letter and the accompanying literature about the Niagara Disabled Young Artists both touching and impressive.

We will be happy to contribute to this worthwhile cause and add it to our list of charitable organizations. For now, enclosed is our check for $2,000.

We certainly wish you the best of luck in your endeavor to have these young artists realize their full potential and become self-sufficient.

Sincerely,

William O. Williams

Tips and Comment:

Businesses are asked to contribute to charities and nonprofit organizations as a matter of course during fund drives. An affirmative reply should state the circumstances and amount of the gift, in addition to the pleasantries.

Alternative A:

I am pleased to respond to your letter of the 23rd, asking for a contribution to the United Homeless Fund.

Enclosed is a check for $5,000.

There is no greater cause in our community or our nation than the homeless, and we are proud to be able to respond with this contribution.

Alternative B:

Enclosed is a check for $500 as our contribution to the Fund for Excellence.

I wish it could be more, but we are a small company with a limited amount of resources.

Your Fund has done wonderful work during its first year, and I sincerely wish you the best of continued success. Your efforts are improving the quality of life here.

Alternative C:

We are happy to renew our pledge to the Fund for another year. As in the past, we believe your work has done a great deal to improve our community.

In fact, we often point to your efforts when we are recruiting new personnel.

If we can be of further help, please let us know.

Thank You for Charitable Donation

WELCOME, INC.
P.O. BOX 56
WILMINGTON, DE

July 12, 19—

Mr. Kelly James
123 Delaware Avenue
Wilmington, DE

Dear Mr. James:

On behalf of the Children's Fund, I thank you for your recent contribution.
Your kind gift will go far toward helping the Fund provide healthy outdoor
activities for gradeschool children during the summer months.
Of course, the gift is tax deductible, and a receipt for your records is
enclosed.
Thanks again.

Yours truly,

Hilda Ferguson
President

Tips and Comment:

Volunteer fundraisers may send thank you acknowledgments of charitable gifts on their own business letterhead. The letter is sincere but relatively routine and may be set up as a repeatable, standard letter, especially if a large volume of similar letters is required.

Alternative A:

It was a pleasure to learn you have contributed to the Community Fund for yet another year. Your help in this fine effort is deeply appreciated.

The money will go toward a variety of worthy local causes.

Your generosity will touch many people in our community. Thanks.

Alternative B:

Thank you for your recent donation to the Save the Children Campaign.

This is a vital effort and I'm very pleased to say a successful one, thanks to people like you who give time and money.

We'll keep you informed during the coming year of projects supported by the Campaign.

Alternative C:

Thanks for the contribution.

We have worked hard to establish the Fund as a vital part of the community, and it is gratifying to see so many local businesses respond to our appeal.

The money collected will help support the new wing of the recreational center and provide opportunities for hundreds of retired people in the city.

Thanks again.

Invitation to Charity Event

CVC COMPUTER CORPORATION
345 TOWANDA DRIVE
BIG BEND, KS

November 15, 19—

Mr. Joe Young
President
Young Fiber Optic, Inc.
23 West 4th Street
Big Bend, KS

Dear Joe:

This is an invitation to you and Betty to join Helen and me at the 4th Annual Save the Prairie dinner and fundraiser, to be held at the Galton House at 6:30 P.M. on Friday, December 3.

The tickets are $100 each, and proceeds go to the Save the Prairie Fund (all donations are tax deductible).

I know you have been interested in the project in the past, and I'm counting on your support again this year.

The Save the Prairie Fund has been able to purchase and protect 2,000 acres of virgin prairie land in the four-county area, thus assuring the survival of this rich historical and environmental heritage.

The dinner will kick off our fund drive for the year.

Please let me know if you can make it.

Sincerely,

Ansel Williams
CEO

Tips and Comment:

Business people often take the lead in promoting community events, such as this sample fundraiser and dinner for a worthy local cause. The invitation is made in a letter rather than as a formal "card" style invitation so that a firm pitch for participation can be included. The style is somewhere between a business letter and a personal letter and may be tilted to account for the degree of association between writer and recipient.

Alternative A:

The annual potluck for the Children's Hospital is next week, and I want you and your husband to join us.

We use the potluck—which is really a gourmet affair, despite the homey name—to kick off the campaign for funds.

Since you are new to the community, I'd like to make this a personal invitation with the hope you will add your support to this vital local project. The hospital treats about 500 kids a year from our efforts.

Alternative B:

We are heading into the holiday season, and that means the annual gathering at the Coliseum on behalf of Operation Bootstrap. I want to invite you to attend.

As you know the project has helped several dozen local families over the last few years to improve their living conditions. The idea is to raise enough support in the form of money and donated services so that families can either upgrade their homes or actually build new houses.

We think this is one of the most effective means of working toward a better community and we want your support.

Alternative C:

Please plan to attend the Charity Fund Ball at 8:00 P.M. on Saturday, December 4, at the Rialto Ballroom.

This is an event sponsored by the Downtown Association in support of local charities and is the primary way we fund our activities throughout the year.

I know you will enjoy the event and will want to assist in our charity efforts.

Refusal to Lend Name

APEX REALTY CO.
445 CARRIAGE HILL RD.
NORTH ESSEX, MA

December 12, 19—

Mr. Mark Beson
Allied Cancer Fund
324 West 45th Avenue
North Essex, MA

Dear Mr. Beson:

Regretfully, I can't comply with your request to use my name in your fundraising drive.

I have allowed my name to be used for this purpose by a number of nonprofit organizations, and whatever beneficial effect it could have has already been diluted to a great extent. Consequently, as a matter of policy, and even though the Cancer Fund is a most worthy cause, I'm limiting the use of my name to groups with which I already have an agreement.

Nonetheless, I wish you great success in your drive.

Sincerely,

Benjamin K. Powers
President

Tips and Comment:

Not every cause is worthy of support, and special circumstances may prevent even lending a name to an organization. The letter of refusal may properly explain why the group is being turned down. Be polite but firm.

Alternative A:

I am sorry to tell you that I cannot let you include my name on the list of supporters for the advertisement to run in next week's paper.

My company has a strict policy of prohibiting corporation executives from such activities since it may conflict with our highly integrated corporate charity drive.

I'm sorry that I cannot help, but I wish you well.

Alternative B:

You may *not* add my name to your board of directors. I do not believe in the principles of your organization and I decline to support its goals.

Why you had my name is a mystery, since I have stated my opposition many times in the past.

Alternative C:

It is with much regret that I must decline your inquiry about allowing my name to appear as a sponsor of this year's fund drive.

I do not think it would be fair to you or to the Health Care Fund, which has had my full support for the last decade. I do not wish to split whatever influence I have in the community between the two organizations, and my long-standing commitment to HCF takes preference.

I do wish you success however, and I suggest that you might ask Fred Hinson at the First National.

Asking for Help for Cultural Activities

BLACK CONSTRUCTION CORPORATION
90 DELAWARE AVENUE
GOSHEN, MD

September 3, 19—

Mr. Oliver Greiner
Greiner Enterprises
23 Pennsylvania St.
Goshen, MD

Dear Oliver:

The Arts Council is ready to begin another year, and the Executive Committee is now recruiting new blood for the Board.

They have asked me to inquire if you would be willing to serve. I know that you have supported the Council and its annual fund drives in the past and that you have a strong interest in the local arts community.

We need people like you on the Board, especially since the fundraising environment has gotten so tight. You are influential among other businesspeople and would make a strong advocate.

Moreover, we need energy and new ideas, and I think you could provide both.

The Board meets once a month, on the second Tuesday, usually for lunch.

Please let me know how you feel about this. I hope you will say "yes."

Sincerely,

James D. Black
President

Tips and Comment:

Local arts groups rely on the business community to supply volunteer management. Often, those who serve on arts boards are given the task of recruiting others in the business world to join them, as in this sample letter. The tone is direct, confident, and complimentary without being fulsome. The writer alludes to the history of the recipient's involvement in community arts, points to the benefits of having his counsel, and is specific about the time required.

Alternative A:

You have been generous in the past with your monetary contributions to the Chamber Music Guild, and we certainly want you to continue when we ask.

However, we want something even more precious—your time and skills.

We have an opening on the Board of the Guild that we want very much for you to fill. The Board is charged with administering the program of the Guild, working through the staff, and we need people such as yourself with solid business experience.

I hope you will accept.

Alternative B:

Will you serve on the Arrangements Committee for the Ballet Company?

I know you are as busy as the rest of us, but we desperately need someone of your background to help this year since we are planning a 25th Anniversary Gala in April.

As far as I can tell, we would meet about once a month for the first few months, and then increase to once every two weeks.

I think you would enjoy the association with the other committee members, and I know we would benefit from your presence.

Alternative C:

When we on the Board of the Arts Fund began to plan our efforts for the coming year, your name came up repeatedly.

Will you be willing to help us with the Fund campaign? We think some new ideas are needed, since the Fund has reached a plateau over the last few years.

Please give this serious thought and let me know.

Urging Volunteer Participation

TRENDS, INC.
P.O. BOX 45
OKRAVILLE, KS

July 5, 19—

Ms. Patrice McManus
Future Realty, Inc.
34 Asher Street
Okraville, KS

Dear Ms. McManus:

The Okraville Board of Realtors is supporting the community-wide effort to promote better housing in the county, and we need your help.

This is strictly a volunteer effort, but it is clearly in the best interests of the real estate community to get behind this drive.

We hope you will participate and give generously of your time and energy.

Thanks.

Sincerely,

Jim Klater
Chairman

Tips and Comment:

Trade associations and business affinity groups are good vehicles to help influence the social betterment of the local community, which also often has a positive effect on the economic health of those involved. This letter asks for volunteer participation in the name of a trade association. Such an appeal will provide the community project with a ready-made pool of supporters and practical workers with a knowledge of the problem and how to solve it.

Alternative A:

The local Committee of Retail Merchants is asking all its members to join in the city's effort to promote the annual Fourth of July parade through downtown.

This will mean posting signs in your store windows and including a notice of the parade in any retail print ads you run between now and the holiday.

While this is purely a volunteer effort, it will help make the Parade a success.

Alternative B:

On Saturday, June 4, the Merchants Association will conduct a volunteer effort to clean up the stretch of Highway 68 between Buffalo Trace Road and East Fourth Street.

This is part of the city's "Adopt-a-Street" program which has been so successful in the past.

We need your participation in the cleanup. Please show up at the Buffalo Trace end of the highway at 9:00 A.M. We will provide all the equipment needed.

We anticipate good media coverage.

Announcing a Community Scholarship

HUGHES REALTY, INC.
98 DOVER DRIVE
BENTONSPORT, OH

April 23, 19—

Ms. Glenda F. Pound
45 Seabrook Lane
Bentonsport, OH

Dear Ms. Pound:

I am very pleased to inform you that you have been selected as the recipient of the Hughes Scholarship, a grant of $2,000 awarded annually to an outstanding graduating senior from Bentonsport High School.

You may use the stipend to defray educational expenses beyond the level of your high school diploma.

Your selection was based on a nomination made by your school and the recommendations of your teachers and others in the community.

We would like you and your family to attend a presentation dinner at the Bentonsport Country Club at 6:30 P.M. on Tuesday, May 1.

Congratulations!

Sincerely,

Wanda K. Hughes
President

Tips and Comment:

The practice of awarding scholarships to outstanding young people of the community is widespread and a good community relations tool in addition to the intrinsic value of such acts. A letter announcing the award should be specific about the amount and the conditions, and it should set up future goodwill publicity for the business funding the scholarship.

Alternative A:

Congratulations...you have been chosen to receive this year's Young Businessperson's Fellowship.

The Fellowship is in the amount of $1,000 and can be used for education. It goes to the outstanding member of the Young Businessperson's Club at the local high school.

Please call me at my office and make arrangements for photographs and a press release.

Alternative B:

It is my pleasure on behalf of the Board of Directors to announce you are the recipient of the $500 Manufacturers' Scholar Award.

The Award goes annually to a sophomore student at University College who is majoring in Industrial Technology.

We would like to use your name in announcing the award to the local media. Please get in touch with my office immediately.

Alternative C:

You have been selected to receive the first ever Booksellers' Scholarship, an award of $1,500 made possible by the local Bookseller's Association.

The scholarship may be used at any state institution of higher education within the next three years.

We plan to announce the award to the press next week.

Letter to Community Neighbors

SUNDRY GOODS, INC.
123 NORTH FOURTH AVENUE
DODGETOWN, IL

March 23, 19—

Dear Neighbors:

Over the coming weeks, we will begin construction of an additional building at the north end of our property on North Fourth Avenue.

The activity associated with construction will be, no doubt, an inconvenience for those of you who live and work nearby.

Please bear with us during the construction. We will make every effort to complete the project as rapidly as possible and with a minimum of disruption to the neighborhood.

If you have specific problems at any time during the coming weeks, please don't hesitate to let me know, and I'll try to help.

Thanks for your patience and understanding.

Truly yours,

George Fern
President

Tips and Comment:

Good community relations may mean nothing more than keeping neighbors or others informed of your plans and activities. A simple notice of what's happening will disarm criticism and complaints in many cases. Note that the sample letter assumes goodwill on the part of the neighbors and presents a completely friendly and reasonable attitude.

Alternative A:

Due to a changeover in our plant procedures, we will be shutting down the water supply to our plant and several surrounding blocks for much of the day on June 4.

We regret the inconvenience this will cause some of you, but we will try to keep the disruption as short as possible.

Please make arrangements to accommodate the cutoff.

Alternative B:

This is to let you know that we have filed an application for a permit to construct low-density apartments in the 400 block of Maple Street on the site formerly occupied by the Bestor Corporation.

As you know, this site has been vacant for the last year and was rapidly becoming a problem for the community.

We feel confident that the new housing will revitalize the area and attract new people.

Alternative C:

I am happy to let you know that we have received Historic Site designation from the State Department of Historic Property for our building at 494 Fern Street.

This means that the entire ten-block area will now be eligible for both tax breaks and direct funding to preserve the historic nature of the neighborhood.

I'd be happy to share information on this.

Letter to Chamber of Commerce

ALLIED DEVELOPMENTS, INC.
34 SPENDER LANE
SEA BREEZE, WA

April 23, 19—

Mr. Jerry Thompson
Executive Director
Chamber of Commerce
Sea Breeze, WA

Dear Jerry:

The good news has finally come through—Allied will begin work in May on the $35 million Sea Breeze Mall project.

As you know, this has been in the works for a long time, and we are looking forward to moving into the construction phase.

We received word today from Amalgamated Stores that they will take the anchor slot in the mall. This will assure us of the level and kind of occupancy we needed.

I think we should make a joint announcement of the project before the week is out. Can you have your PR people call my office to get things rolling on a media announcement?

Your help in standing behind the project has been immense. We couldn't have done it without you. Thanks!

Yours truly,

Bill

Tips and Comment:

The local Chamber of Commerce serves as a focal point for may kinds of business activity in most communities. Depending on the situation, it may be a good idea to keep close contact with the offices of the Chamber and to work with Chamber officials when large projects that may involve the entire community arise. The Chamber can serve as a buffer and a mouthpiece.

Alternative A:

We are contemplating a new project in the Avondale neighborhood and would like to sound out the Chamber on where it is likely to stand.

The project would include a large share of low-income housing, which would be something new for this part of the city. We don't anticipate any problems, but we'd like to stay ahead of the publicity curve on this one.

Please call to schedule a meeting.

Alternative B:

I'd be happy to take ad space in the directory for next year. From our point of view, the directory has served a good purpose, and we want to continue to support it.

I hope you are taking the advice of some of last year's advertisers, however, and plan to include more pages in full color.

Alternative C:

I'd be pleased to serve on the selection committee for the Chamber's "Small Business of the Year Award."

This is a good program that has put the spotlight on many fine businesses in the community.

When do we meet to begin to look over the nominations?

15

COURTESY:
SOCIAL AND PERSONAL LETTERS

The letters and communications in this chapter are not strictly business, but they are business-related. Because the line between business life and social life is often blurred, a successful business executive should be at ease when writing on social matters—a fact that will reflect well on the executive in other situations more directly related to commerce. The following examples show how to deal with several social situations. Some are formal and call for a fairly strict adherence to custom and convention; others allow more leeway of expression.

Formal Invitation

Mr. and Mrs. James K. Lee

request the pleasure of your company

for cocktails and a light buffet

Friday, the sixth of June

at six o'clock

23 Oak Drive

Kansas City, Missouri

The favor of a reply is requested.

Tips and Comment:

The style of formal invitations never varies. Each line is specifically devoted to one part of the invitation: nothing should be altered and nothing should be left out.

the names of hosts

"request" line

description of event

date line

time of day

street address

city and state

reply request

Formal invitations should be printed or hand-written on special stationary (never on business letterhead). There are no alternative versions if the invitation is truly formal.

Informal Invitation

You are cordially invited

for cocktails and a light buffet

on Friday, June 6

at 6 o'clock

23 Oak Drive

Kansas City, Missouri

Jim and Janet Lee

Please reply
555-1212

Tips and Comment:

Informal invitations include exactly the same information as formal invitations, but there is more freedom in style and form of expression. The allotment of information to specific lines is similar to formal invitations, but the actual wording is less rigid. Informal invitations should be printed or written on special stationary.

Alternative A:

We want you to attend
a cocktail party
in honor of Jane Graves
Thursday, January 23
7:00 P.M.
56 Forest Lane
Clives, New York

George and Helen Manners
Please reply: 555-1212

Alternative B:

You are invited
for Dinner
on Saturday, the Tenth of October
at 6:30
133 Randall Street
Lawrence, Delaware

Larry and Margie Polters

Alternative C:

Please attend
an informal reception
on December 2, 19—
at 4 o'clock, P.M.
89 West Second
Minneapolis, Minnesota

Mr. and Mrs. Fred C. Dobbs

Accepting a Formal Invitation

Mr. and Mrs. Kenneth Jones

accept with pleasure

the invitation of

Mr. and Mrs. James K. Lee

to be present for cocktails and a light buffet

at six o'clock

23 Oak Drive

Kansas City, Missouri

Tips and Comment:

A formal invitation calls for a formal acceptance, whose format is just as rigid as the invitation. Each line of the acceptance should mirror the arrangement of the invitation. Acceptances should be on personal stationary, such as note sheets or note cards. The use of the third person echoes the formality of the invitation. No alternatives are suggested.

Accepting an Informal Invitation

RENNE ROGERS
21 EAST DRIVE
KANSAS CITY, MISSOURI

May 31, 19—

Dear Jim and Janet,

I am delighted to accept your invitation for cocktails and buffet on June 6 at six o'clock at your home.

Thanks.

Renne

Tips and Comment:

Accepting informal invitations calls for less rigidity than accepting formal invitations. The proper response may be made on the phone if the original invitation gives a number, but a brief hand-written note on personal stationary is just as good. There is no need to use the third person style in this case.

Alternative A:

We will be happy to attend the dinner at your home on Thursday at 6:30.

Thanks for including us.

Alternative B:

Nothing would give us more pleasure than to attend the reception at your summer home at 5:30 on July 4.

We look forward to celebrating the occasion with you and your other guests.

Alternative C:

Thanks for the invitation. We are happy to accept and will be at the dinner at 7:00 P.M.

Declining an Invitation

RENNE ROGERS
21 EAST DRIVE
KANSAS CITY, MISSOURI

May 31, 19—

Dear Jim and Janet,

Thank you for your kind invitation for cocktails and a buffet on June 6.
Unfortunately, I will be out of town during that week and so am unable to
attend.
I appreciate that you thought of me.

Sincerely,

Renne

Tips and Comment:

Some etiquette mavens say that declining a formal invitation calls for the same degree of rigid formality as issuing or accepting one; however, it seems socially correct to use the same style in turning down either a formal or informal invitation. A hand-written note is, perhaps, best. It is also a good idea to give the reason for declining.

Alternative A:

I am sorry to tell you that Mary and I will not be able to have dinner with you on the third.

We have to be in Nebraska on that date for our daughter's wedding.

Alternative B:

Thank you so much for the invitation to dinner on the fourth; unfortunately I am scheduled for dental surgery that morning, so it is unlikely I could be much of a dinner companion.

I'll regretfully decline at this time.

Alternative C:

Despite wishes to the contrary, we will not be able to attend your reception next week.

Please think of us again.

Thanks for Gift

JOHN G. WENTWORTH
21 DONNER'S PASS ROAD
SACRAMENTO, CA

October 25, 19—

Dear Francis,

Thank you so much for the lovely gift of flowers for my opening.
Your thoughtfulness added much to the occasion, and I appreciate the gesture.
The arrangement added a great deal to the festive look of the office.

Truly yours,

John

Tips and Comment:

A personal or semi-personal gift calls for a polite thank you note in return. Depending on the circumstances or the relationship, such notes may be more or less formal. A hand-written message on informal stationary (even personal notes) may be the most appropriate.

Alternative A:

Thank you for the potted plant. We much appreciate your thought and care in sending this gift.

Please stop by whenever possible.

Alternative B:

It was a very nice touch to send everyone who attended last week's conference the gift of a desk set.

I personally find it not only handsome but extremely useful.

Accept my thanks.

Alternative C:

Your professional skills are exceeded only by your thoughtfulness in sending the leather portfolio.

I will use it daily as a reminder of our relationship.

Holiday Greetings

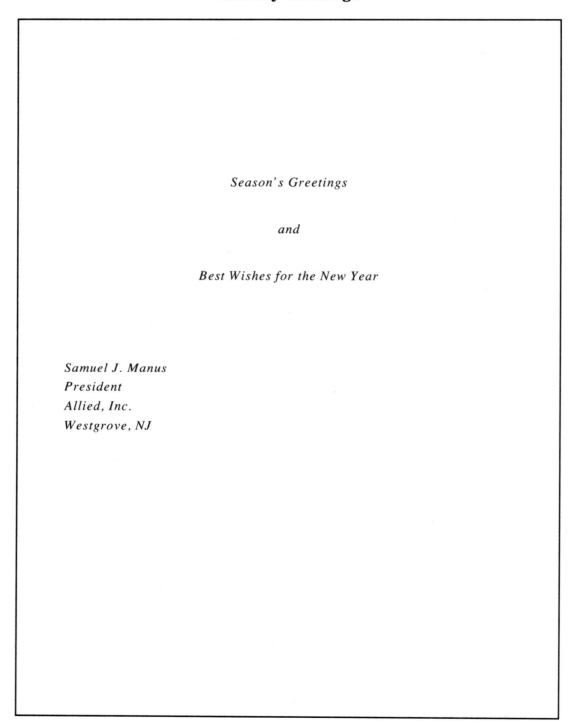

Season's Greetings

and

Best Wishes for the New Year

Samuel J. Manus
President
Allied, Inc.
Westgrove, NJ

Tips and Comment:

It is standard procedure for businesses or individuals within businesses to send holiday greetings to clients and business associates. Although it is quite proper to express religious sentiments at holidays when writing strictly as a private person, business greetings, even from individuals, should be neutral and generic. The greetings may be sent on specially prepared greeting cards with the name and business printed on the card, or commercial cards may be adapted.

Alternative A:

Season's Greetings
from
The Allied Company
to
all its valued clients

Alternative B:

Our best wishes
at this
joyful holiday season

Alternative C:

Wishing you
a prosperous and happy
holiday season

Change of Address

ROBERT K. OBERST
123 AMERICAN AVENUE
FRIENDLY, OK

January 4, 19—

Dear Friends:

As of February 1, my new address will be:

Robert K. Oberst
34 Kennet Street
Dallas, TX

I am moving to Dallas to take a position as president of Amalgamated Products, Inc.

Regards,

Robert K. Oberst

Tips and Comment:

Few practical matters when moving are more important than to alert everyone in your personal and professional network that you are changing addresses. A brief, semi-personal note such as the one on page 380 will serve several functions and can be sent to business acquaintances as well as personal friends. Be certain to get the notice in the mail well ahead of the move.

Alternative A:

On June 1, I will move my business and my home to West Orange. The new home address will be:

34 Rest Haven Road
West Orange, MS
The business address will be:
13 Industrial Park Road
West Orange, MS

Alternative B:

Please note that as of June 24, I will have a new home address:

45 Turner Drive
Sanders, TX

I hope to hear from you at my new place.

Alternative C:

I am moving to Salt Lake City to take over our new plant there and my new home address after February 3 will be:

34 Western Avenue
Salt Lake City, UT

Personal Congratulations on Achievement

GEORGIA B. SAMUELS
98 SEA MEADOWS DRIVE
CANFORD, WY

September 12, 19—

Dear Fred,

Hearty congratulations on your impending B.A. degree.
I know how hard you have worked for this achievement and how much you deserve it.
Accept my best wishes for your accomplishment and for the future.

Yours truly,

Georgia

Tips and Comment:

A personal note of congratulations for personal achievement, such as graduation, winning an award, or getting a promotion, should be brief, sincere, and appropriate to the occasion and the degree of relationship. Notes can be written on official letterhead or personal stationary as the situation demands.

Alternative A:

Please accept my congratulations for winning the Peabody Award for this year.

This is a great achievement and one richly deserved. It is a pleasure to see others acknowledge your professional skill.

I'm delighted for you.

Alternative B:

I was very happy to learn that you have recently been made Vice-President. Accept my congratulations and good wishes for the future.

I'll look forward to talking to you soon.

Alternative C:

Congratulations on your adoption. I understand how long you have waited and hoped for this day.

After being your friend, I know that you will make wonderful parents.

Let me know when your schedule will allow us to get together.

Congratulations on Personal Anniversary

JONES
56 THIRD ST.
EVANSVILLE, IN

May 3, 19—

Dear Janet and Harry,

Your forthcoming 25th anniversary is a wonderful milestone in life—Congratulations!

I'm happy to have known you all these years and to have been able to share many memories with you.

I'm sorry that I won't be able to make it for the celebration, but you know my thoughts will be with you on the big day.

Good wishes for many more.

Truly yours,

Jerry

Tips and Comment:

Personal anniversaries call for personal notes of congratulations. The style is conventional, but may be enlivened by individual touches. Such notes should probably be sent in hand-written form on personal stationary whenever possible.

Alternative A:

Congratulations on the anniversary of your ordination to the priesthood.

I share the feelings of all your parishioners in rejoicing in your ministry and wishing you many years more.

We are fortunate to have you as part of our community.

Alternative B:

Happy anniversary!

It is difficult to believe that you walked down that aisle ten years ago and that we are all growing older (but, one hopes, wiser).

Janet and I will be in your area in August, and we hope to be able to stop for a dinner with you.

Alternative C:

Congratulations on the first anniversary of your adoption of Kevin. Your joy at the event has not been forgotten here, and we wanted to let you know we remembered.

We know you will continue to grow and prosper as a family.

Letter of Condolence

LINWOOD KNITTING MILLS, INC.
50 HARRISON AVENUE
JOHNSTON, IN

June 4, 19—

Mrs. David Jones
378 Younkers Drive
Johnston, IN

Dear Mrs. Jones:

I was greatly shocked yesterday to learn of your husband's death. Please accept my sincere condolences.

I met Dave when he joined our company sixteen years ago, and we enjoyed a close and friendly association.

Dave had the respect and admiration of his colleagues, many of whom were his friends as well. His cheerful disposition was an inspiration to all of us. He will be greatly missed by his co-workers and friends here at the company.

If I can be of any help to you, please let me know.

Sincerely yours,

Robert G. Hardy

Tips and Comment:

The death of a friend or business associate does not demand a condolence letter just for the sake of form; rather, such letters should be motivated by genuine emotion and concern. These are not strictly business letters and should properly reflect more personal feelings.

Alternative A:

Please know that you have my sympathy and good thoughts during this time of loss.

Dave was a long-time associate, and I will miss him a great deal. He was ever kind to me when I first began in the business, and his kindness ripened to a good friendship.

Let me know if I can be of assistance in the days ahead.

Alternative B:

Although we have never met, I was a business associate of your wife, and I am writing to express my sorrow at her passing.

Those of us who met her in the course of business never failed to admire her intelligence and energy. She made life more pleasant for everyone who was fortunate enough to work with her.

Please accept my condolences.

Alternative C:

It is very hard to believe that I can no longer pick up the phone and talk to Dave. We had spoken so often that I felt as if I knew him well, although we had never met face to face.

I had no notion that he was ill, and his death was a great shock.

Expressing Personal Concern

TRANSATLANTIC AIR CARGO
4000 TUPPER BLVD.
GREAT ISLET, NJ

July 5, 19—

Mr. Pete Unger
St. Kline Hospital, Rm. 203
Great Islet North, NJ

Dear Pete:

Since I had lunch with you only last week, I was surprised when I learned this morning that you are in the hospital. However, I was relieved to hear that the operation was successful and you are on your way to a complete recovery.

I know the hospital is not the most pleasant place to be, but try to take advantage of the chance to rest.

In any case, take care, and if I can do anything or if you need anything, phone me.

Best wishes,

Jim

Tips and Comment:

When illness or injury strike a colleague, a note expressing concern may speed recovery or at least lift spirits. By their nature, such letters are appropriately informal and personal.

Alternative A:

I guess that will teach us all to not go down the basement stairs without turning on the light and looking first.

I'm really sorry you ended up with a broken leg, but at least this will be a good time to catch up on your fly-tying in preparation for our trip in July.

I'll try to stop by later this week and see how things are going. Give Sally my sympathy, since she is probably doing all the heavy lifting at your house right now.

Alternative B:

I was certainly distressed to learn from Dave that you are on extended sick leave.

You have my good wishes for a speedy recovery and a quick return to work.

Pay attention to your doctor's advice and let me know if I can do anything.

Alternative C:

One watches the nightly news with its scenes of injury and destruction with routine interest, but you never expect to see a report on a friend. It was horrible to watch the coverage of the wreck and to see the ambulance carry you away.

I'm much relieved after talking to Phyllis. She says the prognosis is good and that your recovery may be swift.

I think I'll just stay out of the road for the time being, but as soon as you are out of the hospital and able to see people comfortably, please let me know.

Business Hospitality

CENTURY ELECTRONIC DEVICES
CENTURY PARK
BROOKS, MA

January 12, 19—

Mr. Hubert Yount
A G. Roberts Co.
700 Crestview Ave.
Dennis, IL

Dear Mr. Yount:

I want to thank you and the A. G. Roberts Co. for your gracious hospitality
in allowing me to present our desktop computer color graphics package to
your engineering department.

The response from your staff was gratifying. Moreover, the questions after
the presentation were challenging. I couldn't have asked for a better
audience.

If you or your staff have any additional questions about our desktop
system, please don't hesitate to call.

Sincerely,

Andrew Stewart
Sales Manager

Tips and Comment:

A "thank you" note for hospitality from a business associate presents a good opportunity to drive home the message of the meeting. Common courtesy combines with business purpose.

Alternative A:

Thank you for your hospitality in showing me around your plant last week.

I was much impressed with the state of the equipment and the obvious efficiency of your production staff. They seemed to know their business and have the right tools.

I will pass on my impression to our purchasing department for their consideration.

Thanks again.

Alternative B:

Thank you for the delicious lunch yesterday and the opportunity to get to know you better.

I look forward to discussing the merger issues further within the next week.

Perhaps you could join me for dinner on Thursday? Please let me know.

Alternative C:

I can scarcely tell you how much I appreciate the kindness and attention you showed me during my time in Minneapolis.

It is inevitable that a good deal of strain and fatigue accompany such a high-pressure meeting, but your attention to my transportation needs made everything much easier.

Thank you.

Personal Introduction

GENERAL CONSTRUCTION AND ENGINEERING
56 HENLEY DRIVE
WOOSTER, VT

April 8, 19—

Mr. Theodore DiPaglia
DiPaglia & Sons
400 DiPaglia Building
Noonan, VT

Dear Ted:

This letter will introduce you to Alan Berry, a fine engineer with whom I have had the privilege of working on many projects.

Alan is considering a move into the road construction business and is seeking information. Since you are so experienced, I thought you would be a good source for him to talk to.

I will certainly appreciate any help you can give him, and I will be happy to reciprocate at any time.

Kindest regards,

Daniel DeMotte
President

Tips and Comment:

Letters of introduction are, to some degree, personal no matter what their business purpose. The writer is giving the person introduced a stamp of approval and asking a friend or associate to extend courtesy and help. It is always a tricky question whether to give a copy to the person discussed, but in any case, care should be taken to not overstate the situation.

Alternative A:

I want to introduce Jane Travis, who has just moved from Lesterville to Hobart. Jane worked closely with our firm during her years here, and I found her help of considerable benefit.

Please give her every courtesy when she calls on you.

Thank you.

Alternative B:

I have just learned that George Herbert has just been transferred by his company to Chicago and will be servicing your region.

I want to introduce you to George and to say that he has my complete confidence, based on years of close association. In my opinion he is one of the most knowledgeable men in our field.

I know you will enjoy getting to know George.

Alternative C:

This is a personal letter of introduction for Heloise Jenkins, who is a recent graduate of Wellesley. She is seeking employment in your area, and I would appreciate it if you could speak to her about opportunities there.

Notwithstanding the fact that she is my wife's niece, Heloise has a superior record from college and shows every promise of developing into an asset for whoever hires her.

Thank you for your consideration.

16

PART OF THE PROFESSION: LETTERS ABOUT PROFESSIONAL ACTIVITIES

Participation in a professional organization is typical of many businesspeople, and as executives approach the highest rungs of their professions the demands on their time and talents from such organizations will increase. The following examples show how to write the proper letter in these situations. Clarity and firmness are the hallmarks of these kinds of letters, as the models demonstrate.

Program Arrangements

AMERICAN MANUFACTURING, INC.
56 TOTENBURG AVENUE
WADLEY, NJ

August 15, 19—

Mr. Jorge H. Jenkins
ABC Corporation
45 Benson Drive
Newburgh, PA

Dear Mr. Jenkins:

The upcoming annual meeting of the National Circuitry Manufacturers Association in Portland on October 25-30, will feature a session on integrated chip making.

The Program Committee would like you to appear as part of a panel discussion that will cap off the session.

The panel will be comprised of six manufacturers and six users with the general topic to be discussed from individual viewpoints.

Because of your long experience in the field, we think you could make a good contribution to the panel.

Please let me know if you are willing to take part.

Yours truly,

Tracy Roberts
Program Chair

Tips and Comments:

Annual meetings and programs are the lifeblood of many professional associations, and it is frequently the duty of association leaders to put together program sessions. This sample asks for participation in the meeting and outlines briefly the scope of the session and the planners' hopes for its content.

Alternative A:

The Association hopes that you will agree to present a paper on management of scarce resources at the next meeting. Your comments to several members of the program board were very stimulating, and we'd like you to share them with the full membership.

The session we have in mind would be at 10:00 A.M. on Monday morning, just before the plenary meeting. We have tentatively scheduled an hour for your presentation.

Please let me know right away if you can take on the assignment.

Alternative B:

Your slide presentation at the regional meeting was impressive and well received.

Will you be able to give it again at the full NMA meeting in June? I have suggested this to the program committee and they have asked me to inquire.

We have a spot open on the program for Tuesday afternoon.

Let me know, and I'll send you more details.

Alternative C:

In putting together our program for the forthcoming annual session in Las Vegas, we have decided to concentrate on the theme, "Ideas for Tomorrow."

In this regard, we would like your company to present the same show you did last August in Tampa.

I assume this will be no problem, since the presentation is ready to go.

Meeting Arrangements

DENVER ASSOCIATES
1942 56TH AVENUE
BENTONVILLE, GA

November 4, 19—

Ms. Laura Black
Runnymede Agency
45 Florence Place
Bentonville, GA

Dear Laura:

Thank you for volunteering to help out with the arrangements for the next Womens' Business Seminar. The program committee last year decided to make this particular meeting the special focus of efforts to attract new members, so you are doing good work.

I have been in contact with Phyllis Glazer, the speaker, and am enclosing the details of her itinerary while in Bentonville.

I will rely on you to meet her at the airport and see that she gets to the hotel in good order. There should be at least an hour and a half between her arrival downtown and the beginning of the seminar.

If you need any more information, please give me a call.

Sincerely,

Grace Balch
Chair, Womens' Business Seminars

Tips and Comment:

One of the obligations of leadership in a professional association is to spend a good deal of time and energy in handling association affairs. While the phone is a time-saver, it is often a good idea to make arrangements for formal meetings by letter, thus providing everyone a record of what to do and when to do it.

Alternative A:

This is to confirm our agreement for use of the ballroom next Wednesday for a meeting of the Associated Designers' Club.

As we discussed, we will need a bar open at least a hour before the scheduled meeting time of 7:00 P.M. The dinner will be served at 8:30 P.M.

Thanks for your help.

Alternative B:

Thanks for taking on the assignment of speaking to our next meeting on your favorite topic, statistical process control.

The club members are looking forward to hearing your discussion, since almost all of them have some involvement in manufacturing.

As you well know, SPC is the latest thing to hit the industry.

I'll pick you up at your office at 11:45 A.M. on May 12.

Alternative C:

Please make certain that you have the printed materials ready by noon on May 19. I will bring all the other material with me to the meeting room, and we can correlate everything then and there.

It is really a big help to have you take responsibility for this part of the meeting.

Thanks again.

Invitation to Committee Membership

FINANCIAL COUNSELING, INC.
222 WEST REED AVENUE
WALLACE, AZ

December 5, 19—

Mr. Thomas Gonzales
President
Advice Unlimited, Inc.
345 Davis Drive
Sacramento, CA

Dear Tom:

As the newly appointed chair of the Program Committee, I am recruiting people to serve during the coming year.

I hope you will agree to be one of the five members of the committee and help us plan the meeting scheduled for September in Wallace.

This will be a big job, so there is no use telling you it is just an honorary position. We intend to work hard to make this the best meeting program ever.

Right now I plan at least four meetings, beginning next month.

Each committee meeting will take at least two days, so you should be ready to commit this time.

Your experience and wide acquaintances throughout the financial planning industry and the Association will be invaluable, and I hope you will say "yes."

Please let me know as soon as possible.

Sincerely,

Wade F. Longworthy
Program Chair

Tips and Comments:

Professional associations typically conduct most of their work through volunteer committees made up of members who donate their time and energies. A letter asking a member to serve on a committee must be both an informational message and a recruiting tool. The example here states the time requirements and makes it clear that the recipient of the letter will be a valued member of a working committee.

Alternative A:

I am asking you to serve on the Nominating Committee for the Annual Meeting.

As you know, this is an important post, since the Nominating Committee selects the slate of potential officers for the next two years.

You have been around the Association in key spots for a long time and have a good notion of who is capable, so your help will assure we get a good set of nominations.

Please let me know if you will serve.

Alternative B:

The Executive Council of the Association has set up a special committee to work on a revision of the by-laws, and I would like you to serve as chair.

I know this is a big responsibility and it will take a lot of time to do the job properly, but we can think of no one better qualified than you.

The committee is charged to examine the current by-laws and make any changes it sees fit.

Alternative C:

I have been given the task of staffing the Rules Committee for next year, and my first act is to ask you to be a member.

This is not one of the more glamorous appointments in the Association, but it is an important one. We will be reviewing the rules by which the Association is governed, which may affect the immediate future of the group.

I'd like to have our first meeting in May in Chicago. Please let me know if you can join us.

Accepting Committee Nomination

ADVICE UNLIMITED, INC.
345 DAVIS DRIVE
SACRAMENTO, CA

December 10, 19—

Mr. Wade F. Longworthy
Financial Counseling, Inc.
222 West Reed Avenue
Wallace, AZ

Dear Wade:

Thanks for the invitation to the Program Committee.

I'll be pleased to serve, and I look forward to the chance to help mold the meeting for next year.

I assume that we should have a theme, and I'd like to suggest "Cutting Through the Bull," as a general approach to the program.

I know this is a little drastic (maybe we can find a softer way of putting it), but it is something that we desperately need to consider if the industry is going to thrive.

Let me know when the first meeting is scheduled.

Truly yours,

Tom

Tips and Comment:

Accepting a committee membership is simple and clear cut. The affirmative answer may be amplified with ideas or suggestions for the work of the committee, as in this sample letter. The logistics of meeting times and places should be seen to in such letters, so there are no surprises as the work unfolds.

Alternative A:

I'll be happy to serve as a member of the Nominating Committee.

I already have several good candidates in mind, and I'll think of more over the coming weeks.

When do we need to get together? My schedule for the next six months is tight, so I'll need to know soon.

Alternative B:

I know that revising the by-laws is going to be a tough job, but I am willing to help out.

The biggest consideration will be to come to an agreement on what should stay and what should be changed, so I suggest we do some preliminary study before meeting.

Let me know what you think.

Alternative C:

Somebody has to do the foot-slogging soldier work for the Association, and it might as well be us.

I'll serve on the Rules Committee as you requested.

What dates in May did you have in mind?

Declining Committee Nomination

TROWBRIDGE COMPANIES
89 OWENBORO ROAD
NEW BERNSTADT, TN

January 23, 19—

Mr. Lawrence C. Hancher
President
National Association of Importers
222 Fourth Avenue, NW
Washington, DC

Dear Larry:

Thanks for the invitation to serve on the Executive Committee. I know how important these spots are, and I'm flattered to have been asked.

However, we are in the midst of a restructuring and reorganization program right now that will take all of my time for at least the next three months.

As much as I would like to help, it is not possible to spend any time or energy away from the office.

Please give my regrets to the staff.

Yours truly,

Samuel Johnson
Executive Vice-President

Tips and Comment:

A polite letter declining a committee appointment should be direct in tone. If possible, explain briefly the reasons why the appointment must be turned down, and try to leave avenues open for the future.

Alternative A:

I'm sorry to have to decline the chance to serve on this year's Nominating Committee.

The work of the Association is important to me and has meant a great deal in the past, but I am absolutely committed to a major project here that will consume all of my time for at least another six months.

Please think of me again.

Alternative B:

I must respectfully decline the nomination to the Planning Committee.

As much as I would like to help you, it will be impossible to get away for the committee meetings.

I think you will be better served to ask someone less occupied.

Alternative C:

After giving this a lot of thought, I am afraid I must turn you down.

I have spent many years working on Association committees, and I think at this stage I need to start to wind down my involvement.

I hope you understand.

Officer Nomination

AMERICAN ENTERPRISES, INC.
23 PLACER STREET
SAN FELIPE, CA

August 12, 19—

Mr. David F. McRee
President
Allied-Techno, Inc.
147 Fifth Avenue
Chicago, IL

Dear David:

It is my pleasure to let you know that the Association's Nominating Committee would like to place your name on the ballot for the office of vice-president.

As you know, the vice-president automatically succeeds to the presidency the following year.

Your service to the Association and your place in the industry make you an obvious choice.

Please let me know as soon as possible if you will accept the nomination.

The election of officers will take place at the Annual Meeting in Dallas in November.

Truly yours,

John J. Epting

Tips and Comment:

It is both courteous and practical to inform candidates for office that they have been nominated. In fact, it is usually necessary to ask if they will serve if elected, as in the case of this sample letter. The writing of such a letter is not complex, but be certain to state all the necessary facts and use some flattery if needed to convince the nominee.

Alternative A:

After meeting last week in Houston, the Nominating Committee selected a slate of official candidates for Association offices.

Your name appears as a candidate for treasurer.

If you will accept the nomination (to be officially voted on in May), please let me know immediately.

Alternative B:

Harvey and I got together last week to select candidates for the official balloting for officers.

We would like you to stand for secretary, based on your enthusiasm for the work of the Association.

As you know, there is always the chance of a nomination from the floor and a genuine fight for the office, but usually the official candidate is selected without much fuss.

Call me if you will accept the nomination.

Alternative C:

This is to let you know that the outgoing officers of the Association, who act as a nominating committee, have put forth your name for the next president.

Before we go ahead and print up the meeting program for Denver, we'd like to know if you will agree to serve if elected.

Please call me.

Accepting Officer Nomination

ALLIED-TECHNO, INC.
147 FIFTH AVENUE
CHICAGO, IL

August 14, 19—

Mr. John J. Epting
Chief Executive Officer
American Enterprises, Inc.
23 Placer Street
San Felipe, CA

Dear John:

I am pleased to accept the nomination to the vice-presidency of the Association.

This is a very flattering gesture by the committee, and I will try hard to live up to its confidence in me if elected.

Let me know if there is anything else I should do at this stage. If not, I'll look forward to the Dallas meeting.

Sincerely,

David F. McRee
President

Tips and Comment:

Unless there are unusual circumstances, a letter accepting a nomination to office in an association may be brief. The main point is to give assent and express suitable sentiments about the honor.

Alternative A:

I am flattered to have been nominated for the office of treasurer, and I accept willingly

Please give my thanks to the other members of the committee.

Alternative B:

I'm delighted to accept the nomination for secretary.

As you said, there are sometimes nominations from the floor, but I haven't heard any inkling of such for this year.

I'll stay in touch as the meeting time draws closer.

Alternative C:

What an honor to be nominated for the presidency!

I will, of course, accept and look forward to the meeting in Denver.

Declining Officer Nomination

FIRST NATIONAL BANK
BANK PLAZA
MOUNTAIN GROVE, MT

June 9, 19—

Mr. James Freehold
Director
Professional Bankers Association
33 West Randolph
Missoula, MT

Dear Mr. Freehold:

Thank you for the offer to nominate me as president of the Western Division of the Professional Bankers Association.

It is indeed an honor, but I must respectfully decline.

I already have more civic and professional responsibilities than time to meet them. As much as I would enjoy the work with the association, it is just not in the best interests of my position here at the bank or of my family.

Thanks for considering me.

Truly yours,

Lance N. Conyers
President

Tips and Comments:

A turn-down for office in a professional association should be sincere but firm. Let the association know you are pleased to have been considered and state your reasons for the refusal. There is no need for elaboration if you do not feel it necessary to leave a door open for future consideration.

Alternative A:

It was a great honor to learn you want to put my name in for the vice-president's position, but I don't think it a good idea at this juncture.

As you may not have known, my wife and I have just adopted a baby girl, and the new parental responsibilities are absorbing all my time and energy outside the office.

Please continue to think of me in the future, however.

Alternative B:

I'm sorry to have to turn down the chance to serve the Association.

My work with you in the past few years has meant much, but I am now making a mid-course correction in my career and planning to leave the field entirely.

Please give my best to the committee.

Alternative C:

It was good of you to think of me, but I must decline.

My full-time work here makes it impossible to spare the time for outside activities.

Professional Award Nomination

UNITED INDUSTRIES, INC.
23 WESTERN AVENUE
CHICAGO, IL

June 12, 19—

Mr. Edward F. Greiner
Executive Director
Association of Allied Industries
23 Roamer Road
Indianapolis, IN

Dear Mr. Greiner:

I want to nominate James V. Balankamp for this year's Outstanding Industrialist Award.

Jim is Executive Vice-President of United Industries and holds responsibility for day-to-day operations for the entire corporation.

He has been in this position for fifteen years, during which the company has become the leader in the field, with more than a 20 percent market share.

Moreover, Jim has been active in the AAI since 19—, serving as chairman of the membership committee twice.

He is well-known and well-liked by his colleagues all over the country.

I'm enclosing a detailed history of Jim's career and his involvement in professional affairs.

Please let me know if I can supply more details or additional information.

Truly yours,

Harold T. Young
Chair

Tips and Comment:

Most professional associations hand out honors and awards to outstanding members. A letter of nomination for such an award should be both enthusiastic and informative. Give the basic outline of the nominee's career and state your reasons for the nomination. The letter should be backed up with more detailed information and perhaps further references.

Alternative A:

In response to the committee's call for nominations, I am submitting the name of Jane Francis for the annual Contractor of the Year award.

Jane has worked long and hard for the association, and I believe she should be granted this honor. She has served on at least three committees and held office as treasurer.

Her own professional record is sterling: she began as an administrative assistant and is now the president of her own company.

Few people in our industry have more to recommend them.

Alternative B:

I am nominating Henry Trent for Realtor of the Year honors.

Henry has consistently been a million-dollar producer, and he is one of the spark plugs of our local Board of Realtors.

I'm including his résumé and a clipping from the local paper that summarizes his career.

Alternative C:

I think it is time we recognized Jim Kerns for his work in the Association.

Jim is due to retire in a couple of years, and we should give him an honor before that takes place. His work both in the profession and in our association will be sorely missed.

For the last ten years Jim has served in one or another of the major association offices and is always available for any assignment.

Accepting Membership in an Association

LEONARD INDUSTRIES, INCORPORATED
21 OVERLOOK DRIVE
WESTCHESTER, IA

May 5, 19—

Ms. Juanita Stubbins
Association of Electrical Engineers
444 Fifth Avenue
New York, NY

Dear Ms. Stubbins:

It is with great pleasure that I accept the invitation to join AEE. The Association has proved itself to be one of the foremost organizations in the country advocating for electrical engineers in the industrial setting.
I hope to be able to contribute to the activities and the future of AEE.
Please let me know if I can be of immediate service.

Truly yours,

Jane M. Fenster
Vice-President

Tips and Comment:

Accepting membership in a professional association calls only for a concise letter, confirming the situation. If the person is willing to take on responsibilities within the organization, this might be a good time to say so.

Alternative A:

I'm happy to respond to your query about the Engineer's Club. I have thought often in the past of joining, but for no good reasons have put it off.

I'd be pleased to submit an application now, particularly since you have shown so much interest in having me become part of the organization.

Let me know what I should do.

Alternative B:

It is indeed gratifying to learn of my election to the Chamber of Associated Deputies. This is a great honor and one that I deeply appreciate.

If I can do anything to assist the group, please let me know.

Alternative C:

What a pleasant surprise to open the mail and find your invitation to become a member. I know how much you have enjoyed your association with the group, and I'm certain I will also.

Of course, I accept.

Thanks, and I'll look forward to my first meeting.

Resignation Association

JOHN B. NUTTING
23 DANNING AVENUE
WESTBROOK, IN

March 23, 19—

Mr. Kenneth Illford
Director
National Association of Engineers
22 North Drive
Silver Spring, MD

Dear Mr. Illford:

This is to inform you that I am resigning from the National Association of Engineers and do not wish to renew either my membership or the subscription to the journal.

I have withdrawn from the practice of engineering in order to pursue other interests.

Thanks for your help in this matter.

Sincerely,

John B. Nutting

Tips and Comment:

As with all letters of resignation, in the case of withdrawing from a trade association the message should be delivered directly. Stating the reasons for the resignation is optional.

Alternative A:

This is my resignation from the Association of Managers.

I am not happy with the service provided and think my money could better be spent elsewhere.

Kindly remove my name from your mailing list.

Alternative B:

I am afraid that I must withdraw membership from the Conference. I am moving to the Northeast within the month and will no longer be in contact with the group.

I have enjoyed the association however, and wish you well in the future.

Alternative C:

Please take me off your membership rolls and stop sending me dues notices. I no longer have any desire to be a member of the Association.

Cooperation with Another Association

T&W INDUSTRIES, INC.
12 WEST ROVER STREET
CLEVELAND, OH

June 5, 19—

Mr. John G. Frenning
President
Allied Technologies, Inc.
Kammerston Road
Fayetteville, AR

Dear Mr. Frenning:

I am writing on behalf of the American Association of Industrial Manufacturers, of which I am currently president, to ask whether the National
Federation of Widget Makers would be interested in holding a joint meeting in Washington sometime this fall.

My association has voted to make a maximum effort to push through SB
123 during the next session, and it appears that the Federation might also
be interested in the goal.

If so, I think we could make a stronger appeal to the Senate if we presented
a united front. The meeting would be to plan and approve our lobbying
efforts.

Please let me know if you think this a wise course.

Truly yours,

Thomas Manning
CEO

Tips and Comments:

This sample letter broaches a cooperative effort between two distinct but related professional associations. It goes right to the point and makes a case for cooperation on a topic of considerable interest to both groups. The writer has taken a confident tone that assumes both professional courtesy and common sense.

Alternative A:

Since both NASC and NAMM have voted to approve the joint statement on accounting rules, it appears to me that we should explore the possibility of making a dual public announcement.

I think adding the prestige of both groups to the announcement would get us wider attention and better coverage.

If you agree, please call me as soon as possible.

Alternative B:

This is to solicit the cooperation of the Association of Retail Owners in the trade fair to be sponsored by the Merchants Association in Chicago next year.

We think this will prove to be a major opportunity to open new markets, and we'd like to include your members.

Please sound out your governing board and let me know if you are interested.

Alternative C:

A recent study by our staff in Washington shows that the number of regulatory rulings by the EPA has increased steadily over the last six months.

Have you any analysis of this trend from your people in New York?

I'd be happy to share information on this.

Professional Certification

ACE ENGINEERING, INC.
23 FERN STREET
OKLAHOMA CITY, OK

June 12, 19—

Mr. Harold J. Lewis
Lewis Engineering, Inc.
12 Davidson Drive
Dallas, TX

Dear Harold:

Enclosed is my most recent draft of the "Advanced Engineer Standards."

As the committee suggested at the meeting last month, I have changed the section on CAD to reflect the most recent trends in that area. Jane Peters was a great help in this, since she is on top of developments.

If we can move this through the review and editing procedures within the next six weeks, I think we can have it ready for a vote of the full membership of the Association in September.

As you know, we want to get all these requirements in place by the new year so we can begin certification for Advanced Engineer status.

Let me know as soon as possible if you have any suggestions.

Truly yours,

George

Tips and Comment:

One of the responsibilities accepted by members of professional associations is to set standards for certification of professionals. Associations play a vital role in putting the public at ease about the qualifications of their members, and they rely on established practitioners to provide the precise knowledge needed to set certification standards.

Alternative A:

I am happy to let you know that I am appointing you to the State Board of Watchmakers as the Association's representative.

As you know from your participation in last year's review, the Association is responsible for helping the State Board to set standards for licensing watchmakers in the state.

We hope to upgrade the standards for watchmakers over the next four years, so please keep in touch with the office.

Alternative B:

I am writing to request your help in putting together a set of quality standards for the new Real Estate Appraiser designation in the state of Alabama.

Since the state board is moving to establish a formal certification of appraisers, it is up to the Association to make its influence and experience felt.

Let's try to get together next week to begin.

Alternative C:

Thanks for the report on the last certification meeting. I was happy to see that the rate of certification has improved, and I judge that to be the result of the Association's new education program.

I assume you have been following the debate in the legislature over removing the state's role in certification. This is a dangerous situation for us, and we need to keep up the pressure in the capitol.

I'll let you know when we plan our next visit to the Hill.

17

GREAT LETTERS FROM THE PAST

This final chapter presents actual letters from the past, most by subsequently famous people, which give the modern business executive some insight into the key elements of great letter writing.

A Military Engineer Successfully Applies for a Job

* * *

Milan, 1482

To Ludovico Sforza

Having, most illustrious lord, seen and considered the experiments of all those who pose as masters in the art of inventing instruments of war, and finding that their inventions differ in no way from those in common use, I am emboldened, without prejudice to anyone, to solicit an appointment of acquainting your Excellency with certain of my secrets.

I can construct bridges which are very light and strong and very portable, with which to pursue and defeat the enemy; and others more solid, which resist fire or assault, yet are easily removed and placed in position; and I can also burn and destroy those of the enemy.

In case of siege I can cut off water from the trenches and make pontoons and scaling ladders and other similar contrivances.

If by reason of the elevation or the strength of its position a place cannot be bombarded, I can demolish every fortress if its foundations have not been set on stone.

I can also make a kind of cannon which is light and easy of transport, with which to hurl small stones like hail, and of which the smoke causes great terror to the enemy, so that they suffer heavy loss and confusion.

And if the fight should take place on the sea I can construct many engines most suitable either for attack or defense and ships which can resist the fire of the heaviest cannon, and powders or weapons.

In time of peace, I believe that I can give you as complete satisfaction as anyone else in the construction of buildings both public and private, and in conducting water from one place to another.

I can further execute sculpture in marble, bronze, or clay, also in painting I can do as much as anyone else, whoever he may be....

Leonardo da Vince

* * *

This and the following letters are from *A Treasury of the World's Great Letters* Max L. Schuster. Simon & Schuster.

A Business Proposal

Comment: Anne Becu, who called herself "Rancon" at the time of writing this letter, eventually took the name Madame Du Barry and became the most famous courtesan of eighteenth-century France and a glittering ornament of the last days before the Revolution. Born in 1746, she was working as a salesgirl in a Parisian millinery shop when she wrote this proposal to an early admirer. Later, she became the mistress of the Comte Du Barry and eventually of King Louis XV. She died by the guillotine in 1793.

* * *

Paris

April 6, 1761

Dear M. DuVal:

Yes, my dear friend, I have told you, and repeat it: I love you dearly. You certainly said the same thing to me, but on your side it is only impetuosity; directly after the first enjoyment you would think of me no more. I begin to know the world. I will tell you what I suggest, now: pay attention.

I don't want to remain a shopgirl, but a little more my own mistress, and would therefore like to find someone to keep me. If I did not love you, I would try to get money from you; I would say to you, You shall begin by renting a room for me and furnishing it; only as you told me that you were not rich, you can take me to your own place. It will not cost you any more rent, not more for your table and the rest of your housekeeping.

To keep me and my headdress will be the only expense, and for those give me one hundred livres a month, and that will include everything.

Thus we could both live happily, and you would never again have to complain about my refusal.

If you love me, accept this proposal; but if you do not love me, then let each of us try our luck elsewhere. Good-bye, I embrace you heartily.

Ranco

* * *

An Unsuccessful Application For Employment

Comment: Although posterity recognizes Franz Schubert as a great composer, his fortunes were bleak during his own lifetime. He lived in constant poverty and was never lucky in finding a patron or a lasting position. None of his troubles prevented an astonishing flow of music from his pen, however. In 1826, two years before his death at age 31, he conducted a desperate letter-writing campaign to find a permanent job. This letter, which gives Schubert's résumé, was addressed to the Austrian Emperor, Franz II, but apparently was never answered.

※ ※ ※

Vienna, 1826

Your Majesty!
Most gracious Emperor!

With the deepest submission the undersigned humbly begs Your Majesty graciously to bestow upon him the vacant position of Vice-Kapellmeister to the Court, and supports his application with the following qualifications:

(1) The undersigned was born in Vienna, is the son of a schoolteacher, and is 29 years of age.

(2) He enjoyed the privilege of being for five years a Court Chorister at the Imperial and Royal College School.

(3) He received a complete course of instruction in composition from the late Chief Kapellmeister to the Court, Herr Anton Salieri, and is fully qualified, therefore, to fill any post as Kapellmeister.

(4) His name is well known, not only in Vienna but throughout Germany, as a composer of songs and instrumental music.

(5) He has also written and arranged five Masses for both smaller and larger orchestras, and these have already been performed in various churches in Vienna.

(6) Finally, he is at present time without employment, and hopes in the security of a permanent position to be able to realize at last those high musical aspirations which he has ever kept before him.

Should Your Majesty be graciously pleased to grant this request, the undersigned would strive to the utmost to give full satisfaction.

Your Majesty's most obedient humble servant,

Franz Schubert

※ ※ ※

Turning Down A Relative's Request For A Loan

✳ ✳ ✳

Dec. 24th, 1848

Dear Johnston:

Your request for eighty dollars, I do not think it best to comply with now. At the various times when I have helped you a little, you have said to me, "We can get along very well now," but in a very short time I find you in the same difficulty again. Now this can only happen by some defect in your conduct. What that defect is, I think I know. You are not *lazy*, and still you are an *idler*. I doubt whether since I saw you, you have done a good whole day's work, in any one day....

This habit of uselessly wasting time, is the whole difficulty; it is vastly important to you, and still more so to your children, that you should break this habit....

You are now in need of some ready money; and what I propose is, that you shall go to work, "tooth and nail," for somebody who will give you money for it.

Let father and your boys take care of things at home...and you go to work for the best money wages, or in discharge of any debt you owe, that you can get. And to secure you a fair reward for your labor, I now promise you that for every dollar you will, between this and the first of May, get for your own labor...I will then give you one other dollar.

Now if you will do this, you will soon be out of debt, and what is better, you will have a habit that will keep you from getting in debt again. But if I should clear you out, next year you will be just as deep in as ever. You say you would give your place in Heaven for $70 or $80. Then you value your place in Heaven very cheaply, for I am sure you can with the offer I make you get the seventy or eighty dollars for four or five months' work....

You have always been kind to me, and I do not now mean to be unkind to you. On the contrary, if you will but follow my advice, you will find it worth more than eight times eighty dollars to you.

Affectionately,

Your brother,

A. Lincoln

✳ ✳ ✳

Accepting A Government Appointment

Comment: In the 1800s, the job of small-town postmaster was usually regarded as a plum, and appointments seldom went to anyone who was not an ardent supporter of the national political party in power. Bill Nye, at the time an obscure newspaper editor and later to become one of the nation's most popular satirists, took his appointment less than seriously, however.

⁂

Office of the *Daily Boomerang*
Laramie City, Wy.

August 9, 1882

Postmaster Gen. Frank Hatton
Washington, D.C.

My Dear General:

I have received by telegraph the news of my nomination by the President and my confirmation by the Senate, as postmaster at Laramie, and wish to extend my thanks for the same.

I have ordered an entirely new set of boxes and post office outfit, including new corrugated cuspidors for the lady clerks.

I look upon the appointment, myself, as a great triumph of eternal truth over error and wrong. It is one of the epochs, I may say, in the Nation's onward march toward political purity and perfection. I do not know when I have noticed any stride in the affairs of state which so thoroughly impressed me with its wisdom.

Now that we are co-workers in the same department, I trust that you will not feel shy or backward in consulting me at any time relative to matters concerning post office affairs. Be perfectly frank with me, and feel perfectly free to just bring anything of that kind right to me. Do not feel reluctant because I may at times appear haughty and indifferent, cold or reserved. Perhaps you do not think I know the difference between a general delivery window and a three-m quad [a typesetting term], but that is a mistake. My general information is far beyond my years.

With profoundest regard, and a hearty endorsement of the policy of the President and Senate, whatever it may be,

I remain, sincerely yours,

Bill Nye, P.M.

⁂

The Art Of The Deal

Comment: Modern-day entrepreneurs are not the first to wheel and deal. P.T. Barnum was a consummate businessman and showman and ever ready to grab headlines with his proposals. The following was written to Civil War hero and former U.S. President Ulysses S. Grant, who was disastrously in debt following a bank failure. The sums involved were mind-boggling at the time. Grant declined the offer.

* * *

New York, January 12, 1885

To General U.S. Grant,
Twice President of the United States, etc.

Honored Sir: The whole world honors and respects you. All are anxious that you should live happily and free from care. While they admire your manliness in declining the large sum recently tendered you by friends, they still desire to see you achieve financial independence in an honorable manner. Of the unique and valuable trophies with which you have been honored, we all have read, and all have a laudable desire to see these evidences of love and respect bestowed upon you by monarchs, princes and people throughout the globe.

While you would confer a great and enduring favor on your fellow-men and women by permitting them to see these trophies you could also remove existing embarrassments in a most satisfactory and honorable manner. I will give you one hundred thousand dollars cash, besides a proportion of the profits, if I may be permitted to exhibit these relics to a grateful and appreciative public, and I will give satisfactory bonds of half a million dollars for their safe-keeping and return.

I have the honor to be truly your friend and admirer,

P.T. Barnum

* * *

A Letter Of Recommendation

Comment: The authors of this letter of recommendation were well-known at the time as two of the world's foremost scientists. Their strong endorsement of a younger colleague won him a post at the Institute.

⁂ ⁂ ⁂

1911

To: Federal Institute of Technology
    Zurich, Switzerland

Herr Einstein is one of the most original minds that we have ever met. In spite of his youth he already occupies a very honorable position among the foremost savants of his time. What we marvel in him, above all, is the ease with which he adjusts himself to new conceptions and draws all possible deductions from them. He does not cling to classical principles, but sees all conceivable possibilities when he is confronted with a physical problem. In his mind this becomes transformed into an anticipation of new phenomena that may some day be verified in actual experience....The future will give more and more proofs of the merits of Herr Einstein, and the University that succeeds in attaching him to itself may be certain that it will derive honor from its connection with the young master.

Henri Poincaré

Madame Marie Curie

⁂ ⁂ ⁂

MASTER CHECKLIST FOR LETTER WRITING

The following points (listed in alphabetical order) make up a master checklist for the executive letter writer. Compare your letters to the checklist, and you will be assured that you have covered the basics.

1. *Address Form*

Proper address form must be used in business letters. See the charts in Appendix C for the correct forms of address for people with titles or positions, and use them whenever writing to someone in these categories.

Less formal letters also require the proper form of address, however. The rule is to list the name, title, company, street and city address—in that order, each on a separate line. For example:

> Mr. James Keener
> Executive Vice-President
> Hiland Manufacturing Company, Inc.
> 303 West Third Avenue
> Overbrook, NH 03777

When addressing a letter to a woman, use the "Ms." form unless you know for certain that the woman prefers another style:

> Ms. Janice Keener
> Executive Vice-President
> Hiland Manufacturing Company, Inc.
> 303 West Third Avenue
> Overbrook, NH 03777

It is becoming more and more acceptable in business letters to eliminate the *Mr.*, *Mrs.*, *Miss*, or *Ms.* altogether, and to begin with the recipient's first name only.

In general, avoid using abbreviations, except for the name of the state, although abbreviations are acceptable for the outside envelope address. (Postal Service rules for outside addresses are discussed in Appendix B.)

If a title or a company name is unusually long, use two lines, with the second line indented:

> Mr. John Keener
> Chairman of the Board
>   and Chief Operating Officer
> Hiland Manufacturing Company, Inc.
> 303 West Third Avenue
> Overbrook, NH 03777

2. *Complimentary Close*

The complimentary close, which comes after the text of the letter and before the signature, has become almost ritualized and no longer really conveys much genuine meaning. The standard forms now are: "Truly yours," "Yours truly," "Sincerely," or "Sincerely yours." In the case of some high officials, it is still proper to use "Respectfully yours" (these cases are noted in Appendix C).

3. *First Sentence*

Play special attention to the first sentence and try to make it the best one in the entire letter.

The first sentence of a letter is the grabber: it should set the tone and define the purpose of the letter as well as get the reader's attention.

Depending on the subject of the letter and the impact you want to have on the reader, the first sentence may be provocative, factual, challenging, or a statement of a social amenity, but it must be effective and appropriate. The first sentence prepares the reader for the rest of the communication.

Examples:

"I read your editorial of October 29 with increasing dismay and alarm."

"I'm pleased and honored to join the town's citizens who are participating in the mayor's campaign to fight juvenile delinquency through affirmative action."

"You may be able to repair a damaged heart valve with your eyes closed, but how well do you cope with worker unemployment compensation or managing office cash flow?"

"We have been patient in asking for the amount you owe us, but patience has run out."

"We wish to replace our electronic typewriters with a complete word processing system, and we would be interested in getting detailed information."

4. *Format*

The format of a letter should please the eye, and it should mesh with the production requirements of your office. Strive to use a standard format, one of those proven over time to be effective. Be certain the format fits the way you plan to produce it, for example by a word-processing computer that has special spacing requirements. In general, it is best to stick to one of the usual formats (discussed in detail in Appendix B) since the appearance of these formats signals the reader that you are a serious businessperson, ready to do serious business. If you employ an unusual format, be certain you have a good reason, such as a special need to get attention.

5. *Last Sentence*

The final sentence of a letter is nearly as important as the first. The last sentence should reinforce and seal the message you wish to get across to the reader. Make it clear and powerful, leaving no doubt as to what you wanted to communicate. Examples:

"We ask that you correct this mistake as soon as possible."

"Please give all your workers our sincere thanks and appreciation."

"We are happy you have decided to join our organization, and we are confident that both you and the firm will benefit."

"A representative will phone you within the next few days to answer any questions."

"Please let me know what you wish to do."

"Unless otherwise instructed, your proxy will be voted in accordance with the judgment of the proxy holders named by you."

6. *Paragraphs*

The arrangement of your message into paragraphs is important to how the letter is received and understood.

The traditional rule is to organize complete subpoints of your message as individual paragraphs; however, this rule is too vague for many writers to follow effectively. A better guide in letter writing is to keep the paragraphs short so that the reader doesn't get bogged down.

It is even permissible, and perhaps desirable, to make each sentence a separate paragraph, especially if the letter itself is short.

At its best, paragraphing is an art to be mastered. In everyday, practical situations strive for paragraphs that reinforce the clarity and power of your letter.

7. *Salutation*

The form of the salutation depends on the relationship between you and the recipient and on the tone of the letter. If the letter is a piece of formal business correspondence, the salutation should follow the traditional guidelines (discussed in Appendixes B and C). If the letter is informal, more latitude is permissible.

The safest is a simple "Dear" followed by the formal title of the recipient. For example: "Dear Mr. Jones" or "Dear Ms. Smith."

If you know the person well, use a less formal mode, even in a business letter: "Dear Jim" or "Dear Edna," for example.

A significant problem has developed, however, in addressing letters to a company or group that you do not know. In days past, the solution was to make the salutation a simple "Gentlemen." This is no longer standard, since it is likely to be inaccurate. However, no gender-neutral formula for impersonal salutation has yet been devised.

8. *Signature*

Your signature on a business letter consists of your written signature above your typed name and business title, and the name of your division or department, if appropriate. Business titles and degrees follow the typed signature. (See Appendix B for more details.)

For example:

> Paul Stewart, President
>
> Paula Stewart, Ph.D.
>
> James Fall, Director
>
> Jane Fall, CPA

9. *Style*

The style of your letter should reflect your personality. It is no crime to let the reader know that a real person is writing to them. Whether the letter is formal or informal, try to avoid stiffness and stilted language.

Don't hide behind trite phrases you have read elsewhere or try to imitate a style you think might be appropriate but doesn't really express your personality.

Let your personality shine through and your letters will be a pleasure to read.

10. *Tone*

Just as the tone of your voice reflects the mood you are in, the tone of a letter mirrors your attitude toward the reader. If you feel condescending, the tone of the letter will probably sound that way. If you are genuinely friendly, that tone will emerge.

The best tone accurately conveys what you really feel and think, so strive to be sincere and honest in the tone of your letter writing. Anything else results in artificiality and poor communication.

FORM AND MECHANICS OF BUSINESS CORRESPONDENCE

The appearance of a business letter determines much of its effect, and the physical document that arrives in the hands of the reader forms an instant impression for either good or ill.

The image of the writer and impact of the message will depend to a large degree on the visual style, feel, neatness, and format of the letter.

There is no excuse for sloppy-looking letters. In the past, it was a hallmark of serious business to send beautifully typed letters, which indicated the presence of a skilled typist who was able to bring to bear training and experience to produce a perfect text in perfect form. Today, the same effect can be achieved by nearly any business, large or small, through the use of word processors and a little care and attention. In fact, word processing equipment (usually a computer wedded to a printer) is capable of producing an endless stream of letters in perfect form.

By carefully setting up the form and mechanics of correspondence, a business will improve its image and amplify the impact of its messages.

FORM

Good business letters employ conventional forms for a simple reason: to make the message clear. Using an unconventional style will only distract the reader from the all-important message and give a less than desirable impression of the writer.

There are several acceptable format styles from which to choose, but all business letters have basic elements in common:

- company letterhead (usually printed)
- date line
- inside address
- salutation
- body
- close
- signature
- envelope (outside) address.

In some cases, a letter also requires optional elements such as reference lines, attention lines, subject lines, and identification initials.

Company Letterhead

The company letterhead may be plain or fancy, but it is a key element for two reasons. First it gives a graphic impression of the company and the individual sending the letter. It is an official statement about what the company is and how much effort and money it is willing to invest in creating an image of itself.

While there are no hard and fast rules about what makes a good letterhead design, no serious business can do without a well-considered and well-printed official letterhead. The most effective letterheads are employed over a long period of time to establish a firm public image.

The second reason for a printed letterhead is practical: it saves time by giving all the essential data of name, address, and phone number automatically on each letter. The information should include the exact form of the company's name, the street and city mailing address, and phone number or numbers. It is becoming increasingly common to include telex or fax numbers. Some letterheads also have the name and title of the company official or the department, although this is a matter of choice and internal perogative.

If it is temporarily impossible to use a printed letterhead, the best course is to type a similar block of information in letterhead style at the top of the page.

Date Line

Every letter must be dated, and the date usually appears as one of the first elements of the letter. The simplest form of date is the most desirable, giving the month, day, and year in a clear manner. Do not spell out the numbers or use the ordinal form (2nd, 5th). Two styles are acceptable:

> January 2, 19—
>
> 2 January, 19—

Anything else is superfluous and creates confusion.

Inside Address

The inside address is at the top of the page in most styles of business correspondence and includes the individual's name, title, company name, street, city, and state address. It is one of the most formal elements of a letter, and care should be taken to make certain it is correct in all details, including punctuation of the company name.

Each of the elements of the inside address begins with a new line. If the title or name of a company is too long for a single line, then indent when beginning the second continuation line.

Be very careful to reproduce exactly the names, titles, and numbers of the addressee. Note, for example, if a company name uses an ampersand (&) instead of the spelled-out *and* or whether the firm uses the abbreviation *Inc.* Mistakes can be avoided by referring to the addressee's previous correspondence for exact spellings and stylings.

Although abbreviations are correct on the envelope address as a space-saving measure, spell out every option in the inside letter address. The one exception to the preference for spelling out is the name of the state, which should be abbreviated according to the official Postal Service two-letter forms (without periods):

Alabama	AL
Alaska	AK
Arizona	AZ
Arkansas	AR
California	CA
Colorado	CO
Connecticut	CT
Delaware	DE
District of Columbia	DC
Florida	FL
Georgia	GA
Hawaii	HI
Idaho	ID

Illinois	IL
Indiana	IN
Iowa	IA
Kansas	KS
Kentucky	KY
Louisiana	LA
Maine	ME
Maryland	MD
Massachusetts	MA
Michigan	MI
Minnesota	MN
Mississippi	MS
Missouri	MO
Montana	MT
Nebraska	NB
Nevada	NV
New Hampshire	NH
New Jersey	NJ
New Mexico	NM
New York	NY
North Carolina	NC
North Dakota	ND
Ohio	OH
Oklahoma	OK
Oregon	OR
Pennsylvania	PA
Rhode Island	RI
South Carolina	SC
South Dakota	SD
Tennessee	TN
Texas	TX
Utah	UT
Vermont	VT
Virginia	VA
Washington	WA
West Virginia	WV

Wisconsin	WI
Wyoming	WY
American Samoa (no abbrev.)	
Guam	GU
Puerto Rico	PR
Virgin Islands	VI

The Salutation

The salutation is a polite preliminary to the actual message of the letter. It almost always begins with "Dear" and, if possible, includes the name of a specific person. The most conventional and usual form is "Dear Mr. Doe," "Dear Ms. Doe," etc. ("Ms." is discussed in Appendix C.) In business correspondence, the salutation is punctuated with a colon rather than a comma.

If the addressee is not known by name, some neutral form may be used, but this has become complicated by the increased presence of women in the executive workforce. The old styles of "Dear Sir" or "Gentlemen" are no longer appropriate or accurate. However, there is, to date, no acceptable substitute, except the rather lame "Dear Sir or Madam."

The use of titles is illustrated in Appendix C.

The Body

The body of the letter is arranged according to the dictates of whichever style has been selected. Of course, a pleasing arrangement on the page is one of the major goals. (See "Format Style" on page 443.)

The Close

The close is also a polite form, which expresses some degree of social warmth or emotion, even if artificial. In previous days, these closings were often ornate and orotund. In modern business correspondence, the norm is to use simple closings such as "Yours truly" or "Sincerely" with little more ado. (See Appendix C for more discussion.)

The Signature

The signature line is important information, especially if the penmanship of the signer is hard to read. The form should follow the appropriate level of formality and might even be omitted in a letter between close business friends. It is also customary to include the signer's title after the name, although if the printed letterhead has this information, it may be omitted.

Envelope (Outside) Address

The outside address on the mailing envelope must include a return address, which in most business correspondence is presumably accounted for by a printed block in the upper left-hand corner similar to the company letterhead.

The recipient's address should be positioned slightly below the midpoint of the envelope and slightly to the the right (at least one inch from the bottom of the envelope).

The Postal Service regulations call for a strict order of elements in an outside address:

      1. Name of individual addressee

2. Name of company

3. Street number and name *and* suite, apartment, or room number

4. Post office box number

      5. City, state, and Zip Code.

Any extraneous elements, such as attention lines or reference numbers, should be placed above the individual addressee's name.

Technically, the Postal Service prefers either a street address or a post office box number, but it will deliver mail that includes both. However, the specific delivery address given on the next to the last line (the line just before the city, state, and Zip Code) is the official address in the eyes of the Postal Service, and that is where the Service will attempt delivery.

The Postal Service also prefers that addresses be typed in block capital letters with no punctuation, which eases automated sorting of envelopes. And, of course, the Postal Service demands at least the five-digit Zip Code and urges mailers to use the Zip plus 4 version, if possible.

It is permissible to use standard abbreviations for the outside envelope address, since space is limited.

Other Elements

Some letters need additional elements such as reference, attention, or subject lines, which provide specific information to the addressee. These are placed according to the format selected for the letter in general. When a letter is typed by another person, it is also a long-standing custom to include the initials of the typist at the bottom of the letter, although this practice is disappearing rapidly under the impact of word processing machines.

Format Style

There are several common, acceptable format styles for the body of a business letter. The following illustrate the block, semi-block, indented, official, and casual styles. Each has its own specifics, and it matters little which is chosen, except one style should be followed consistently within a single letter. Overall, a style may be selected and installed as the standard, and the word processor programmed to produce the desired style.

Block Style

PRENTICE HALL INC.
ENGLEWOOD CLIFFS, N.J. 07632
Telex No. 13-5423

July 16, 199—

Ms. Sheila Jones
The Modern School for Secretaries
12 Harrington Place
Greenpoint, N.Y.

Dear Ms. Jones:

In reply to your request for examples of current business letter styles, this letter is an example of the block style letter which is the standard at Prentice Hall. We have reproduced it in our Employee Manual so that everyone is familiar with the form and the instructions for its use.

Since Prentice Hall is a leading exponent of modern business methods, they naturally use the most efficient letter form. This style saves time and energy.

As you can see, there are no indentations. Everything, including the date and the complimentary close, begins at the extreme left.

Our dictaphone typists always use this form, unless the dictator instructs otherwise.

Sincerely,

Martha Scott
Correspondence Chief
MS:cf

Block Style with Reference Line

PRENTICE HALL INC.

ENGLEWOOD CLIFFS, N.J. 07632

Telex No. 13-5423

July 16, 199—

Your reference 12:-3:1

Ms. Sheila Jones
The Modern School for Secretaries
12 Harrington Place
Greenpoint, N.Y.

Dear Ms. Jones:

You asked me if there is any one style of setting up a letter that is used more than the others. Probably more business concerns use the block style of letter than any other style, because its marginal uniformity saves time for the typist. This letter is an example of the block style.

As you can see, the inside address is blocked and the paragraph beginnings are aligned with the left margin. Open punctuation is used in the address.

The date and reference lines are flush with the right margin. The date line is two spaces below the letterhead, and the reference line is two spaces below the date line. The complimentary close begins slightly to the right of the center of the page. Both lines of the signature are aligned with the complimentary close.

As the dictator's name is typed in the signature, it is not considered necessary to include his or her initials in the identification line.

Sincerely yours,

Martha Scott
Correspondence Chief
Accounting
Department

cf

Semi-Block Style

PRENTICE HALL INC.

ENGLEWOOD CLIFFS, N.J. 07632

Telex No. 13-5423

July 16, 199—

Ms. Sheila Jones
The Modern School for Secretaries
12 Harrington Place
Greenpoint, New York

Dear Ms. Jones:

Subject: Business Letter Styles

Most companies have a definite preference as to letter style. Many leading business corporations insist that all letters be typed in semi-block style. This style combines an attractive appearance with utility. Private secretaries, who are not usually concerned with mass production of correspondence, favor it.

This style differs from the block form in that the first line of each paragraph is indented five or ten spaces. As in all letters, there is a double space between paragraphs.

The date line is flush with the left margin, two or four spaces below the letterhead. The complimentary close begins slightly to the left of the center of the page. All lines of the signature are aligned with the complimentary close.

Very sincerely yours,

Martha Scott
Correspondence Chief

MS/cf

Indented Style

PRENTICE HALL INC.

ENGLEWOOD CLIFFS, N.J. 07632

Telex No. 13-5423

July 16, 199—

Ms. Sheila Jones,
   The Modern School for Secretaries,
      12 Harrington Place,
         Greenpoint, New York

   Dear Ms. Jones:

   This is an example of the indented style of letter which many conservative organizations still use. The indented style is correct, however, for any type of firm.

   Each line of the address is indented five spaces more than the preceding line. The beginning of each paragraph is indented the same as the third line of the address, which is ten spaces. The complimentary close begins a few spaces to the right of the center of the page, and the lines of the signature are aligned with the complimentary close. Closed punctuation is used in the address but not in the signature.

Very truly yours,

Martha Scott
Correspondence Chief

Ms:cf
Enc.

Official Style

PRENTICE HALL INC.

ENGLEWOOD CLIFFS, N.J. 07632

Telex No. 13-5423

July 16, 199—

Dear Ms. Jones:

Every correspondence manual should include a sample of the official style. It is used by executives and professional individuals when writing personal letters, and it looks very well on the executive-size letterhead.

The structural parts of the letter differ from the standard arrangement only in the position of the inside address. The salutation is placed two to five spaces below the date line, depending upon the length of the letter. It establishes the left margin of the letter. The inside address is written in block form, flush with the left margin, from two to five spaces below the final line of the signature. Open punctuation is used in the address.

The identification line, if used, is placed two spaces below the last line of the address.

Sincerely yours,

Martha Scott
Correspondence Chief

Ms. Sheila Jones
The Modern School for Secretaries
12 Harrington Place
Greenpoint, New York

MS/cf

Casual Style

PRENTICE HALL

ENGLEWOOD CLIFFS, N.J. 07632

Telex No. 13-5423

July 16, 199—

Ms. Sheila Jones
The Modern School for Secretaries
12 Harrington Place
Greenpoint, New York

Dear Ms. Jones:

This is an example of a short letter. The style differs from the previous sample letters in that the lines are double-spaced, and the beginning of each paragraph is indented five or ten spaces.

As you can see, the date is typed in the conventional position, and the complimentary close and the signature below it start a few spaces to the right of the center of the page.

Very truly yours,

Martha Scott
Correspondence Chief

MS:cf

MECHANICS

Word Processing

Word processors have revolutionized the mechanics of business correspondence. Anyone with a word processing system—either a "smart" typewriter or a computer and printer combination—is able to produce perfectly typed and formatted letters with a minimum of effort.

However, great care must be exercised to set up the word processing system so that the final product meets the highest standards. This requires attention to electronic formatting and vigilance.

Most computer word processing systems have their own peculiarities in how the software may be used to manipulate the format of letters. Some, for example, impose restrictions on line spacing within a document. The best idea is to explore fully the possibilities of using the software at hand. The great advantage is that time invested in formatting will serve again and again with little or no further effort. The vision of a benighted typist spending hours redoing letters is gone.

Ironically, the goal of a word processing system is to produce something that looks as if the skilled labor of an accomplished typist had been employed (this is rather like the way furniture makers go to great lengths to make plastic look like wood). Even though the recipient of a business letter these days must know in the fore part of the brain that it came from a computer, the unconscious psychological impact of a perfectly produced letter is still powerful.

Therefore, care should be taken that the printout part of the system really is "letter-quality" (a revealing term used by the manufacturers of word-processing systems). Never send a letter produced on a poor-quality, low-density dot-matrix printer. A daisy-wheel, impact printer is still the standard for high-quality letters, although fewer and fewer offices have such printers, since they are technically very slow. A good 24-pin matrix printer will produce acceptable "letter quality."

The laser printers now appearing in many offices produce the best image of all. In fact, the laser image is technically superior to even the daisy-wheel impact style printer image. It is tempting to use the electronic and graphic tricks available with most laser printers when dealing with letters; however, a business is best advised to leave the fancy typefaces and zippy formats for reports or company newsletters. Even if a system can produce a document with bells and whistles, a conventional document is preferred.

Paper

Not to be overlooked is the matter of choosing the right paper for letters. The usual paper is called "bond," and is a specialized product of the paper industry. In general, business correspondence uses 8½-by-11-inch bond with Number 10 envelopes.

Bond comes in several grades and finishes. The grades are industry standards, although they are so arcane as to make them difficult to understand. Basically, the higher the cotton content of a bond, the higher the grade. Twenty-five percent cotton bond, for example, has that percentage of cotton fiber and correspondingly less wood pulp. The higher cotton content usually gives a better feel and appearance to the paper. Weight is also a consideration. Bond is usually sold in 20 pound and 24 pound weights, with the higher having more thickness and feeling more substantial (in theory at least).

In practice, the many paper companies make a wide range of special letter bonds with a mind-boggling variety of feel, weight, and color. The best method is to examine samples closely and choose whatever seems most appropriate and pleasing.

A new wrinkle in the already complex business of choosing paper has been introduced by word processing technology. Most office printers use continuous form paper that passes through the machine by means of a tractor feed. Therefore, for greatest efficiency in an office with a high volume of letters, the company letterhead should be available in a continuous form version. Before ordering such continuous form letterhead, check to be certain the perforated edges between the sprocket holes and the actual sheet are smooth and neat when the reproduced letter is separated from the tractor feed.

The ability of a specific letter bond to take printing must also be considered, since most companies will want to have the letterhead printed, sometimes in several colors of ink. And, you should carefully consider the actual color of the paper itself—even "white" paper comes in several shades, running from the blue end of the scale to the beige. Remember that choosing a dark colored letterhead paper will make photocopying difficult and unsightly.

A special note of caution is necessary in choosing letterhead to be used in a laser printer. The extremely high temperatures used by laser technology will melt the raised type lettering popular with some letterhead designers.

Of course, envelopes in the standard Number 10 business correspondence size should be ordered to match the letterhead. Printers or paper companies can supply envelopes in the same paper stock and with the same printed letterhead. Most businesses will also wish to order larger envelopes (9" x 12") and self-sticking mailing labels as well.

FORMS OF ADDRESS

Address forms are very important in business correspondence. Proper forms may seem like only nagging details, but they are part of creating a positive reception for your letter.

As the formality of the relationship between the letter writer and the recipient increases, so does the need to use the proper address form.

Honorifics and titles are meaningful to those who bear them, and in order to get the best possible hearing for letter, it is wise to observe the formalities. On the other hand, in recent decades there has been a tendency in the United States to move in the direction of a little less formality, even in official letters to people who are not personal friends.

In some cases, formality is always advised, no matter what the relationship—if the letter deals with company or public business and is likely to become part of the "official" record, then full formality is in order. For example, even if the writer is a life-long best friend of the President of the United States, an official letter to the nation's Chief Executive should employ official usage.

The following list provides forms of address that are recommended for all impersonal, formal correspondence. The list is divided into these categories:

- United States Government
- United States State and Local Government
- United States Judiciary

- United States Diplomatic Corps
- Foreign Officials
- United States Military
    —Army
    —Navy
    —Other branches
    —Other ranks
- Clergy and Religious Leaders
    —Protestant
    —Roman Catholic
    —Jewish
- College and University
- United Nations
- Organization of American States
- Canadian Officials
- British Peerage, Baronets, and Knights
- British Government
- Miscellaneous

Included in each case are the proper forms for the inside and envelope address, and the proper salutations. Since there are often acceptable degrees of formality even in official correspondence, both formal and informal salutations are sometimes listed (the most formal given first). In general, the most formal salutation is "Sir" or "Madam," with the "Dear Mr.____" and "Dear Ms.____" suggested as less formal. The old form of "My Dear____" is no longer in wide use.

At one time, it was a simple matter to assume all officials would be male, but this is clearly no longer the case, so forms of address for women must be taken into account. As a rule, in the United States the use of "Ms." is appropriate in most cases, unless the recipient has made known a preference to the contrary for "Mrs." or "Miss." The old style of addressing a woman by the married form of her husband's name ("Mrs. Tom____") is no longer in favor except among the most antiquarian letter writers. The routine use of "Ms." has the advantage of covering up the problem of guessing whether the woman addressed is married or single. In the case of some honorifics, the problem is not so easily solved. The traditional use of "Esq." after lawyers' names, for example, is still a matter of debate when the attorney is a woman. "Esquire" is a medieval title that was exclusively masculine, but many women lawyers insist it is appropriate today no matter what the sex of the person addressed.

In the following examples, male and female recipients alternate, with both forms given in the salutations.

While there is considerable variation in the proper salutation, the customary closing is usually "Truly yours" or "Sincerely yours," with the latter considered slightly less formal.

U.S. GOVERNMENT OFFICIALS

The President

Address:	The President The White House Washington, DC
Salutation:	Mr. President Dear Mr. President
Close:	Respectfully yours

Former President

Address:	The Honorable John R. Doe (local address)
Salutation:	Dear Mr. Doe
Close:	Respectfully yours

Vice President

Address:	The Vice President of the United States United States Senate Washington, DC
Salutation:	Dear Mr. Vice President
Close:	Respectfully yours

First Lady

Address: Mrs. Jane R. Doe
                    The White House   Washington, DC

Salutation: Dear Mrs. Doe

Close: Truly yours

Speaker of the House

Address: The Honorable John R. Doe
                    Speaker of the House of Representatives
                    Washington, DC

Salutation: Sir or Madam
                    Dear Mr. or Ms. Speaker

Close: Truly yours

Former Speaker of the House

Address: The Honorable John R. Doe
                    (address)

Salutation: Sir or Madam
                    Dear Mr. or Ms. Doe

Close: Sincerely yours

Cabinet Officer

Address: The Honorable John R. Doe
                    Secretary of State
                    Washington, DC

Salutation: Sir or Madam
                    Dear Secretary; Dear Madam Secretary

Close: Truly yours

Attorney General

Address: The Honorable John R. Doe
                The Attorney General
                Washington, DC

Salutation: Sir or Madam
                Dear Mr. or Ms. Attorney General

Close: Truly yours

Former Cabinet Officer

Address: The Honorable John R. Doe
                (local address)

Salutation: Dear Sir or Dear Madam
                Dear Mr. or Ms. Doe

Close: Sincerely yours

Postmaster General

Address: The Honorable John R. Doe
                The Postmaster General
                Washington, DC

Salutation: Sir or Madam
                Dear Mr. or Ms. Postmaster General

Close: Truly yours

Under Secretary

Address: The Honorable John R. Doe
                Under Secretary of Labor
                Washington, DC

Salutation: Dear Mr. or Ms. Doe

Close: Truly yours

U.S. Senator

Address: The Honorable Jane R. Doe
                    United States Senate
                    Washington, DC

Salutation: Dear Senator Doe

Close: Truly yours

Former Senator

Address: The Honorable John R. Doe
                    (local address)

Salutation: Dear Senator Doe

Close: Truly yours

Senator Elect

Address: The Honorable John R. Doe
                    Senator Elect
                    (local address)

Salutation: Dear Mr. or Ms. Doe

Close: Truly yours

Committee Chair (Senate)

Address: The Honorable John R. Doe
                    Chairman
                    Committee on Foreign Affairs
                    United States Senate
                    Washington, DC

Salutation: Dear Mr. or Madam Chairman
                    Dear Senator Doe

Close: Truly yours

U.S. Representative

Address: The Honorable Jane R. Doe
                    House of Representatives
                    Washington, DC

Salutation: Dear Representative Doe
                    Dear Ms. or Mr. Doe

Close: Truly yours

Former Representative

Address: The Honorable John R. Doe
                    (local address)

Salutation: Dear Mr. or Ms. Doe

Close: Truly yours

Territorial Delegate

Address: The Honorable John R. Doe
                    Delegate of Puerto Rico
                    Washington, DC

Salutation: Dear Mr. or Ms. Doe

Close: Truly yours

Heads of Independent Federal Offices or Agencies

Address: The Honorable John R. Doe
                    Director, United States Information Agency
                    Washington, DC

Salutation: Dear Mr. or Madam Director
                    Dear Mr. or Ms. Doe

Close: Truly yours

Librarian of Congress

Address: The Honorable Jane R. Doe
                            Librarian of Congress
                            Washington, DC

Salutation: Dear Mr. or Ms. Doe

Close: Truly yours

Other High Officials

Address: Mr. John R. Doe
                            Comptroller General
                            of the United States
                            Washington, DC

Salutation: Dear Mr. or Ms. Doe

Close: Truly yours

Secretary to the President

Address: The Honorable Jane R. Doe
                            Secretary to the President
                            The White House
                            Washington, DC

Salutation: Dear Ms. or Mr. Doe

Close: Truly yours

U.S. STATE AND LOCAL GOVERNMENT OFFICIALS

Governor

Address: The Honorable John R. Doe
                            Governor of New York
                            Albany, NY

Salutation:	Sir or Madam Dear Governor Doe
Close:	Respectfully yours

Lieutenant Governor

Address:	The Honorable Jane R. Doe Lieutenant Governor of Illinois Springfield, IL
Salutation:	Madam or Sir Dear Ms. or Mr. Doe
Close:	Respectfully yours

Secretary of State

Address:	The Honorable John R. Doe Secretary of State of Iowa Des Moines, IA
Salutation:	Mr. or Ms. Secretary
Close:	Truly yours

Attorney General

Address:	The Honorable John R. Doe Attorney General of Ohio Columbus, OH
Salutation:	Mr. or Ms. Attorney General
Close:	Truly yours

President of the Senate

Address:	The Honorable Jane R. Doe President of the Senate of the State of Virginia Richmond, VA

Salutation: Dear Mr. or Ms. Doe

Close: Truly yours

Speaker of the House (lower legislative chamber)

Address: The Honorable John R. Doe
                       Speaker of the Assembly of the
                       State of New York
                       Albany, NY

Salutation: Dear Mr. or Ms. Doe

Close: Sincerely yours

Auditor, Comptroller, or Treasurer

Address: The Honorable Jane R. Doe
                       Auditor of the State of Idaho
                       Boise, ID

Salutation: Dear Ms. or Mr. Doe

Close: Truly yours

State Senator

Address: The Honorable John R. Doe
                       The State Senate
                       Trenton, NJ

Salutation: Dear Senator Doe

Close: Truly yours

State Representative

Address: The Honorable Jane R. Doe
                       House of Representatives
                       Frankfort, KY

Salutation: Dear Ms. or Mr. Doe

Close: Truly yours

District Attorney

Address: The Honorable John R. Doe
                 District Attorney, Taylor County
                 Bedford, IA

Salutation: Dear Mr. or Ms. Doe

Close: Sincerely yours

Mayor of a City

Address: The Honorable Jane R. Doe
                 Mayor of Shelbyville
                 Shelbyville, IN

Salutation: Dear Mayor Doe

Close: Truly yours

President of a Board of Commissioners

Address: The Honorable John R. Doe, President
                 Board of Commissioners
                 City of Buffalo
                 Buffalo, NY

Salutation: Dear Mr. or Ms. Doe

Close: Truly yours

City Attorney

Address: The Honorable Jane R. Doe
                 City Attorney
                 San Francisco, CA

Salutation: Dear Ms. or Mrs. Doe

Close: Truly yours

Alderman or Council Member

Address:	Alderman John R. Doe (Councilman John R. Doe) City Hall Denver, CO
Salutation:	Dear Mr. or Ms. Doe
Close:	Truly yours

U.S. JUDICIARY

Chief Justice of the U.S. Supreme Court

Address:	The Chief Justice of the United States The Supreme Court of the United States Washington, DC
Salutation:	Dear Mr. Chief Justice
Close:	Respectfully yours

Associate Justice of the U.S. Supreme Court

Address:	Mr. Justice John R. Doe (or Ms. Justice Jane R. Doe) The Supreme Court of the United States Washington, DC
Salutation:	Dear Mr. or Ms. Justice
Close:	Respectfully

Retired Justice of the U.S. Supreme Court

Address:	The Honorable John R. Doe (local address)
Salutation:	Dear Justice Doe
Close:	Truly yours

Chief Justice of a State Supreme Court

Address: The Honorable Jane R. Doe
                  Chief Justice of the
                    Supreme Court of Minnesota
                  Minneapolis, MN

Salutation: Dear Mr. or Ms. Chief Justice

Close: Truly yours

Associate Justice of State Supreme Court

Address: The Honorable John R. Doe
                  Associate Justice of the
                    Supreme Court of Minnesota
                  Minneapolis, MN

Salutation: Dear Justice Doe

Close: Truly yours

Presiding Justice

Address: The Honorable Jane R. Doe
                  Presiding Justice, Appellate Division
                    Supreme Court of New York
                  New York, NY

Salutation: Dear Justice Doe

Close: Truly yours

Judge of a Court

Address: The Honorable John R. Doe
                  Judge of the United States District
                    Court for the Southern District of
                  California
                  Los Angeles, CA

Salutation: Dear Judge Doe

Close: Truly yours

Clerk of a Court

Address: John R. Doe, Esq.
                    Clerk of the Superior Court
                    Boston, MA

Salutation: Dear Mr. or Ms. Doe

Close: Sincerely yours

U.S. DIPLOMATIC CORPS

Ambassador

Address: The Honorable John R. Doe
                    American Ambassador
                    London, England
                    (If the ambassador holds a military rank,
                    that may be used as a substitute, e.g.
                    General John R. Doe)

Salutation: Dear Mr. or Madam Ambassador

Close: Truly yours

Minister

Address: The Honorable John R. Doe
                    American Minister
                    Bucharest, Rumania

Salutation: Dear Madam or Mr. Minister

Close: Truly yours

Charge d'Affaires

Address: John R. Doe, Esq.
                    American Chargé d'Affaires
                    (address)

Salutation:	Dear Mr. or Ms. Doe
Close:	Truly yours

Consul General, Consul, Vice-Consul

Address:	Jane R. Doe, Esq. American Consul General Warsaw, Poland
Salutation:	Dear Ms. or Mr. Doe
Close:	Truly yours

High Commissioner

Address:	The Honorable John R. Doe United States High Commissioner to Argentina Buenos Aires, Argentina
Salutation:	Dear Mr. or Ms. Doe
Close:	Truly yours

FOREIGN OFFICIALS

Ambassador to U.S.

Address:	His Excellency, Erik Doe Ambassador of Norway Washington, DC (Custom varies from country to country in the use of additional honorifics, such as titles, special courtesies, etc.)
Salutation:	Dear Mr. or Madam Ambassador
Close:	Respectfully yours

Foreign Minister to the U.S.

Address: The Honorable Georges R. Doe
                      Minister of Mauritania
                      Washington, DC

Salutation: Dear Mr. or Madam, Minister

Close: Respectfully yours

Prime Minister

Address: His Excellency, Jawaharlal Doe
                      Prime Minister of India
                      New Dehli, India

Salutation: Dear Prime Minister

Close: Respectfully yours

President of a Republic

Address: His Excellency, Juan Doe
                      President of the Dominican Republic

Salutation: Dear Mr. or Madam President

Close: Respectfully yours

Premier

Address: His Excellency, Charles Doe
                      Premier of the French Republic
                      Paris, France

Salutation: Dear Mr. or Madam Premier

Close: Respectfully yours

Foreign Chargé d'Affaires

Address: Mr. Jan Gustaf Doe
Chargé d'Affaires of Sweden
Washington, DC

Salutation: Dear Mr. or Ms. Doe

Close: Respectfully yours

U.S. MILITARY

ARMY

General of the Army

Address: General of the Army
John R. Doe, U.S.A.
(local address)

Salutation: Dear General Doe

Close: Truly yours

Other General Officers (Lt. Gen., Major Gen., etc.)

Address: Lieutenant General John R. Doe, U.S.A.
Fort Leavenworth, KS
(The designation *U.S.A.* means Regular Army;
the designation *A.U.S.* means Reserve)

Salutation: Dear General Doe

Close: Truly yours

Other Officers

Address: Colonel John R. Doe, U.S.A.
Fort Dix, NJ
(Substitute correct rank)

Salutation: Dear Colonel Doe

Close: Truly yours

Chief Warrant Officer

Address: Mr. John R. Doe, U.S.A.
                        Fort Dix, NJ

Salutation: Dear Mr. Doe

Close: Truly yours

Chaplain

Address: Chaplain John R. Doe
                        Captain, U.S.A.
                        Fort Sill, OK

Salutation: Dear Chaplain Doe

Close: Sincerely yours

NAVY

Fleet Admiral

Address: Fleet Admiral John R. Doe, U.S.N.
                        Department of the Navy
                        Washington, DC

Salutation: Dear Admiral Doe

Close: Truly yours

Other Flag Officers (Admiral, Vice Admiral, etc.)

Address: Admiral John R. Doe, U.S.N.
                        United States Naval Academy
                        Annapolis, MD
                        (The designation *U.S.N.* means regular
                        service; the designation *U.S.N.R.* means
                        Reserve)

Salutation:	Dear Admiral Doe
Close:	Truly yours

Senior Officers (Commodore, Captain, Commander, Lt. Commander)

Address:	Commodore John R. Doe, U.S.N. U.S.S. Iowa San Diego, CA (Substitute correct rank)
Salutation:	Dear Commodore Doe
Close:	Truly yours

Junior Officers (Lieutenant, Lieutenant J.G., Ensign)

Address:	Lieutenant John R. Doe, U.S.N. U.S.S. Spruance San Diego, CA
Salutation:	Dear Mr. Doe
Close:	Sincerely yours

Chief Warrant Officer, Warrant Officer

Address:	Mr. John R. Doe, U.S.N. U.S.S. Aurora Passcagula, MS
Salutation:	Dear Mr. Doe
Close:	Truly yours

Chaplain

Address:	Chaplain John R. Doe Captain, U.S.N. (address)
Salutation:	Dear Chaplain Doe
Close:	Truly yours

AIR FORCE

Air Force titles are the same as the Army. The designation *U.S.A.F.* is used for regular service, and *A.F.U.S.* for the reserve.

MARINE CORPS

The Marine Corps titles are the same as the Army, except for the top grade, which is Commandant of the Marine Corps. *U.S.M.C.* means regular service; *U.S.M.R.* means reserve.

COAST GUARD

Coast Guard ranks are the same as the Navy, without a Fleet Admiral. *U.S.C.G.* means regular service; *U.S.C.G.R.* means reserve.

OTHER RANKS

Ranks below warrant officer in the armed forces, such as sergeant, petty officer, etc., are addressed by rank and name. For example:

Address:	Chief Petty Officer Jane R. Doe, U.S.N. (local address)
Salutation:	Dear Chief Petty Officer Doe
Close:	Truly yours

CLERGY AND RELIGIOUS LEADERS

PROTESTANT

Anglican Archbishop

Address:	To His Grace The Lord Archbishop of Canterbury Canterbury, England
Salutation:	Dear Archbishop

Close: Respectfully yours

Presiding Bishop of the Episcopal Church in America

Address: The Most Reverend John R. Doe
                       Presiding Bishop
                       (address)

Salutation: Dear Bishop Doe

Close: Respectfully yours

Anglican Bishop

Address: The Right Reverend
                       The Lord Bishop of Salisbury
                       Salisbury, England

Salutation: Dear Bishop

Close: Respectfully

Methodist Bishop

Address: The Reverend John R. Doe
                       Methodist Bishop
                       Phoenix, AZ

Salutation: Dear Bishop Doe

Close: Respectfully

Episcopal Bishop

Address: The Right Reverend John R. Doe
                       Bishop of West New York
                       Buffalo, New York

Salutation: Dear Bishop Doe

Close: Respectfully

Episcopal Archdeacon

Address:	The Venerable John R. Doe Archdeacon of Bethlehem Bethlehem, PA
Address:	Dear Archdeacon
Close:	Respectfully

Episcopal Dean (head of cathedral or seminary)

Address:	The Very Reverend Jane R. Doe Dean of the Cathedral Louisville, KY
Salutation:	Dear Dean Doe
Close:	Truly yours

Episcopal Canon

Address:	The Reverend Canon John R. Doe Cathedral of St. Mark's Minneapolis, MN
Salutation:	Dear Canon Doe
Close:	Truly yours

Episcopal Priest

Address:	The Reverend Jane R. Doe St. Swithin's by the Sea Carmel, CA
Salutation:	Dear Ms. or Mr. Doe
Close:	Truly yours

Protestant Minister

Address:	The Reverend John R. Doe Cavalry Baptist Church Elmyria, OH
Salutation:	Dear Mr. Doe
Close:	Sincerely yours

ROMAN CATHOLIC

The Pope

Address:	His Holiness The Pope Vatican City
Salutation:	Your Holiness
Close:	Respectfully

Apostolic Delegate

Address:	His Excellency, The Most Reverend John R. Doe Apostolic Delegate (address)
Salutation:	Your Excellency
Close:	Respectfully yours

Cardinal

Address:	His Eminence, John Cardinal Doe Archbishop of New York New York, NY
Salutation:	Your Eminence
Close:	Respectfully yours

Archbishop

Address:	The Most Reverend John R. Doe Archbishop of Baltimore Baltimore, MD
Salutation:	Dear Archbishop Doe
Close:	Respectfully

Bishop

Address:	The Most Reverend John R. Doe Bishop of Cincinnati Cincinnati, OH
Salutation:	Dear Bishop Doe
Close:	Respectfully

Abbot

Address:	The Right Reverend John R. Doe Abbot of Westmoreland Abbey Washington, DC
Salutation:	Dear Father Doe
Close:	Respectfully

Canon

Address:	The Reverend John R. Doe (local address)
Salutation:	Dear Canon Doe
Close:	Respectfully

Monsignor

Address:	The Right Reverend Mgsr. John R. Doe (local address) (May be *Very Reverend*, depending on rank)
Salutation:	Dear Monsignor Doe
Close:	Respectfully

Brother

Address:	Brother John R. Doe (local address)
Salutation:	Dear Brother Doe
Close:	Truly yours

Priest

Address:	The Reverend John R. Doe St. Stephen's Church Wadley, AL
Salutation:	Dear Father Doe
Close:	Truly yours

Sister Superior

Address:	The Reverend Sister Superior (abbreviation of order, if used) Convent of the Sacred Heart Sacramento, CA
Salutation:	Dear Sister Superior
Close:	Truly yours

Sister

Address:	Sister Jane Doe Covington Catholic High School Covington, KY
Salutation:	Dear Sister Jane Doe
Close:	Truly yours

JEWISH

Rabbi

Address:	Rabbi John K. Doe (local address)
Salutation:	Dear Rabbi Doe
Close:	Respectfully

COLLEGE AND UNIVERSITY OFFICIALS

President of College or University

Address:	Dr. John R. Doe President, Columbia University New York, NY (If no doctorate, use *Mr.* or *Ms.*) The Very Reverend John R. Doe (If Roman Catholic priest)
Salutation:	Dear Dr. Doe Dear President Doe Dear Father Doe
Close:	Sincerely

Chancellor

Address:

Dr. Jane R. Doe
Chancellor, University of Tennessee
Knoxville, TN

Salutation:

Dear Dr. Doe

Close:

Sincerely

Dean or Assistant Dean

Address:

Dean John R. Doe
School of Law
University of Iowa
Iowa City, IA
or
Dr. John R. Doe
Dean, School of Law

Salutation:

Dear Dean Doe
Dear Dr. Doe

Close:

Truly yours

Professor

Address:

Professor Jane R. Doe
Department of Classics
Swarthmore College
Swarthmore, PA
or
Dr. Jane R. Doe
Professor of Classics

Salutation:

Dear Professor Doe
Dear Dr. Doe

Close:

Truly yours

Associate or Assistant Professor

Address: Dr. John R. Doe
                      Associate Professor
                      Department of History
                      Grinnell College
                      Grinnell, IA
                                or
                      Mr. John R. Doe

Salutation: Dear Dr. Doe
                      Dear Professor Doe

Close: Truly yours

Instructor

Address: Ms. Jane R. Doe
                      Department of Computer Science
                      MacAlaster College
                      St. Paul, MN
                                or
                      Dr. Jane R. Doe

Salutation: Dear Ms. Doe
                      Dear Dr. Doe

Close: Sincerely

UNITED NATIONS

Secretary General

Address: His Excellency, John R. Doe
                      Secretary General of the United Nations
                      New York, NY

Salutation: Dear Mr. Secretary General

Close: Sincerely

Under Secretary

Address:	The Honorable John R. Doe Under Secretary of the United Nations New York, NY
Salutation:	Dear Mr. Doe
Close:	Sincerely

Foreign Representative to U.N.

Address:	Her Excellency, Juanita Doe Representative of Uruguay The United Nations New York, NY
Salutation:	Dear Madam or Mr. Ambassador
Close:	Truly yours

U.S. Representative to the U.N.

Address:	The Honorable John R. Doe United States Representative to the United Nations New York, NY
Salutation:	Dear Mr. or Madam Ambassador
Close:	Sincerely

U.S. Representative to a U.N. Council or the General Assembly

Address:	The Honorable Jane R. Doe (specific title)
Salutation:	Dear Ms. or Mr. Doe
Close:	Truly yours

ORGANIZATION OF AMERICAN STATES

Secretary General

Address:	The Honorable John R. Doe Secretary General of the Organization of American States Washington, DC
Salutation:	Dear Mr. Secretary General
Close:	Sincerely

Assistant Secretary General

Address:	The Honorable John R. Doe Assistant Secretary of the Organization of American States Washington, DC
Salutation:	Dear Mr. Doe
Close:	Truly yours

Foreign Representative to OAS

Address:	His Excellency, Juan R. Doe Representative of Brazil on the Council of the Organization of American States Washington, DC
Salutation:	Dear Mr. or Madam Ambassador
Close:	Truly yours

U.S. Representative to OAS

Address: The Honorable John R. Doe
                        Representative of the United States on the
                        Council of the Organization of American States
                        State Department
                        Washington, DC

Salutation: Dear Mr. or Ms. Doe

Close: Sincerely

CANADIAN OFFICIALS

Governor General

Address: His Excellency
                        General The Right Honorable
                        The Earl of Glouchester
                        Governor General of Canada
                        Ottawa, Canada

(There are complex rules for personages with military titles and titles of nobility when they occupy the office of Governor General. Military titles are placed as shown, and if there is a noble title, it appears as shown. If the person is without military or noble rank, the proper form is simply: His Excellency, The Right Honorable, etc.)

Salutation: Excellency
                        Dear Governor General

Close: Respectfully

Prime Minister

Address: The Right Honorable
                        John R. Doe
                        Prime Minister of Canada
                        Ottawa, Canada

Salutation: Dear Mr. Prime Minister

Close: Respectfully

BRITISH PEERAGE, BARONETS, AND KNIGHTS

The rules for British titles of nobility call for the eldest son of a peer to assume the next highest family title below the father. Wives of eldest sons assume appropriate similar titles. Thus, the eldest son of Duke may be styled a Marquess. Younger sons are called by their full name, preceded by "Lord," as in Lord John Doe.

Duke

Address:	The Duke of Omnium (local address)
Salutation:	Dear Duke
Close:	Sincerely

Duchess

Address:	The Duchess of Omnium (local address)
Salutation:	Dear Duchess
Close:	Sincerely

Younger Son of a Duke

Address:	The Lord John Doe (local address)
Salutation:	Dear Lord John
Close:	Sincerely

Wife of a Younger Son of a Duke

Address:	The Lady John Doe (local address)
Salutation:	Dear Lady John
Close:	Truly yours

Daughter of a Duke

Address: The Lady Jane Doe
                    (local address)

Salutation: Dear Lady Jane

Close: Sincerely

Widow (or divorced wife until she remarries)

Address: Jane, Duchess of Omnium
                    (local address)

Salutation: Dear Duchess

Close: Truly yours

Marquess

Address: The Marquess of Queensbury
                    (local address)

Salutation: Dear Lord Queensbury

Close: Truly yours

Marchioness

Address: The Marchioness of Queensbury
                    (local address)

Salutation: Dear Lady Queensbury

Close: Sincerely

Earl

Address: The Earl of Oxbridge
                    (local address)

Salutation: Dear Lord Oxbridge

Close: Sincerely

Countess (wife of an Earl)

Address: The Countess of Oxbridge
                      (local address)

Salutation: Dear Lady Oxbridge

Close: Truly yours

Younger Son of an Earl

Address: The Hon. John R. Doe
                      (local address)

Salutation: Dear Mr. Doe

Close: Sincerely

Wife of a Younger Son of an Earl

Address: The Hon. Mrs. John R. Doe
                      (local address)

Salutation: Dear Mrs. Doe

Close: Truly yours

Viscount

Address: The Viscount Doe
                      (local address)

Salutation: Dear Lord Doe

Close: Sincerely

Viscountess

Address: The Viscountess Doe
                      (local address)

Salutation: Dear Lady Doe

Close: Sincerely

Daughter of a Viscount

Address: The Hon. Jane Doe
                  (local address)

Salutation: Dear Miss Doe

Close: Truly yours

Baron

Address: The Lord Doe
                  (local address)

Salutation: Dear Lord Doe

Close: Truly yours

Baroness

Address: The Lady Doe
                  (local address)

Salutation: Dear Lady Doe

Close: Truly yours

Baronet

Address: Sir John Doe, Bart.
                  (local address)

Salutation: Dear Sir Doe

Close: Sincerely

Wife of a Baronet

Address   Lady Doe
                  (local address)

Salutation: Dear Lady Doe

Close: Sincerely

Knight

Address:	Sir John Doe (local address)
Salutation:	Dear Sir John
Close:	Truly yours

Dame (female equivalent of Knight)

Address:	Dame Jane Doe (local address)
Salutation:	Dear Dame Doe
Close:	Truly yours

BRITISH GOVERNMENT OFFICIALS
(British usage always abbreviates Hon. and Rt. Hon.)

Prime Minister

Address:	The Rt. Hon. Jane Doe Prime Minister No. 10 Downing Street London, England or (if title) The Rt. Hon. Dame Jane Doe
Salutation:	Dear Miss, Mrs., or Mr. Doe Dear Dame or Sir Doe
Close:	Respectfully

Secretary of State for Foreign Affairs

Address:	The Rt. Hon. John R. Doe Secretary of State for Foreign Affairs London, England
Salutation:	Dear Mr. Doe
Close:	Truly yours

Lord Chief Justice

Address:	The Rt. Hon. The Lord Chief Justice of England London, England
Salutation:	Dear Lord Chief Justice
Close:	Truly yours

Lord Chancellor

Address:	The Rt. Hon. The Lord High Chancellor London, England
Salutation:	Dear Lord Chancellor
Close:	Sincerely yours

Member of the House of Lords

Address:	The Rt. Hon. The Earl of Oxbridge House of Lords London, England
Salutation:	Dear Lord Oxbridge
Close:	Sincerely

Member of the House of Commons

Address: The Rt. Hon. John Doe, M.P.
                        House of Commons
                        London, England

Salutation: Dear Mr. Doe

Close: Sincerely

Privy Councillor

Address: The Rt. Hon. John Doe
                        (local address)

Salutation: Dear Mr. Doe

Close: Truly yours

Lord Mayor

Address: The Rt. Hon. The Lord Mayor
                        of London
                        London, England

Salutation: Dear Lord Mayor

Close: Truly yours

British Ambassador

Address: His Excellency
                        The Rt. Hon. Sir John Doe
                        British Ambassador
                        London, England

Salutation: Dear Mr. or Madam Ambassador

Close: Truly yours

Governor General of a Dominion or Colony

Address:	His Excellency, The Rt. Hon. John Doe Governor General of New Zealand
Salutation:	Dear Mr. Doe
Close:	Respectfully

MISCELLANEOUS

Attorney

Address:	Ms. Jane R. Doe, Attorney-at-Law Ms. Jane R. Doe, Esq.
Salutation:	Dear Ms. Doe
Close:	Truly yours

Physician

Address:	John R. Doe, M.D. Dr. John R. Doe
Salutation:	Dear Dr. Doe
Close:	Truly yours

Dentist

Address:	Jane R. Doe, D.D.S. Dr. Jane R. Doe
Salutation:	Dear Dr. Doe
Close:	Sincerely

Certified Public Accountant

Address:	John R. Doe, C.P.A.
Salutation:	Dear Mr. Doe
Close:	Truly yours

Veterinarian

Address:	Jane R. Doe, D.V.M. Dr. Jane R. Doe
Salutation:	Dear Dr. Doe
Close:	Sincerely

Engineer

Address:	John R. Doe, P.E.
Salutation:	Dear Dr. Doe
Close:	Sincerely

INDEX